ANNOTATIONS

NAHUM DIMITRI CHANDLER

ANNOTATIONS

....

On the Early Thought of W. E. B. Du Bois

DUKE UNIVERSITY PRESS *Durham and London* 2023

© 2023 DUKE UNIVERSITY PRESS
All rights reserved
Text design by Matthew Tauch
Cover design by Franc Nunoo-Quarcoo
Typeset in Garamond Premier Pro
by Westchester Publishing Services

Library of Congress Cataloging-in-Publication Data
Names: Chandler, Nahum Dimitri, author.
Title: Annotations : on the early thought of W. E. B. Du Bois / Nahum Dimitri Chandler.
Other titles: On the early thought of W. E. B. Du Bois
Description: Durham : Duke University Press, 2023. | Includes bibliographical references and index.
Identifiers: LCCN 2021046024 (print)
LCCN 2021046025 (ebook)
ISBN 9781478015796 (hardcover)
ISBN 9781478018421 (paperback)
ISBN 9781478023029 (ebook)
Subjects: LCSH: Du Bois, W. E. B. (William Edward Burghardt), 1868–1963—Political and social views. | African Americans—Civil rights—19th century. | African Americans—Social conditions—To 1964. | United States—Race relations. | BISAC: PHILOSOPHY / Movements / General | LITERARY CRITICISM / American / African American & Black
Classification: LLC E185.97.D73 C436 2023 (print) | LC E185.97.D73 (ebook) | DDC 323.092—dc23/eng/20211230
LC record available at https:// lccn.loc.gov/2021046024
LC ebook record available at https:// lccn.loc.gov/2021046025

Cover art: W. E. B. Du Bois at home at 409 Edgecombe Avenue (Hamilton Heights/Sugar Hill, Harlem) in New York City, 1948. Photograph by Bernard Cole. W. E. B. Du Bois Papers (MS 312). Courtesy of the Special Collections and University Archives, University of Massachusetts Amherst Libraries.

DUKE UNIVERSITY PRESS GRATEFULLY ACKNOWLEDGES THE HUMANITIES COMMONS OF THE SCHOOL OF HUMANITIES AT THE UNIVERSITY OF CALIFORNIA, IRVINE, WHICH PROVIDED FUNDS TOWARD THE PUBLICATION OF THIS BOOK.

CONTENTS

vii	*Preface*
xv	*Acknowledgments*
xvii	*Note on Citations*
1	**PART I** On Paragraph Four of "The Conservation of Races"
81	**PART II** On the Question of the Illimitable in the Thought of W. E. B Du Bois
145	*Afterthought*
147	*Notes*
161	*References*
173	*Index*

PREFACE

....

I

This book is an expression of my thought that W. E. B. Du Bois was one of the most committed, gifted, hard-working, and accomplished thinkers of our era, from the late nineteenth century to the early twenty-first century, in America and across the world in general.

It is likewise my judgment that in order to challenge and determine in what way we may go beyond his accomplishments we must first take an acute and knowledgeable measure of his thought. Above all such a determination requires a reading of his writing with a commitment to be or become responsible in our thinking for what is most at stake therein, his thought, as given and exemplified in his practice, of thinking in writing.

This book is one expression of my own efforts in such critical engagement, that is to say, with Du Bois as a thinker.

II

Across the duration of the past half century, the practices of a relatively unprecedented critical accounting, sifting, and judgment in contemporary thought—within the discourses and disciplines of the study of politics, history, literature, artistic practice and architecture, forms of engineering, discourses of law and legality, and philosophical discourses as well as the interpretive dimensions of the disciplines of the human sciences—emerged and enabled the inception of an ongoing reconfiguration of the worldwide context for leading edge work in such practices. On the one hand, we may remark on the tendentious generalization of critical practice, that is, a reflection and astringent judgment within thought on the very terms, that is to say the conditions and limits, of its own possibility. On the other hand, during those same decades, throughout all of the domains just noted, the articulation of theory has emerged as essential, necessary, and general for any practice of thought that would be radical with regard to any and all that is at stake within it. We can thus surmise in our own time that the past several decades of critical reflection have rendered the general condition that for thought to approach the possibility that it may be commensurate with the problematization that has brought it forth, it must become theoretical, even practical theoretical—that is to say, it must ceaselessly proceed by always, no matter whatever else it undertakes in general, by asking after its own possibility.

III

Yet, too often engagement with the work of a thinker-writer from among folks or people of "color," to maintain and stake Du Bois's metaphor of "the problem of the color line," has meant that criticism has relentlessly approached the practice of such a thinker as ultimately, or perhaps only, a determined expression of a context, whether that context is understood as social, political, economic, or a discursive and theoretical horizon.

The writing and legacy of the extraordinary Frantz Fanon, because there is so much at stake in his superb example, may help to make clear my thought here. It may be that Fanon, in all senses of reference, has been appropriated, in part, over the past several decades because it has seemed apparent to many that one could imagine that more clearly than ever he could be situated in relation to already assumed, perhaps hegemonic or leading, theoretical dispositions, specifically a context such as psychoanalysis (however diverse and contested) or, more generally, a broad context such as mid-twentieth century French thought (of the social, cultural, or aesthetic) that rose to new international recognition and engagement during those same years. As well, his work and example may seem to offer the potential that by way of such references it could be assimilated to, or understood as existentially continuous with, emergent forms of political and economic concern and discourse, notably all that has recently been evoked under the heading of the postcolonial. Yet, it may well come to light that no such appropriation of Fanon's legacy ought be understood as radical for future thought in general. In likewise regard, a notice of such approaches with regard to C. L. R. James may be at once apposite and illuminating, by contrast, perhaps (for in terms of the circumstance of historical conjuncture and timing Du Bois was in fact of an entirely other generational reference from those I have mentioned here), efforts from the 1960s through the 1980s to enfold Du Bois under a Marxist banner, such as has been done with James, for example, gradually became incoherent, despite the older thinker's great regard for Karl Marx as a practical theoretical thinker. Then, in like manner, it was discovered in the 1990s that one could not so easily place Du Bois as a pragmatist philosopher. Nor could one carry out in a successful manner what has been repeatedly attempted since the 1960s: to simply declare Du Bois a certain traditional sociologist; that limit in the contemporary engagement with the thought of Du Bois remains, despite his own great aspiration, and his pioneering contributions to sociological thought, as discipline and even as an institution. Nor likewise has it been decisive during these same decades for contemporary scholars and thinkers to approach Du Bois as if he were and ought to be understood first or ultimately, in his historiographical practices, as an exemplary academic empiricist historian

What has remained elusive is a careful, sustained, supple, and generous reading of the internal emergence and theoretical articulation of Du Bois's own thought in his writing practices. It would seem that many have so far remained uncertain that such an approach could be realized.

In this book, I read Du Bois as a generative and original thinker whose thought may be understood to offer another context for modern and contemporary theoretical practice, as much as it may itself be submitted to critical contextualization.

To establish this argument, I deliberately move with a certain close regard for the rhythms of enunciation and registers of discourse given in a handful of early texts by Du Bois, as best that I can recognize and respond to them, such that, in turn, a reader may be able to find, and to recognize, a distinct articulation of values and judgments from a standpoint that is first situated within Du Bois's own manner of thinking in writing. I believe this closeness will at once challenge readers in their initial engagement and yet also sustain them, holding them close to the argument and the potential contributions of Du Bois's discourse, his practice in thought, in the common pursuit with me of an ongoing and somewhat new inhabitation of Du Bois's thought and example: that is, another understanding, by way of this address of his example, of the traditions that may now be understood anew of African American intellectual and theoretical production in critical thought.

The approach I take in this study is in contrast to that of most contemporary approaches to Du Bois, both in comparison to others (such as figures who have followed after him that I have noted above simply as examples or references—that is, Fanon or James), and in the most direct approaches that seek to situate him as a figure of legacy, whether in affirmation or in negation. The key thought I propose herein may be understood in quite simple and direct terms. In this book, I do not apply theory to the reading of Du Bois. Rather, I understand, approach, and elaborate (in a critical sense) Du Bois's work as itself theoretical. That is to say, Du Bois's own work can be understood to adduce, indicate within its engagement, a questioning of the conditions and possibility of its own conception and its enunciation. It can be studied and reengaged according to such terms. If so, Du Bois's text, in a general but quite practical sense, may be approached as a problem for those who would seek to understand it, as a solicitation rather than as a solution of any kind.

IV

In a manner of speaking, this work is a philosophical study—by way of a close reading of a key text by W. E. B. Du Bois from the second half of the last decade of the nineteenth century, that is to say: proximate to the turn to the twentieth century. The principal text in question is "The Conservation of Races," first presented in public on the March 5, 1897. In that essay, Du Bois sought to produce a truly general understanding of the historicity that announced the African American as a form of social and historical human being. My study addresses two primary aspects of this work. The initial consideration concerns the concept of race, of which he gave a distinctive critical account. The further consideration offered here is Du Bois's conceptualization of the historicity attendant to matters African American, in general. These considerations are each tethered to the other; one is at stake in the other, in mutual and reciprocal implication. This study thus undertakes (1) to provide a theoretical annotation of Du Bois's complex engagement with the concept of race (which is nothing other than the problem of the concept of the human as an *historial* entity) and (2) to cultivate and elaborate from the premises of Du Bois's early thought a distinct approach, in a theoretical sense, for thinking about the historicity in which matters African American are produced. On the latter, Du Bois sought to cultivate a conception that might account for the emergence of matters African American—as world historical—that is, the context of modern history on a planetwide scale of reference.

It must also be noted, however briefly, that there is at least one fundamental domain of Du Bois's concern at the turn to the twentieth century—the other principal one in my estimation, along with the concept of race (or the human) and the conception of modern historicity—that is not addressed in this study. That matter is the question of the genesis, character, and historical organization of forms of subjectivity that constitute the social and historical experience of African Americans. This is the question addressed by Du Bois's inimitable concept metaphor of "double-consciousness" and its attendant tropes, concepts, metaphors, and lexemes, the most notable of which is "second sight." This dimension of Du Bois problematization produces such a fundamental dimension of his itinerary—perhaps the most sedimented and fundamental—that it may be rendered legible and resonant for us in virtually every major reference at multiple levels of his writing and activity. Likewise, it articulates with contemporary horizons of thought in such a manner that the magnitude of the references to thought worldwide since the eighteenth century that it places at stake always remain exorbitant to any nominal critical engagement with them. Thus, Du Bois's practice on this order of problem yields for me a demand that it be considered in a study devoted to its critical elaboration on its own terms, of context and understanding; thus, I have determined to do so elsewhere.

V

The study manifests two distinct kinds of annotation. The first form of annotation is a work of theoretical desedimentation, if you will. Part I is focused on one paragraph in Du Bois's essay "The Conservation of Races." It attends to the logic, in the general sense, of the claims made therein in relation to thetic propositions of the paragraph. The second form of annotation is a kind of theoretical elaboration. This manner of proceeding is given in part II. It is an effort to recognize by way of my own theoretical narrative a principle of narration that is exemplified in Du Bois's practice across the middle paragraphs of this same essay. In those middle paragraphs of his text, Du Bois produces an account of the past of human existence according to the premise that he had formulated with regard to the idea of race (which I annotate in part I, here), that is to say in accordance with his critical re-conceptualization of such idea.

The principle of narration in Du Bois's thought that I, in turn, adduce in part II, by way of a kind of theoretical narrative of my own, may be given a concise general prefatory formulation. To adduce the status of an historical entity, a form of being whose futural standing is not given, Du Bois was led to cultivate a theoretical sense of *an alogical logic* as a way to address in knowledge and discourse the organization and operation of social genesis, that is as the constitutive (infra)structure in the processes of idealization, in the development, formation, and organization of values. In the understanding that I propose here, Du Bois cultivates such a thought to account for the historial status of the form of social being that goes under the heading of the Negro or African American. In part II of this study, I propose that such genesis may indeed be characterized by the phrase *the alogical logic of the second time*.

The work of the late pianist and composer Cecil Taylor provides exemplary reference and guidance for my elaboration of this thought. Likewise, I annotate the work of Jacques Derrida, of the same generational cohort as Taylor. Yet, still, it is Taylor's practice that I signal here, for what is most at stake is given in the practice of art; it is otherwise than a mathesis, a genealogy, an archaeology, or even a possible new thought of a grammatology. If anything, it might be a call for a new inhabitation of all that we might put at stake under the heading of a music*s* (Chandler 2018).

It is my hope that the reader might recognize a theoretical through line across the whole of this study. Du Bois is seeking to formulate a conception of history for those he would nominalize as African American. Yet, he ultimately seeks to realize this theoretical objective, not by the declaration of a finality but as the formulation of a problem, for thought, or thought as action, or action as always already of the thoughtful. The first stage of his effort, an account of which is given in part I here may be understood as an adjudication or analytical determination of the terms of his own thought on the matter. The second stage, an approach to which is offered in part II here might well be understood as a kind of speculative claim—of his thought as of the pertinence and provenance of his theorization, certainly for those who might be understood as African American, in part by the exemplarity of that form of example, but also, somewhat surreptitiously, as of pertinence and provenance for those who might be understood as persons or peoples committed to the futural efflorescence of all manner of difference amongst humans, in general.

Whereas part I of this study is an effort to dislodge some of the sedimentation that has embedded our understanding of Du Bois's work on a decisive seme, the idea and concept of race, in modern thought. On its submerged face, this seme and engagement of it addresses our very idea and concept of the human and historicity, in general. Thus, I consider part II of this study an elaboration of his work toward a re-inscription of the terms of our understanding of historicity and dispositions toward historical narration. The respective forms of the two parts of this study are thus somewhat distinct. One may be understood as an effort in the patient sifting and working through of layers of conceptual formulation. The other might be understood as a re-inscription of the terms of reference thus rendered available for a certain recognition and theoretical re-interpretation. Although I am hopeful that it may be understood as a reasonably supple approach, in that it is an address of the records of a specific locution given by Du Bois, it is my hope that the reader may find value and pertinence in the very necessity, as I see it, of the diversity of the two forms of annotation offered herein.

VI

It is thus that I offer here some brief considerations of the thought of W. E. B. Du Bois on the human and historicity at the turn to the twentieth century.

Although the text of this study was completed by the end of the last day of the year 2007, at the inception of the direct institutional expression of the massive worldwide calamity in economic and social well-being attendant to the last years of the opening decade of the twenty-first century, these few prefatory paragraphs by which I make reference to the contexts in critical practice that have enabled my own formulation of problem in thought in this study, written almost as a lapidary postscript proposing a retrospective perspective on the work I have attempted in this study, these prefatory paragraphs acquired their shape almost a short generation later, during the last weeks and days of that momentous and fateful year 2020, as we stood again amidst worldwide calamity, which became, for a time, at once catastrophe and disaster. The passages of this text are thus articulated amidst an incipient ongoing shifting, sliding, colliding, collapsing—that is to say, radical reformation—of long held sedimentations of episteme and practical theoretical projection. Yet, too, I hope that the perspective I have sought to adduce within these prefatory paragraphs along with this book as a whole may be understood also to maintain an abiding and tenacious hope that the rising generations may find buried herein an untimely yet ongoing resonance for their own imagination, both now and in the future, that is to say, in the imagination of another past—through its renewal—as another future, in thought, in all senses of this word.

ACKNOWLEDGMENTS

Throughout the preparation of this work, the ongoing support of friendship has been fundamental within my own sense of the world, most especially for my sense of hope therein—essential, thus, to this book's realization. Along with many others, who shall remain unnamed, I wish to thank Scott Michaelsen, Peter Cowan, Satoshi Ogihara, Christine Council, Brad Bonneville, Lewis Ricardo Gordon, Kimiyo Murata-Soraci, Ben Barker, and Yasuhisa Kitamura, for their friendship. I am most grateful for the support of Maria Phillips and Franc Nunoo-Quarcoo, which has been perennial over the decades and years. Of the several dozen whom I hold, across the generations, as family, two are *of* each day; thus, my wife and son are, always, the opening of my gratitude, for the gift that is care, for so opened the space by which this discourse could find its way forth.

It is my pleasure to be able to share here my appreciation for Ryan Kendall and to thank Jessica Ryan and Matthew Tauch, along with Lisl Hampton and Leslie Watkins, each of Duke University Press, for their considerate attention to the production of this text as a book. It is my honor and gratitude to acknowledge here the generous editorial guidance and affirmation of Ken Wissoker, throughout, especially for the duration of the final stages of the preparation of this study for publication.

NOTE ON CITATIONS

I

While I have taken scholastic reference to the original publication or to the unpublished manuscript of texts by W. E. B. Du Bois, in every case of his writings engaged in this study, with citations noted within the text, where possible or appropriate, I have also without exception consulted the versions of all published texts included in the thirty-seven volumes of the *Complete Published Works of W. E. B. Du Bois* issued from 1973 to 1986 by the Kraus-Thomson Organization and edited and introduced by the late Herbert Aptheker as well as the six volumes of Du Bois's texts published by the University of Massachusetts Press (1973–1985), also edited and introduced by Aptheker, which include three volumes of selected correspondence and three of selections of other texts, including previously unpublished texts and documents. The bibliographical details of those texts edited by Aptheker, if cited herein, are listed in the reference list at the end of this book.

II

The Souls of Black Folk: Essays and Sketches is cited herein from the first edition of its original publication (Du Bois 1903c). A full-text version of the second edition, which has no major changes from the first, is available in electronic form through the University of North Carolina's Documenting the American South project, available as an open access online text at https://docsouth.unc.edu/church/duboissouls/dubois.html (Du Bois 1903d). I consider that presentation of the book (based on its second edition, June 1903) an accurate and reliable work of scholarship. The pagination is the same in the first and second editions. In-text citations are given below in parentheses with the relevant page number(s), the chapter number, and the paragraph number(s) within the chapter. For example, the in-text cite (Du Bois 1903c, 213, chap. 11, para. 13) indicates *The Souls of Black Folk: Essays and Sketches*, page 213, chapter 11, paragraph 13, according to the pagination of the first edition of the book, issued in 1903.

III

With *The Philadelphia Negro: A Social Study* of 1899, when quoting or referencing specific passages of the text, I cite from its original publication (Du Bois and Eaton 1899).

IV

The early essay by Du Bois that is our main focus of interpretation in this study—"The Conservation of Races"—is always cited by an abbreviated title, CR, the page number in the original publication of the text and paragraph number, with the paragraph enumeration determined according to the original publication (Du Bois 1897a). For example, the in-text cite (CR 5, paras. 1–3) refers to the original publication of "The Conservation of Races" issued in 1897, page 5, paragraphs 1–3. Notably, however, this essay is also included in *The Problem of the Color Line at the Turn of the Twentieth Century: The Essential Early Essays*, a collection that I prepared in support of the present work as well as additional studies that I have carried out on Du Bois's early writings. As the edited and annotated edition of "The Conservation of Races" in that book includes the paragraph number in the margins of the text, although I give citations to only the original 1897 publication, attentive readers with that collection at hand may find the relevant passage simply by reference to the paragraph number of this essay in the 2015 publication (Du Bois 2015e). That collection includes complete versions of essential early essays by Du Bois as originally published or as extant in his unpublished papers, edited and annotated, with paragraph enumeration thoughout, according to contemporary scholarship.

V

Finally, I occasionally refer to material that may be found only among the W. E. B. Du Bois Papers of the Special Collections and University Archives at the University of Massachusetts Amherst Libraries, housed in the W. E. B. Du Bois Library (MS 312). (Occasionally, such material is referenced according to the microfilm version of those papers [Du Bois 1980a]). These papers have been digitized under the University of Massachusetts Amherst Libraries online repository Credo and are now available as open access material at https://credo.library.umass.edu/view/collection/mums312. Additional bibliographic detail for some notable specific citations from among these papers may be found in the notes or in the reference list at the end of this book. The original papers were compiled and edited by Herbert Aptheker, whereas the microfilm edition was supervised by Robert C. McDonnell.

PART I

For Robert Bernasconi

On Paragraph Four of "The Conservation of Races"

I. THE PROBLEMATIZATION

THE DENIGRATION OF AFRICA

The status of Africa in the metaphysical discourses of Europe and the Americas across the modern period stands in the background of all of the writings of W. E. B. Du Bois on the situation of the Negro in the United States at the turn to the twentieth century.

If the Negro American intelligentsia and political leadership withdrew from the idea of race at the end of the nineteenth century, it was no doubt due to the eventuality of the devolution and implication of that idea in the massive denigration of the *historial* entity known as Africa and of those persons understood as African—the peoples of the continent that bears this name and the descendants thereof, in every sense, who are spread across the whole of the planet earth—within modern Western economic, political, and intellectual practices during the past half millennium. Such denigration should be understood to include the centuries from 1441 to 1883, characterized by the forced conscription of "Africans" into enslavement; the incipit of the colonization of the continent by European nation-states in the making, of which the 1884–1885 Berlin conference would be the late nodal culmination in economic, political, and military terms of a centuries-long eventuality; and the great modern discursive formation in the West, as a modern *historial* articulation—from philosophy to literature, from travel accounts to legal documents, from religious discourse to a nascent science (experimental as well as theoretical)—of a predominantly negative understanding, beyond its variegation, of matters African, stretching across the whole expanse of the modern epoch.

It is the interlaced discursive formations of this general historicity that exhibit the texture or fabric of this denigration in the dominant epistemic orders according to a pattern of semiotic legibility that can be critically inhabited within its own terms by way of a dialogic principle. That is, such formations necessarily announce within their promulgation a reflexive gesture that is the rendering of historicity as the very terms of its enunciation and legibility. At the very least, that is to say, it can occur only in the necessarily interwoven proposition of an order of distinction and a simultaneous justification or account of the claims, positions, implications, and declarations made therein. It is within the unfolding of this reflexive gesture that the formation of the philosophical concept of race and the discourses of race in Europe and the so-called New World took shape. From the second half of the eighteenth century—in the midst of the European Enlightenment—and across the nineteenth century, the idea and concept of race was elaborated in Europe and in the Americas and in the Caribbean as the fundamental order of distinction—philosophical and scientific, in particular, but also within the horizon of law in general—according to which historial differences among human groups should be understood or the relative status of such adjudicated. It was thus, of course, according to this concept and in this elaboration that the denigration of the Negro or African across the nineteenth century was affirmed within the lead formal and dominant discourses of Europe and the Americas, including the Caribbean.

In a sense that sets in motion the problematization of Du Bois's early discourse, the persistent denigration of the Negro in America—here, the reference is specifically to the United States—should be understood to arise within this frame or horizon: that is, the global level denigration within European practices of the historial figure of "Africa," that is, as historial subject, or as an example of humanity or humanitas, regardless of its own actual promulgation as origin of world and possibility. The denigration of the Negro American, it can then be said, arose as both constitutive part and as determined parcel of this global level disregard of persons, things, and matters "African." We can thus further recognize that a certain general order of epistemic problem comes into legible view: the question of the so-called Negro problems in the United States encodes therein a fundamental question about how the historial entity in question is understood on a global scale in philosophical discourse and scientific knowledge. The problematic named therein is a certain question, sedimented but distinctly legible, concerning the status, in every sense, both ontological and historical, of the Negro American.

THE SOLICITATION OF W. E. B. DU BOIS

It does not surprise, thus, that Du Bois was solicited by its implication and compelled to attempt an intervention on its epistemic-political terrain as the inaugural step in the formulation of a project that would propose to address the so-called Negro problem(s) in the United States. That inaugurating step is given in the essay "The Conservation of Races," presented on March 5, 1897, as an address at the founding session of the American Negro Academy (ANA) held at the Lincoln Memorial Church in Washington in the District of Columbia.

In terms of the archive proper it might be considered a sort of second step. The sense of inaugurating step that I intend here is epistemological, pertaining to the organization of the terms of Du Bois's theoretical enunciation.

"The Afro-American," an essay prepared by Du Bois from sometime in late 1894 or early 1895, could well be taken as a chronological first step in that it is at the inception of a period of time, some three years, in which he was trying to find his sense of way, to clarify his problematic and his vocation (Du Bois 1894[?]; 1975b, 54–55; 1968, 208). This essay has been virtually unknown in the scholarship on Du Bois. It was only recently brought to publication (Du Bois 2015a, 2010). I date the text to the period of time from the last month of 1894 to the first months of 1895, some five to six months after Du Bois had returned to the United States following two years of study in Germany and travel throughout Europe. Du Bois had just taken up his first appointment as a young assistant professor at Wilberforce University. In that essay, he poses the question of the "Afro-American" as an example of a global matter of the so-called Negro problem in which the question of Africa on a global level stands in the background, even as he wished to emphasize that the "American Negro" is not "African" but "American."

T. Thomas Fortune had been the most vocal advocate of the use of the term "Afro-American" by the Negro American intelligentsia and leaders of the time, up to the early 1890s (Fortune 2008). With the title of that early essay, Du Bois may be understood to enjoin Fortune's discourse. Yet, subsequently, notably in the 1897 essay "The Conservation of Races," Du Bois would elaborate his own metonymic yet critical nominalizations of such terms, notably Negro American or American Negro, African American, or Afro-American. Indeed, as I believe that one can affirm from my study, it is precisely the epistemological grounding and theoretical footing of such nominalization that forms the abiding substance of the ruminations from Du Bois's essay "The Conservation of Races."

Briefly, to give an initial characterization of "The Conservation of Races," this responsive incipit can be named on two registers: to rethink the concept of race (if it does in all truth bespeak a necessity, what chance for the Negro in history?); to evaluate the place in human history in the general sense of the figure of "Africa." What has surprised some is that in the former effort, at least at the outset of his itinerary, Du Bois attempted to reformulate and utilize the concept of race. And, in all truth, Du Bois never relinquished throughout the remainder of his itinerary the commitments that guided him in this early example of his practice. This has produced all manner of conundrums for our contemporary reception of his early discourse. It need be said directly here in the light of that history of preemptive and willful engagement that Du Bois's manner of affirmation of a concept that he continued to call race in this early moment is fundamentally at odds with what has generally been claimed about his discourse by those who would presume that they have given a definitive critical rejection of it. Yet what might equally surprise those commentators, in the context of our much-too-easy assumption that we are now beyond that long nineteenth century, is that the enigmas and paradoxes that he faced remain confounded in our own time—even as we find ourselves astride the third decade of the twenty-first century. It can thus be said that Du Bois's practice in this early moment remains, paradoxically perhaps, exemplary in our own time and in a manner that extends beyond the discourses of the Negro or the Negro American. And, with regard to the latter effort, while a global vision is often recognized for Du Bois late in his itinerary, what might well surprise here, when seen from within the terms of his own discourse, is how poor seems our contemporary understanding of the early date of its occurrence for him, its fundamental status and breadth in his discourse, and the persistent manner of his rhetorical efforts in proposing a revaluation of things "African": it arises right at the inception of his attempts to state for himself just what were "the Negro problem(s)" just before the mid-1890s upon his return from doctoral study in Europe, and its appearance in "The Conservation of Races" is thus, in the factual sense, simply its rhetorical maintenance. The status of the *historial* figure of Africa as a problematization of modern historicity on a global scale should be understood as a threshold form of solicitation of Du Bois's itinerary.¹

OUR PROBLEMATIZATION

This general solicitation and the double-layered intervention it calls forth from Du Bois form the warp and weft of our own problematization—in our engagement with his itinerary. For, if we would accede to the most profound possibilities bequeathed therein to us, we must propose a radicalization of the question that we can recognize in this epistemic-political conjuncture. In a radical sense, the question is not whether we agree or disagree with Du Bois's inhabitation of this vortex. Rather, the question is in what way does his example allow us to think with him to the limits of epistemological possibility and thereby recognize within those paths or according to the horizon they render legible the possibilities for a desedimentation of our own grounds of inhabitation and thus the terms of another thought of forms of historical emergence and the elaboration of historicity. This is to say, if the problematic at hand is that "back of most discussions of race with which he ["the American Negro"] is familiar, have lurked certain assumptions as to his natural abilities, as to his political, intellectual and moral status" (CR 1, para. 1), the issue is something more than differences of opinion about the Negro or the African. It is about how we think about historial possibility in general. It is about our understanding of the status of necessity and freedom in the devolution of history with regard to the forms of the human in general. It is about the paradoxes attendant to any concept of truth when the status of any possible response to the question "what is ?" has been radically problematized. Let us say here and now that it is always and already complicated. Doubtless then the value of a decision for or against Du Bois's practice sustains far less interest for us in its eventuality than a labor of desedimentation that may perhaps assist us in dislodging certain encrusted premises that shape contemporary practice—political and intellectual—in this domain. For the status of the human remains a scene of vexation in the thought of our time. Du Bois, thus, enters on this complex and overwrought epistemic terrain—in the scene at hand, the status of difference among the human—and attempts to make possible a rethinking of the given dominant organization of terms as they are announced in the form of the so-called Negro problem.

II. A GENERAL PROBLEMATIZATION

In a theoretical sense, "The Conservation of Races" is organized as a threefold structure headed by a statement of question that amounts to a kind of preamble. Following a three-paragraph ambulatory discourse, Du Bois moves into the development of his argument in the proper sense. In the essay's opening stages, he critically examines the concept of race, outlining its traditional formulation in the discourses of science and proposes a certain reformulation of its infrastructure. In the middle and textually dominate stage of the essay, he outlines a schematic history of the movement and function of "race differences"—in his reformulated sense—in human history. In the final stage of the essay, Du Bois outlines a certain conceptualization and a new program, the project of an "intellectual clearing house" specifically proposed for African Americans in the United States that would serve as an intellectual guide for policy and action—with the aim of enabling the realization of their full historical possibility in terms of the future as its horizon.

In part I, I attend only to the first stages of Du Bois's essay, his ambulatory preparation for his discourse and then his attempt to dismantle and reformulate the concept of race.

In part II, I attempt to maintain a meditation on the middle stages of his essay.

The stakes of Du Bois's vision of the American Negro Academy (ANA) as an "intellectual clearing house" must be reserved for another consideration. For it has its own internal thetic projection and conceptualization in terms of its difference from various other projects among the ANA's founding members. This is most notable with regard to the vision of the senior and initial guiding voice for the group, Alexander Crummell; and then too we situate here his follower John W. Cromwell. Yet it is different as well from other founding figures in the organization, the Grimké brothers Archibald and Francis, in particular, as well as other competing projects of the time, such as the initiatives by Booker T. Washington and William Monroe Trotter, respectively for example. Too, all of these approaches, along with the unfolding of other initiatives of the first two decades of the twentieth century—the Niagara Movement and the National Association for the Advancement of Colored People that issued from it, for example—all of this must be reserved for another passage of reflection that might be elaborated subsequent to the ground work and elaboration proposed in the annotations of this study.

It should be emphasized that the status of this idea—"an intellectual clearing house"—has gone essentially unremarked in the critical literature.

At issue herein—the present study in general—is a somewhat different approach to the same concern: an attempt to follow the formulation of term and (internal) movement of thought by which Du Bois orients himself as an intellectual in the first stages of his maturation as an independent scholar and thinker.

On the one hand, it must be recalled that the fundamental historiographical work on the American Negro Academy (ANA) remains that undertaken by Alfred A. Moss Jr. during the late 1970s (Moss 1981).

On the other hand, with regard to Alexander Crummell specifically, with reference to the late nineteenth-century context, the work of Wilson Jeremiah Moses has been the most sustained (Crummell 1992; Moses 1989, cf. 258–75). Yet, in his early 1990s commentary on the relation of Crummell and Du Bois, in its insistence on the continuity of the thought of the younger thinker with that of the older one, it seems to me that he bypasses the juncture of difference between the two that I remark here (see Moses 1993, esp. 284). To my reading, Du Bois explicitly states his withdrawal from the theological premise (which Crummell held) with regard to the question of the status of the concept of race in an understanding of the ground of the Negro or Negro American as a form of the human.

Du Bois opens his address, "The Conservation of Races," with the following apparently unremarkable words.[2]

> The American Negro has always felt an intense personal interest in discussions as to the origins and destinies of races: primarily because back of most discussions of race with which he is familiar, have lurked certain assumptions as to his natural abilities, as to his political, intellectual and moral status, which he felt were wrong. He has, consequently, been led to deprecate and minimize race distinctions, to believe intensely that out of one blood God created all nations, and to speak of human brotherhood as though it were the possibility of an already dawning tomorrow. (CR 5, para. 1)

The interest of these words must be given retrospectively: by the way in which Du Bois will use them as the rhetorical foil—the deployment of which sustains a statement of conceptual and theoretical problematization—in relation to which he can introduce and delineate the central proposition of his address. He will put forward the apparently antithetical proposition that the African American intelligentsia and leadership should affirm a concept of race in order to properly understand the status of the Negro in America and to establish a firm basis for an approach to policy and a course of action that would realize the groups' ultimate historial possibility.

In this opening paragraph, then, Du Bois outlined a schema of reference by which the status of the Negro American at the turn to the twentieth century was usually adjudicated. That frame of reference is a configuration of ideas gathered under the heading of the idea of race. (And we must note that in terms of the text at hand, "The Conservation of Races," we are not yet speaking specifically of the formal concept—announced in philosophy and science—that takes its shape in terms of this more general horizon of idea.) In this configuration, disposition and determinate judgment, the status of the Negro is referred to as an understanding of the "origins and destinies of races." Based on this reference there are often "assumptions," not only pre-judgments of the Negro's character if you will (as given, say, in an individual example) but also fundamental presuppositions about the "political, intellectual and moral *status*" (my emphasis) of the group as a form of being, of human being, "back of most discussions of race." We might understand such judgment along two lines The first implies a reference to the Negro as a natural being, specifically to an order of being that may be understood (according to discourses that might purport to address an ontological order of attention, concerned with the grounds, possibility, and determinations of being, in fundamental thought) to bespeak a kind of necessity and its determinations. This would be the Negro as a natural entity—as body—certainly. But, second, the real issue concerns the status of such ostensibly determinate order of body for the articulation of the intellectual and moral attributes of the Negro. Such capacity, or such "natural abilities," would name the bequest or absence thereof that would determine the Negro's standing as a moral being—the humanitas of the human—that might realize or exemplify a perfection of such. This second aspect can thus be remarked as the background for any judgment about the Negro as a "natural" being: it is a kind of predetermination of the status of the Negro within an ontological problematic, specifically a certain metaphysical horizon, as a kind of being. It is thus that there is a judgment as to the "status" of the Negro, their "political, intellectual and moral status."

The organization of "assumption" here can be given some specification even if it remains general. The determination given within the idea of race that had become traditional in Europe and America by the end of the nineteenth century is that there is a limit given within nature as to the ability, capacity, or faculty of the group understood as the Negro.[3] Further, the implication would be that such limited dispensation within the orders of nature constitutes the ground for a determination of the status of the Negro, their historial status as a group (ontologically for philosophy and science and historically or socially within the devolution of the political, intellectual, and moral organization of nations, for example, the Negro in the historical project of the United States of America). Although he does not explicitly recall it in this opening paragraph, Du Bois distinctly implies that in such "assumptions" the Negro is judged as inferior to other "racial groups" specifically, but especially such groups understood as "white" or "European."

Given that this general construal of idea articulated the most distinctive idiomatic terms of the social systems in which their historic exploitation and oppression as a group was rendered possible and sustained, it is no surprise that the Negro American intelligentsia and political leadership would disavow the idea of race. On the contrary, nothing could make more emphatic sense in the last years of the nineteenth century. In the face of such an overdetermined idea of the organization of human difference and its bearing in history, the Negro American response had been to deny difference and to affirm the unity of the human by way of the claim of a divine dispensation: that the truth of the supposed unity of that form of being called human is a divine one. Its ultimate source would be the sovereign authority of God. Such premises were then interwoven with the metaphoric idioms of both folk genealogy and the proclamations of the discourses of natural science: that the human as such is birthed "out of one blood." On this metaphorical basis, the Negro American leadership had taken a clear course of action and policy, to minimize the distinction of so-called race and to emphasize the "brotherhood" (with all of the attendant metaphorics of family, lineal kinship, etc.) of different groups of humans. And, in the background, in the shadows of this course of action and policy, stands the resolute but inexplicit presumption of the absolute truth and authority of the inaugural formal ideals of the Republic of the United States of America.

For Du Bois, in this address of March 1897—given in the nation's capital while he is in the midst of the empirical and scholastic research that would yield *The Philadelphia Negro*—this is not enough. Although speaking at the Lincoln Memorial Church to an audience heavily marked by the presence of several of the most prominent African American clergy, such as the prime mover behind the founding of the organization, Alexander

Crummell, or those affiliated with major religious institutions, Du Bois will systematically take leave from this religious authority and justification as the basis of judgment and policy by the Negro leadership. (And, understood in light of the history of the forms of intellectual leadership among African Americans of the eighteenth and nineteenth centuries, this disposition may well be one of the most singular aspects of his intervention.) In its stead, Du Bois proposed the authority of philosophy and science.

In the second paragraph, we see the sharp edge of this claim come glinting into light. Du Bois continues:

> Nevertheless, in our calmer moments we must acknowledge that human beings are divided into races; that in this country the two most extreme types of the world's races have met, and the resulting problem as to the future relations of these types is not only of intense and living interest to us, but forms an epoch in the history of mankind. (CR 5, para. 2)

While in the eventuality of this discourse Du Bois will attempt to mark out his difference from both the historical position of the denigration of the Negro by way of the idea of race and the Negro response to it, here, at this juncture, Du Bois focused on distinguishing himself in terms of the latter.

If, here, Du Bois maintains that the Negro American leadership, despite their understandable withdrawal from it, must nonetheless accept the concept of race and the actuality of "races" as the framework of reference for any sober consideration of the status and social condition of the Negro, it is because he is operating with a conceptual predicate he shares with the discourses of the natural science of his day: that there is in its actuality an order of essence (or, an order of essential distinction or difference) among humans that distinguishes them in a decisive manner (perhaps even categorically) as groups, one from another. The heading given in philosophy and science for this idea is the concept of race. The idea is that the concept of race is an epistemological heading that issues from the supposed order of proper name.

"[That] we must acknowledge that human beings are divided into races" is the premise with which Du Bois begins his whole statement that is "The Conservation of Races." The suggestion is that knowledge—philosophy as science, perhaps—has given us the understanding of a certain truth about human beings. And, we must not fail to notice that in a general sense this claim follows from another premise, that there is such a being called "Man" or the human, or (hu)mankind, understood as a kind of whole. Thus, this whole is "divided into races." "We," the Negro, Du Bois declares, must accept this truth, of understanding as reason, as philosophy and science: acknowledge it, or recognize it, and use it as the basis of or guide to understanding "our" everyday situation.

And here we must offer a fundamental notation: that the announcement of the whole called the human or humankind, human beings as a kind of being, also names simultaneously (and on the same level of ontological status) an essential order of difference within or among this whole. Such an order of essence that would demarcate differences within the human had been announced as knowledge within philosophy and science since the eighteenth century, since the Enlightenment. Its privileged name, of course, has indeed been the nominalization understood as "race."

And then, a further notation: this concept of race was internally confounded from its first formal appearance as a heading for thought. That appearance was in the work of Immanuel Kant—not only his 1784–85 essay "The Determination of the Concept of Race" but most precisely the 1788 essay "On the Use of Teleological Principles in Philosophy" (Kant 2007a, 2007b, 2001c).[4] But, also, it found its articulation in the biological sciences of the late eighteenth century, especially in the productions of Johann Friedrich Blumenbach, the theoretical inheritor of Kant's thought of race among humans, and then across the long nineteenth century, a periodization that references an epistemic formation that may be understood to have stretched well into the twentieth.[5] What should have been taken up as a question—as a form of problematization of existence and thus as a problem for thought—was instead assumed as a given. And, indeed, it can be shown that in the discourses of the eighteenth century, in its dominant formulations, it was operated as a presupposition or construed according to the architectonic position of a principle of reason. From the earliest full formulation his own pathway to a certain thought of the transcendental in 1781, Kant had cautioned (in the "Appendix to the Transcendental Dialectic" of the *Critique of Pure Reason*, for example) against the mistaken apprehension of a regulative idea as a constitutive one (Kant 1998 [1781]). Yet, in the midst of his elaboration of the critical project, Kant nonetheless appears, for example in the subsequent and pivotal essay for his thought from 1788 noted above, very late in that pivotal decade, to do exactly what he earlier warned against. The idea of race is a concept that he had first operated, with only a nascent formalization in his published work in the middle of the 1770s. This conundrum that I remark here showed forth theoretically when he attempted to address again the status of the concept of race, to give a theoretical understanding of its "determination," as he had formulated such a thought (of determination) within the architectonic of his thought as he had announced it in the First Critique. That is to say, in the essay from late in the critical decade he construes the concept according to what he calls "the use of teleological principles in philosophy." He most precisely takes as constitutive what he has cautioned should only be taken as regulative, in the promulgation of reason that would adhere to its own protocols of self-questioning and a certain sobriety in thought (Kant 2001c, 2007b).

What must now be understood is that *at this stage in the discourse* of "The Conservation of Races" Du Bois appears to follow the same procedure as Kant and to risk an uncritical maintenance of the same order of "transcendental illusion," as Kant calls it in the first critique (Kant 1998 [1781]). That is, with reference to Kant's formulation of the term, as it seems Kant himself has projected his own determination of a concept of race, Du Bois in his 1897 text, "The Conservation of Race," appears as if on the cusp of producing what might at best be taken as a regulative idea of race, a hypothesis for thought shall we say, as a constitutive one, a premise, in terms of which one would then claim to recognize the constitution of being and world. And, of course, the further difficulty remains as to the status of "regulative ideas" as Kant calls them. This latter is a question I will leave to the side in the present discussion, reserving it for fulsome engagement elsewhere. One might consider Jacques Derrida's ruminations on this fundamental problematization across his entire itinerary (Derrida cf. 1974, 1978c, 2005). Yet the conundrum that would remain for such a reading of Du Bois is that it might still remain quite legible and demonstrable that he is not in pursuit of a project that would name a pure sovereignty in thought or history—in whatever form—as it might be argued was maintained and pursued by Kant in his endeavors throughout the 1780s and 1790s (across his meditations on history, for example). Thus, it might be supposed that Du Bois is more profoundly understood, instead, as seeking after the terms that might make possible a fundamental or incontrovertible recognition of the heterogeneity of another order of whole—as otherwise than a supposed pure or sovereign entity—as a heading for thought and existence.

Such order of the whole that Du Bois is seeking to put in question would be, on the one hand, the nation-state apprehended under the name "America" and, on the other, that which has been called the human or mankind. Du Bois may seek to affirm a constitutive heterogeneity in each of those examples of a sense of whole. Likewise, he may seek to affirm a maintenance of an incessant difference in the apparition that might posit the realization of any such whole. This study as a whole ought be understood as an elaboration of this theoretical horizon within Du Bois's text, hence as an epistemological consideration and order of attention to his practice in discourse.

So, Du Bois's opening premise is that there are races, that they can be nominalized, and that a kind of typology can be outlined or certain criteria can be specified according to which they can be understood and described as an organized ensemble.

He then proposes that in terms of the order of differences among these groups (by the "criteria" of such we might suggest), the two most different such groups, the most extreme in their differences, are in *relation* in the United States, across its history of course, but in particular at the end of the nineteenth century. The matter of their relation is a problem—difficult—shall we say. The violence, destruction, and negativity of the historical terms of this relation for the Negro American goes unspoken and unnamed here. Perhaps silence is an index of Du Bois's sense of his audience on the occasion of the founding of an "Academy" of and for the American Negro. They, this intelligentsia, would know, always already, as it were.

In the opening paragraph of the essay "The Relation of the Negroes to the Whites in the South," from July 1901, Du Bois characterizes this relation, dramatically and powerfully, with a global horizon in his theoretical eye (Du Bois 1901, 121–22; 2015f, 189–90, paras. 1–3). Yet, it ought to be noted here that when the 1901 essay was republished in April 1903 as the ninth chapter of *The Souls of Black Folk: Essays and Sketches*, it was reissued without its epistemologically frame setting first locution (Du Bois 1903c, 164–65). Perhaps, in 1903, Du Bois understood the frame as provided by the book as a whole, notably its forethought. Perhaps, in 1901, the projected immediate audience of his text, the readers of the *Annals of the American Academy of Political and Social Science*, the forum in which the essay was originally published, would have been in his mind. In that 1901 essay version of our text then, in its first of three ambulatory paragraphs calling for a "joint endeavor to seek the truth" to address the problematization for knowledge that "the world-old phenomenon of the contact of diverse races of men is to have new exemplification during the new century" would bring forth anew, Du Bois then concluded the third ambulatory paragraph with the proposition that this problematization should become the guiding concern of an entire line of study.

> We have in the South as fine a field for such a study as the world affords,—a field, to be sure, which the average American scientist deems somewhat beneath his dignity, and which the average man who is not a scientist knows all about, but nevertheless a line of study which by reason of the enormous race complications with which God seems about to punish this nation must increasingly claim our sober attention, study, and thought, we must ask, what are the actual relations of whites and blacks in the South? and we must be answered, not by apology or faultfinding, but by a plain, unvarnished tale. (Du Bois 1901, 121–22; 2015f, 189–90, paras. 1–3)[6]

This proposition may be understood as the direct epistemological extension, at once of a supposed empirical practice and a theoretical perspective, of the broad epistemological formulation for a "study of the Negro problems," of matters attendant thereto as marked out by two kinds of study: analytical attention to the social group itself and attention to the "peculiar social environment" of that group, respectively (Du Bois 2015h, 71, para. 9; 2015i, 92, para. 43; see also 1903c, 8, chap. 1, para. 9). It is the second category of the study of the "half-named Negro problem" that Du Bois is restating as a problem for knowledge in the opening paragraphs of the 1901 essay, the remainder of which is its elaboration, by reference to the American horizon, notably the American South, which is subsequently articulated as the ninth chapter of the 1903 book of essays. The 1901 essay may be understood as a theoretical companion to the 1900 essay, "The Present Outlook for the Dark Races of Mankind," the latter of which adduced as its guiding thematic the world historical and worldwide context of reference for what Du Bois, which (for the first time with this theoretical production or sense of the lexeme "*problem* of the color line" [my emphasis]) is formulated as the global-level "problem of the color line" that acquired its incipit amidst the fifteenth century (Du Bois 1900, 2015d, 2015c; Chandler 2021). (We ought to note here that in the ninth paragraph of "Strivings of the Negro People" from the summer of 1897, Du Bois wrote of the "half-named" Negro problem, an essay that in 1903 would become the first chapter of *The Souls of Black Folk: Essays and Sketches* [Du Bois 1897b; 1903a].)

Finally, then, Du Bois begins to name a distinctive concept of historicity—according to two forms of temporality—in order to situate this problem in terms of his historical present. In terms of a sense of the present as immediate, the problem is "of intense and living interest" to the "American Negro," to "us" as he says. But, also, Du Bois proposes, it should be understood in terms of another order of historicity that would include a certain past and a possible future; thus, Du Bois writes that the matter of such relation "forms an epoch in the history of mankind." The "epochal" status of such relation might be understood to relate to its character, although Du Bois does not render such a logic here, at least not explicitly or at this time. He will do so over the following years—giving an achieved statement of such a conception only over the course of the second half of the year 1899, after he had released the manuscript of *The Philadelphia Negro: A Social Study* for publication (the epilogue of which addresses exactly this issue), and it is articulated during the time when he was perhaps first seeking to put its implication in some perspective. In the 1899 passage of thought, "the problem of the color line," as it will then be called, is about the presumption of one group of humans to stand as an absolute and sovereign entity over another human group (of whatever kind). The claim, whether explicit in these terms, or not, would propose that one group could stand on the basis of an essential predicate beyond and thus above the limit of historial becoming of the group understood as subordinate. That is to say, this is the conception yielded by his narration of the formation of the "problem" in question. Elsewhere, in a companion work to the present study, I propose an elaboration of this formulation of a sense of world historical problem (Chandler 2022).

Here it may be noted that, perhaps during this latter time, there is a certain deepening and radicalization of Du Bois's understanding of the historial status of "the problem of the color line." For the months in question follow upon the death in May 1899 of his beloved son, his firstborn child. It seems that along with an intensification of his already rather remarkable capacity for work, a certain urgency to make full sense of his place in history, his social and historical situation, along with a new sobriety begins to announce itself even on the surface of his discourse. In the year following, and upon his return from a second visit to Europe, Du Bois attempted his first meditation on African American religion. Its providential question remains at the heart of *The Souls of Black Folk: Essays and Sketches* gathered and published three years later as summarized in the question that prepares the conclusion to the final chapter of the book under the heading "the sorrow songs":

> Through all the sorrow of the Sorrow Songs there breathes a hope—a faith in the ultimate justice of things. The minor cadences of despair change often to triumph and calm confidence. Sometimes it is faith in life, sometimes a faith

in death, sometimes assurance of boundless justice in some fair world beyond. But whichever it is, the meaning is always clear: that sometime, somewhere, men will judge men by their souls and not by their skins. Is such a hope justified? Do the Sorrow Songs sing true? (Du Bois 1903c, 261–62, chap. 14, para. 23)

In the next paragraph of the essay this question turns away from the theological formulation of the question in the "sorrow songs" toward the status of scientific knowledge. Du Bois writes there (Du Bois 1903c, 262–63, chap. 14, para. 24): "So woefully unorganized is sociological knowledge that the meaning of progress, the meaning of 'swift' and 'slow' in human doing, and the limits of human perfectibility, are veiled, unanswered sphinxes on the shores of science." The terrain marked out by these latter formulations of question, as we shall see, encloses in outline the epistemological domain, that is to say the discursive scene or contexts in terms of thought and reflection that inscribe and situate Du Bois's inquiry in "The Conservation of Races."

We can remark this second paragraph of "The Conservation of Races" then in a summary fashion. Du Bois proposes the supposed actuality of races as the beginning of his reflection upon the situation of the "American Negro." It is this apparently real, or actual, fact, according to him, that stands at the root and has yielded the historical and social problem that is the topic of his discussion. The "problem" at hand, which takes its root in this apparent ontological distinction, difference, or "division" of humans into such groups, is that in the United States "the two most extreme types of the world's races have met." It poses, thereby, the question of the relationship between these two groups of humans. Du Bois, indexing the occasion for his discourse, describes this question as one of "living interest to us," that is, the Negro. This is the actual historical question that provokes his discourse. It is a problem of an actual circumstance of lived difference. And yet it is a question that indexes an entire "epoch in the history of mankind." The operative question is how might the supposed "Negro" American and the supposed "White" or "European" American live together in the future. It is this operative question that is the titular source of the more sedimented question of the status of the Negro with regard to the supposed actuality of races and their differences. "The Conservation of Races" is thus, first of all, a conceptual, reflective, discursive response to an existing historical situation.

With this characterization of the problem in mind, in the next paragraph, the third, Du Bois outlines an address of the situation of the "American Negro" that would be fundamentally different than the approach he has presented as typical of the African American intelligentsia and general leadership at the end of the nineteenth century.

> It is necessary, therefore, in planning our movements, in guiding our future development, that at times we rise above the pressing, but smaller questions of separate schools and cars, wage-discrimination and lynch law, to survey the whole question of race in human philosophy and to lay, on a basis of broad knowledge and careful insight, those large lines of policy and higher ideals which may form our guiding lines and boundaries in the practical difficulties of everyday. For it is certain that all human striving must recognize the hard limits of natural law, and that any striving, no matter how intense and earnest, which is against the constitution of the world, is in vain. The question, then, which we must seriously consider is this: What is the real meaning of Race; what has, in the past, been the law of race development, and what lessons has the past history of race development to teach the rising Negro people? (CR 5, para. 3)

The approach entails three phases, if you will, although these "phases" would ineluctably overlap at every practical turn. First, he declares the necessity of a whole epistemic shift of perspective. He proposes another epistemic horizon: "human philosophy." That is to say, he proposes that the basis of judgment be knowledge and not revelation or the assumption of divine dispensation. Second, he suggests that the Negro American leadership should then determine the best, proper, or true "higher" ideals for this group on the basis of the knowledge thereby found (as yielded or attained). Finally, he proposes that such ideals should in turn be used to decide the course of action and policy in the address of the "smaller questions" of the immediate and the "everyday," such as "the questions of separate schools and cars, wage-discrimination and lynch law." This will thus be, for Du Bois, a secular *critical* project; it will be a matter of an institutional projection of the Negro in ongoing critical reflection, judgment, decision, and action.

Du Bois proposes that the assembled Negro intelligentsia begin by thinking the status—ontologically, politically, morally—of the Negro American in the United States according to reason generally and a certain form of rationality in particular. He proposes that the Negro intellectual proceed according to what he apparently understands as the most fundamental and secure path of reason: that is, philosophy and the form of rationality called science. "It is necessary," he writes, that "in planning our movements, in guiding our future development, that at times we rise above the pressing, but smaller questions . . . to survey the whole question of race in human philosophy" (CR 5, para. 3). This is a theoretical, even speculative, point of view. This would be *theoria* as the reflective step that leads to a certain standing above, as from a vantage to overlook a scene or situation, to gather within perspective a horizon beyond the immediately given. From such a position one might take account of science, certainly what had been known as natural science, but also, as we shall see, what would come to be known as social science. And, in the second part of his address, he will propose a narrative that amounts to a sketch of a kind of philosophical history of the development of what he calls, with a specific sense, "races."

It should be emphasized that, for Du Bois, there is a necessity to this approach—surveying the "whole question of race" and apprehending it according to the truths of "human philosophy"—for the order of knowledge here would itself be determined by a necessity given in the order of things: "For it is certain that all human striving must recognize the hard limits of natural law, and that any striving, no matter how intense and earnest, which is against the constitution of the world, is in vain" (CR 5, para. 3). The idea is that there is a fundamental order which is or bespeaks "the constitution of the world." And, in knowledge this yields a certain truth which is given in a doctrine of natural law. Such an order, that is, can be recognized in knowledge and understanding as "the hard limits of natural law." Further, the implication for human practice is that any "striving"—as a group or collective we can suggest—must accord with such "law." That is, to fail to accord with this law and thereby be "against the constitution of the world, is vain": to be without purpose, without meaning, frivolous. This suggests already that the groups that Du Bois calls races are, in his understanding, the proper subject of historicity, of human history.

Beyond this ambulatory discourse, Du Bois declares or asserts this architectonic organization of the relation of the "constitution" of human historicity and the order of knowledge and practical action several times and at essential junctures over the course of the first two theoretical sections of the essay, those examining the concept of race and outlining a speculative narrative of the historicity of race, respectively. First, the next passage of such assertion comes at the opening of the sixth paragraph, after he has profoundly questioned the traditional concept of race as given by natural science, but yet, in the intervening fourth and fifth paragraphs, respectively, he proposes to specify anew and in different terms a proper conception of race. "If this be true, then the history of the world is the history, not of individuals, but of groups, not of nations, but of races, and he who ignores or seeks to override the race idea in human history ignores and overrides the central thought of all history." Second, as the first sentence of the seventh paragraph, just before he will turn, in the eighth paragraph, to directly characterize the organization of races in his contemporary moment according to his own conception of race, he declares: "Turning to real history, there can be no doubt, first, as to the widespread, nay, universal, prevalence of the race idea, the race spirit, the race ideal, and as to its efficiency as the vastest and most ingenious invention of human progress." A few lines later he goes on to describe it as "this ancient instrument of progress." He concludes that seventh paragraph with the claim that the contrary idea, often held by the Negro American, "can not be established by a careful consideration of history." Third, as he turns in the eleventh paragraph to directly address his guiding concern, which will in fact be the topic of the entire closing theoretical section of the essay, a decision and statement about what practical course of policy and action the Negro American leadership should take in its relations with other groups in America to realize its fullest and most high historical possibility, he declares flatly to his audience of Negro intellectuals: "We cannot reverse history; we are subject to the same natural laws as other races." Thus, it can be said that these formulations articulate an abiding concern of Du Bois in this text. This concern is, in fact, one of the deepest and most abiding concerns of all of Du Bois's early work, tumbling forth repeatedly across the writings of the first two decades of his itinerary with a sort of restless urgency, from the early 1890s through to the First World War. They can perhaps be summarized in a formulation given in the fifth paragraph of the essay at hand, "The Conservation of Races": to find a path that might go some way "toward explaining the different roles which groups of men have played in Human Progress." That formulation is echoed almost exactly seven years later in the penultimate paragraph of the last chapter of *The Souls of Black Folk: Essays and Sketches*, "The Sorrow Songs" (quoted in full below, in section IV). (For, as we can confirm, Du Bois was writing the text of this closing chapter of the book across the weeks from the end of January through the first days of March 1903. One can note, for example, the letter of 10 March 1903 from Francis Fisher Browne to Du Bois acknowledging receipt of the final version of the essay and musical epigraphs for the book as a whole [Du Bois 1980a, reel 2, frames 433–518].)

To establish the most radical perspective in addressing such questions, one must take a step that is otherwise than simply an address of the "difficulties of [the] everyday." Only after one has done so could one, first, accede to "the broad knowledge and careful insight" that could provide a secure basis to "lay . . . large lines of policy and higher ideals." And then, further, one might use such general understanding to "form . . . guiding lines and boundaries in the practical difficulties of every day" (CR 5, para. 3). In this sense, to step back or to step aside is to find the means or the path to "rise above the pressing but smaller questions" of everyday maintenance, defense, and survival. Perhaps then one might be able to see or grasp and to "survey the whole question."

Since the eighteenth century, in European philosophy, this has been considered the initial gesture toward the assumption of a transcendental thought. Here we will simply remark and not attempt to adjudicate this proximity of practice. What interests us at this juncture is that by way of this gesture, Du Bois is establishing a distinct position with regard to the discussion of the Negro question. If philosophy is at issue it is on the basis of this organization of problematization and not a concern with the status of pure reason or the *phænomenon* as such (understood at once with reference to both the modern German and the ancient Greek *philosophical* thought, the *phainomenon* in the latter language, encoded in this latinate linguistic lexical reference). And, on the other face of this problematization, it must persistently be recalled that with regard to post-Enlightenment thought in general, this question in all truth arises right in the midst of the critical project and is at stake at every juncture of its elaboration.

Yet if Du Bois would propose as a thetic projection to recognize through such a shift of epistemic perspective an order of the constitution of the world that would thereby announce the determinate possibility of the Negro as a recognizable and distinct form of human being—that is to say, as a race (even in the carefully redefined sense that he will propose)—what his discourse in fact produces is a series of formulations that announce the thought of "natural" history as an essentially open structure of historical process and becoming in which there is no simple, there is no unitary "one" or absolute proper, and the capacity to name such a form of being as human is put into profound problematization. This is first of all by way of the concepts and propositional statements of his discourse. However, more fundamentally, it is also by way of the organization of the entire path of inquiry and questioning in this *text* as open to the implication of the emergence and articulation of heterogeneity and difference. At no point in "The Conservation of Races" does Du Bois attempt to foreclose the recognition and affirmation of difference. On the contrary:

the entire theoretical project is to recognize such. The essay amounts to a philosophical discourse—in the form of an appeal—that would seek to recognize sameness in the organization of the Negro as a historial entity as only the implication of the operations of difference in the "constitution" of being as temporal and thus historial process. This was a gesture as fragile and unstable as it was profound at the horizonal advent of the twentieth century. And, as we are astride the third decade of the twenty-first, so it remains.

It is here, then, finally, that Du Bois names the question that is singular to him on this occasion and which serves as the general theoretical guide for his entire discourse: "What is the real meaning of Race?"

Across the course of the main body of the text, this question is construed according to two temporalities: the present as a yield of the past (a speculative narrative of the formation of "races" and "nations" takes shape here) and the present as the form of an opening toward the future (wherein a radical dilemma of identification shows forth). That is to say, Du Bois is concerned to understand the historical present for the assembled self proclaimed leaders of the "American Negro" with regard to the "race idea." And from this twofold account will issue a specific formulation by Du Bois of the organization of the practical work of "race" leadership—the American Negro Academy as an "intellectual clearing house."

Yet if Du Bois would take over an inherited idea of race—from philosophy or science—how does that idea stand in light of a critical inquiry that would be otherwise than the received dogmas given in answer to the question "what is race?" or "what is the meaning of race"? Perhaps given in the fact that the science of "race" had been so vexed and so uncritical from its inception, Du Bois was led to first undertake a critical account of the infrastructural organization of this concept, so to speak, even before undertaking his reflection on the status of race or race differences in human history. Du Bois had to adduce a critical reflection and account of the epistemological terms by which the supposed objectivity that would be the orientation of his own inquiry—the idea or concept of race among humans—is determined within science. Specifically, his concern must be with how this idea as a general field of thought is adduced as a formal concept in the sciences of race among humans. It is necessary that he do this prior to giving any account that would purport to exhibit the operations of that which is named under this general idea in the processes of history—past, present, or future. If he cannot clarify the conceptual sense of such an objectivity he would run the risk of a certain impertinence to the task at hand or of wandering without a guide across the vast topography of a philosophical history of the human. It is to the task of a certain conceptual clarification that Du Bois turns in the next paragraph—that is, the fourth. In an epistemic sense it is the most decisive passage of thought in the entire discourse of this address.

III. THE PROBLEM OF THE CONCEPT OF RACE

When we thus come to inquire into the essential difference of races we find it hard to come at once to any definite conclusion. Many criteria of race differences have in the past been proposed, as color, hair, cranial measurements and language. And manifestly, in each of these respects, human beings differ widely. They vary in color, for instance, from the marble-like pallor of the Scandinavian to the rich, dark brown of the Zulu, passing by the creamy Slav, the yellow Chinese, the light brown Sicilian and the brown Egyptian. Men vary, too, in the texture of hair from the obstinately straight hair of the Chinese to the obstinately tufted and frizzled hair of the Bushman. In measurement of heads, again, men vary; from the broad-headed Tartar to the medium-headed European and the narrow-headed Hottentot; or, again in language, from the highly-inflected Roman tongue to the monosyllabic Chinese. All these physical characteristics are patent enough, and if they agreed with each other it would be very easy to classify mankind. Unfortunately for scientists, however, these criteria of race are most exasperatingly intermingled. Color does not agree with texture of hair, for many of the dark races have straight hair; nor does color agree with the breadth of the head, for the yellow Tartar has a broader head than the German; nor, again, has the science of language as yet succeeded in clearing up the relative authority of these various and contradictory criteria. The final word of science, so far, is that we have at least two, perhaps three, great families of human beings—the whites and Negroes, possibly the yellow race. That other races have arisen from the intermingling of the blood of these two. This broad division of the world's races which men like [Thomas Henry] Huxley and [Friedrich] Ratzel have introduced as more nearly true than the old five-race scheme of [Johann Friedrich] Blumenbach, is nothing more than an acknowledgment that, so far as purely physical characteristics are concerned, the differences between men do not explain all the differences of their history. It declares, as [Charles] Darwin himself said, that great as is the physical unlikeness of the various races of men their likenesses are greater, and upon this rests the whole scientific doctrine of Human Brotherhood. (CR 6, para. 4, personal names and brackets mine)

If the question that names the epistemic horizon of the essay "The Conservation of Races" as a whole and in terms of that order of thought that can properly be understood as historial and concerned with the supposed ontological is "the origins and destinies of races" (CR 5, para. 1), then the matter that names the order of attention in paragraph four, specifically, focused as it is on the *concept* of race in an epistemic sense on the order of thought which is theoretical, is the question of the determination of "the essential differences of races" (CR 6, para. 4). At this juncture, Du Bois's concern is more specific than the general *idea* of race. It is now tuned to the question of the *concept* as it has been operated in science—natural science in particular.

In an implicit but profound sense that would articulate an entire ontology, the thought of this concept is that a certain order of essence will determine the status and character of difference or the organization of differences among that order or form of being called human. Thus, it can be said that the concept of race as it develops in European and American thought—precisely during the time of the elaboration of the critical thought of the transcendental—produces and maintains a naive or precritical understanding of the problem of the sign or the *phænomenon* as that which organizes the very possibility of its premises. In an abstract sense it would portend to name within the form of the human an order of pure being—a pure essence that would show forth as a form of being. In a practical sense (and the other face of the abstract) it would insist, in a dogmatic fashion, on the status of a form of human being understood under the heading of the "European" (which may often, subsequently, be taken in a synonymic fashion, as a heading, as the figure of a supposed kind of human, understood as "white") as a unique and primordial dispensation within an entire system of metaphysics. And, derivatively, it would concatenate a distribution of other figures of the human in a categorical and hence hierarchical order. It is the organization of this conceptualization that Du Bois engages here in the fourth paragraph in the form in which it was operative within the sciences of the human—natural and social—at the end of the nineteenth century. And, he will question the very principle by which it has determined the concept of the object of its inquiry.

In this sense, from the outset of his discussion, Du Bois will propose the epistemological reduction of a naive ontology. And, over the subsequent paragraphs, it might be said, he will propose, even if in a schematic and (necessarily) unstable discourse, a return to an active theoretical constitution of sense and value, to the theoretical recognition of the activity of a *historial* organization of being as becoming, of emergence, perduration, and possible dimunition or dissipation. In such a thought, ideals of truth and value, if there is such, would be rendered as a form of the organization of life and living as relation—relation to the other, most simply.

However, the realization of this intervention was not and could not be a definitive one: and, this was for essential reasons. This is to say, we cannot expect that Du Bois's efforts in his engagement with this problematic could accede to a wholly uncontradictory perspective and position. Indeed, this practice can be understood to bespeak an order of dilemma that remains intractable in our own time. We still inhabit an epistemic horizon that is—in this domain of historicity—common with Du Bois. We cannot simply assume that certain dimensions of his limits are not our own. It is perhaps apposite to at least outline the contours of the difficulty noted here, for the complication shows forth not only in the discourse of Du Bois but just as fundamentally within our own practice—leaving aside the question of the limits of the "we" inscribed here. The problem, in a word, is that no discourse or practice in general can simply mark or absolutely delimit its own inhabitation of the presumption of essence—and, for essential reasons. There is no simple outside to this difficulty that must be negotiated by any reflexive, critical, or desedimentative theoretical practice. In paragraph four of "The Conservation of Races," Du Bois broaches and begins to negotiate this complex and uneven terrain layered across deeply sedimented strata of existence and forms of metaphysical inhabitation. And, now, we along with him must likewise find our way within a forbidding, indeed unforgiving, terrain and amid an "unhospitable" and discomfiting environment that is at once historical and contemporary (Spillers 2006, 7).

If Du Bois was confronted by a science that operated as if it could accede directly to the truth of its object in a transparent fashion by a reading of the mark as if the operation were a simple denotation, we confront in the history of discourses a practice that proceeds in the reverse direction with regard to its understanding of the status of the mark. In a philosophical sense, the genealogy of the concept of race from the middle of the eighteenth century through to the end of the nineteenth century remains a vexed issue. There has been a remarkable and resolute idealism in the reading of the history of thought. The immanent formation of the concept of race in European discourses and its relation to the most fundamental thought of our time to emerge therein has even into our contemporary moment been relegated to the backwater or the margins of the dominant critical historiography and core philosophical discussion. And, with reference only to what has been called the twentieth century, such disposition was maintained in the midst of a historicity whose pivotal problem would be the negotiation of a global "problem of the color line" in every sense as Du Bois had proposed—and here, we specifically include the attempted destruction of the Jews and the Roma of Europe, notably understood as the Holocaust, along with the legacies of slavery—in the Americas and on the continent of Africa—and the maintenance of the deepest structures of colonial configuration on a global scale. Thus, while the matter in its most radical sense is not so much one pertaining to the textual and discursive sources of the conceptual conundrums that the sciences presented to Du Bois—he will give us some legible traction on the matter, and we can adduce others—it remains that the order of questioning in this domain has always been to treat the problem of the concept of race as a derivative one and thus, for all intents and purposes, as a categorically secondary one. Likewise, thus, rather than recognize that the thought of the transcendental is itself historial in its possibility and becoming (something that such a thought itself in its most radical form yields as its threshold contribution), supposed critical discourse in general has too often persistently proposed a simple and naive form of transcendental reading with regard to historicity in that domain of practice, knowledge, and understanding wherein the concept of race is fundamentally at issue.

This might be understood by way of a reference to some of the most questioning thought of our time concerned with that order of being that would be the privileged example of the gathering of reason. Therein the critique of anthropologism does not extend to an explicit questioning of another order of presumptive essentialism, that of the absolute or ultimate unity of the *form* of what is at stake under the thought of the transcendental in discourses of Europe since the middle eighteenth century—except in its most formalist and linguistic dimensions of literature and other forms of "non-philosophy." Yet, without such an extension, no questioning of the persistent claim of the absolute singularity of the European *eidos* as privileged example of the privileged example ("Man" or the human) otherwise under critique can be rendered, let alone be made radical. It is this limit that accounts for the persistent ignorance within the mainstream discourses of the necessity of ongoing fundamental critical work in this area.

In our contemporary moment, it may not still occasion too much surprise if we notate here the work of Immanuel Kant, G. W. F. Hegel,

Edmund Husserl, or Martin Heidegger. (Most certainly we must note that Heidegger would specifically privilege Germany and the German language in this radical domain. Also, see further brief annotation of this thinker below.)[7]

Yet it can be shown that this problematic also remained confounded throughout the work of Michel Foucault, for example, right in the midst of his critique of the concept of "man" (Foucault 1966, 385–98, esp. 388–90; 1973, 373–86, esp. 376–78; 1999, 113–14; 1978). It perhaps yet remained unresolved in his remarkable and powerful work proposing the thought of "bio-power," which was brought to reserve by his death in the midst of its elaboration (Foucault 1980b, 2003).[8]

To take another example, though not simply one among others in my judgment, as noted above in my reference to Kant's declared protocol of the regulative use of ideas of reason, this question in its broad and fundamental sense worried Jacques Derrida from one end of his itinerary to the other: from the *mémoire* of the early 1950s, across all of the major texts of the 1960s, the engagement with Hegel that was published in the 1970s, in the re-crossings of the discourse of Heidegger in the 1980s, through the meditations on sovereignty of the 1990s and through the last years, such that in his 2002 lectures on the problematic, sovereignty, he would precisely return to the question of Kant's understanding of the interests of reason and the thought of the possible unity of such (Derrida 2003, pt. 4, 153–78; 1978c, 107–17, sec. 8; 1986; 1989, esp. chap. 6, 47–57;1990a; 1987; 1978d, 81–82, 311–12, n. 4; 1978b; 1983; 2002b, esp. 261–62; 1992; 2005). And it is still the case that the dominant receptions of Derrida's work remain for all appearances unaware of the generality and depth of this problematic therein. However, it must be noted that in the midst of the 1960s, no doubt in dialogue with Foucault's turning point text of that decade, which has come into English under the heading *The Order of Things* (Foucault 1966), in his essay "The Ends of Man," explicitly dated by Derrida to that fateful spring of 1968—in which the assassination of the Rev. Martin Luther King Jr. might be recognized as a most useful intellectual mark among possible others (for one of King's most important statements in the months prior to his death was a speech given at Carnegie Hall in New York City on February twenty-third in honor of W. E. B. Du Bois [King 1970])—in a key footnote on the place of anthropologism in Kant's architectonic, the problematic of the European example on the level that we are attempting to situate it here remains unremarked on any explicit register of the text (Derrida 1982b). The terrain here is exceedingly difficult to approach within a discussion that would question—in a manner that we would affirm—the anthropologism of postwar European thought.[9]

Thus, with these two examples as touchstone references, it might be further proposed that for all intents and purposes *none* of the most far-reaching theoretical itineraries that would announce themselves as European or derivative thereof if nothing else and which claim the legacy of a thought of the transcendental or the elaboration of a problematic of immanence in its aftermath, from the middle of the last century through to the opening decades of the current one, itineraries that we inherit, inhabit, or engage in our own time, broach our problematic in any fashion that is commensurate with what is at stake under its heading.

It can also be said a fortiori that the history of ideas and various forms of historicism—respectively (but they can easily coalesce)—remain unable to situate its problematic with regard to the most fundamental questions of philosophy and metaphysics in general.[10]

Yet the question in truth places at stake all that has gone forward in the critique of anthropologism in a manner that is more radical than has perhaps yet been understood in the discourses notated above or those that would claim them as their own in the current moment. Indeed, it concerns the unity of the historicity of the very thought in question.

Hence, in our own moment of practice, we cannot turn for assistance, except with caution, to such discourses as I have just noted here (even as we would maintain and elaborate a profound general affirmation of the problematizations and initiatives that inaugurated their respective interventions in modern thought) in the clarification of what is at stake by way of the ongoing epistemological problematization of the concept of race and the elaboration in our time of a centuries long theoretical reproblematization of the very idea of the human.[11]

It is at precisely this juncture that the example of Du Bois as a thinker—as a thinker in practice, as a thinker of practice—and the texture of his discourse—as practical epistemic bearing statements of concept-metaphor, theoretical proposition, and methodical intervention—becomes apposite for contemporary fundamental critical discourse of any kind that would address the domain of lived and historical difference of the supposed human in the orders of existence.

* * *

It is, thus, that we now attempt, simply, a passage of reception marking our incipit according to the letter of the text.

Perhaps one notices on first reflex that the idea and concept of race that Du Bois proposes to address is not given an explicit general formulation at the outset of this paragraph. And, it is not simply decidable as to why Du Bois forgoes the attempt at such. We can note, however, an essential complication that would arise from proposing such a statement. Although he must pre-comprehend the idea and concept that he would question in order to establish it as an objectivity of which he would give an account, Du Bois precisely does not wish to suggest at the outset of his inquiry—or, indeed, at any moment of this essay—that there is already given—as *a finally accomplished existent* even as idea—a thing called race. The struggle to sustain a thought of this difference of the given as limit and the given as possibility is the scene of a rhetorical torsion that is of the essence of the epistemic question at stake here. It runs throughout, every dimension, the entirety, of the essay.

And then, in the background of this pre-comprehension, is another, the necessary pre-comprehension of the pre-comprehension. This is the question: what is (the) human? Who, or what, is the human, the human being? Who, or what, are those beings gathered under the name human? What is the essential unity of the form of being called human? It is then that the specific question we are following in Du Bois's discourse announces itself. If there is the appearance of difference within such, the human as a form of being, what is its status? What is the sameness, the essence, across the apparent differences among all of the groups that are called human? What is it that makes them belong to the same order of beings? Is it only or primarily a "physical" substrate? Is it otherwise than the "physical" as a determining necessity? With regard to sameness or difference, physical or otherwise, what is the meaning of their apparitional differences?

Here, then, it can be proposed that the question of the differences among humans on the order of a thought of the whole of humankind as a unity arises within the unfolding of this latter thought and is part and parcel of its possibility. Thus, as Du Bois must begin with a pre-comprehension of the concept of race, in the same gesture he must pre-comprehend the idea or thought of the human. While manifesting a certain limitation of his questioning, in both cases it can now be said, it is yet the questions "what is race?" and "what is the human?" that are in fact on the table. In this sense, both questions take shape under the interrogative force of the occasion and the practical theoretical guide of Du Bois's labor of thought in this essay, the question "who, or what, is the Negro?" Specifically, "who, or what, is the 'American Negro'?" Then, is the Negro a race? In what sense does the human include them—especially in its devolution as the historial?[12]

Simply remarking these inexplicit questions that stand at the edge of the incipit of the letter of the text, we can now read that the titular inquiry is a question about "the essential differences of races."

The issue might be translated as the question of whether there are divisions within the unity called the human that should be understood as essential—of or pertaining to an essence? And, if there are such differences, what are they?

And, how might we come to recognize or know them? Specifically, in what way can science as a form of understanding that would claim the status of knowledge—not revelation or simple intuition, but a certain rational use of understanding to apprehend something of the organization of existence in order to gain access to such essence—be certain of its apprehension? Is such possible? And, then, the question might be specified further and more exactly: in what way has scientific inquiry approached this question?

This is already to suggest that in order to ask about the concept of race, Du Bois, along with and following the discourses of race or the sciences of the human, must have a pre-comprehension of the idea of race in general. This necessarily means that he (and we along with him, if we follow his discourse) in asking about it must place it within a certain pre-comprehension of the ontological, of presence as a form. The question is the historically inherited formulation from ancient Greek thought, organized according an emergent heading as philosophy, of logic and its elaboration as concept and conceptuality: "what is . . . ?" That is to say, it is the question of presumptive essence, a possible first question if you will, one that is of the very inaugural gesture of any traditional notion of knowledge as science. This is the classical gesture. Du Bois, as he must do and seems to wish to do, in a sense, will respect it here. For any project of knowledge, the question of essence can only be ignored; it cannot be simply avoided. This is a difficulty that Du Bois's discourse must negotiate. However, one can complicate the necessity with which it is carried or maintained in a discourse and a practice. As we shall see, Du Bois will indeed attempt to displace its position or appurtenance within a gesture of knowledge and practical understanding. He will question the naive or willful presumption of access to the simply given *real or reality* (that is, nature as an order of necessity that determines in an absolute sense the appearance of something, here the form of the human), specifying that such—if anything—is only by way of the reflexive practice of the human as a form of being (whether we call it the sign, the phenomenon, or, in his oft-used contemporary term, "ideals"), and reconstrue the ground of the production of appearance or the mark, proposing thereby a different way or form of science in order to accede to its presumed truth.

So, what is this idea of race, of the forms of difference among humans? Perhaps it can be said that there is a whole theoretical disposition sedimented here. That disposition would propose that there is an order of sensible mark ascribable to the human as a body, ostensibly given in the formal organization of the body, that can stand as a reliable (in principle, certain) basis for an act of judgment that would demarcate and recognize for science discrete groups among humans. Further, it would maintain that such order of mark is expressive of an essential order of the possibility and being of such groups (ontological possibility). Such groups would comprise so-called races among humans. (The lexical term "race" should thus be simply noted here as from the discourses of a general natural history afoot in the late seventeenth century and early eighteenth century and developed specifically with regard to the human within the philosophical discourses of the late eighteenth century and the biological discourses of the late eighteenth and early nineteenth centuries (Bernasconi 2001). The idea is then that such an order of mark may serve as a criterion for the apprehension of this essential order. Methodologically it proposes to operationalize this theory, to render the object, by recognizing within the order of the criterion separate and distinct elements or attributes of the (human) body as a mark. These would—in pluralization—be "criteria." Then, this thought would attempt to coordinate those elements distinguished, or an ensemble of such, with a category or type of human, that is, to coordinate them according to a certain sense of relative whole. The operative inquiry of science is to gather facts and information about "criteria" that would provide a basis for judgments about the existence and character of race groups. It is thus that we would stand within the opening of Du Bois's discourse in paragraph four.

Such an approach would be presumptive in its determination of the ontological status of the supposed criteria. As a lexical figure, this English word in its etymology carries us back into the Greek to *kritérion*, which entails both *kritēs* (to judge) and *krīnein* (to separate). In its semantic layers as understood in English, the word "criteria" can be thought to name an already constituted order of being and as such to serve as the basis for a claim of predication or an act of judgment. In a theoretical projection it would stand as a reference point—whether as principle, condition, standard, or rule—against which some other matter or organization of such can be evaluated. Examples of practical synonymic linguistic markers for criteria here would be standards, measures, or tests of some kind. The logic here is of the sort of presumption that would maintain a theory of the absolute integrity of the monogram, the overlapping or combining of two or more graphemes to form another that is then understood as a symbol. The sciences of race of Du Bois's time of writing presuppose an existential predicate for the concept of race, then propose to find expressions (or indications) of it, and then further to make assertorial statements about the same that would thereby and in turn (re)subsume them under the heading of a general claim about what is understood as the human as an order of being. In the productions of such a thought, above all as concept, a reckoning with the genealogical production of the so-called monogram and the fictions that would be maintained in its name, so to speak, such as the "criteria" for specifying "the essential difference of races," in order for its ontological and existential presumption to be maintained as simply given in an order of necessity must be forestalled or preemptively concluded.

Yet, to engage the discourses of science, the general authority of which he would affirm over and against revelation and simple empirically derived intuition, Du Bois must begin with them as the presumptive arbiter of any judgment of truth. In the past, the various sciences—natural or social—that would address this question have proposed "many criteria of race differences." Du Bois lists four such criteria: "color, hair, cranial measurements and language." His account throughout the fourth paragraph follows these four forms of mark within the supposed unity of the human simply and precisely as the examples of that order that would ostensibly provide a criterion of some kind by which to recognize difference of race among humans. Following, thus, the order of attention of the sciences, to attend to the given form of the object, its ostensibly manifest character, Du Bois accepts, in an initial sense, the fact of patterns of sensible difference among human groups. "And manifestly, in each of these respects, human beings differ widely.... All these physical characteristics are patent enough." So, there is an apparent order of difference among humans. There is variation within the supposed unity of this kind of being. Du Bois generally describes these differences by way of a notation of extremes and the gradations between them (at first explicit, but subsequently implicit): for example, of "color" he writes that such variation goes "from the marble-like pallor of the Scandinavian to the rich, dark brown of the Zulu, passing by the creamy Slav, the yellow Chinese, the light brown Sicilian and the brown Egyptian." After his acceptance and emphasis of the apparent fact of variation, it is this logical organization of the description that I would mark in relief in the context of our discussion, rather than the specific nominal entities or their specific characterization. This rhetorical organization constitutes a theoretical suggestion: that there are types of human and such might be susceptible to a systematic description.

And, likewise, he must cross the terrain of the presumptive logic by which such manifest criteria are understood to render a basis for judgment. This is the theory of agreement of which Du Bois, with such apparent brevity, speaks: "All these physical characteristics are patent enough, and if they agreed with each other it would be very easy to classify mankind." In theory, the elements or attributes recognized therein should be readable and interpretable as specifying a discrete physical type, that is, a certain recurrent concatenation of elements. And, then further, such types have a specific place in an entire ontological schema. Such status is then understood as organized within an entire metaphysical presumption in which a punctually given or available essence is apprehended and comprehended by science. Ostensible attribute would stand as the mark of an entire interlinked chain of more or less explicit and more or less formal presumption: that the natural organization of the physical, here given in bodily character, announces already the organization of *historial* character, the former standing as resolute indication of the latter. The relation of the physical and *historial* would thus be of an ontological order, the *historial* bespeaking thus such order of determination. Such historical character would then name the status of the human group as *historial* being within an entire metaphysics. And, in a manner that references especially the European and American eighteenth century, there would be the scientific yield of a classification, a fixed order, of the groups of the so-called human. And, it must be said, in a reference especially to the nineteenth and early twentieth centuries, it would propose to affirm an existing historical and social ordination of power, authority, and privilege. That is to say, that at its limit it would affirm the military and economic implication of the devolution of modern imperialism on a global scale.

Yet, a claim about the objective articulation of objectivity, the conceptualization of race here proposes more than simply that there is a manifestation of bodily form that should be noted. It implies most precisely the simultaneous claim that there is an order of the common-in-difference (or difference-in-common) in terms of which the putative manifest differences among humans can be rendered meaningful. Thus, although it is nothing different than the recognition of differences that we have just remarked above, it should be understood in the order of discourse and critical reflection according to a whole additional level of epistemic implication. It pertains to the unstable possibility of appearance as such, we might say.

This is because difference, if you will, cannot be understood as such under the category of a thing. Differences, in fact, are thus properly speaking a mark or value of distinction that can be recognized, if at all, only by way of an intentional act (even if such is not a sovereign act with regard to its possibility) whether of understanding in general or of a (more or less formal) project of knowledge. The movement in which differences appear cannot be named in the order of the existent as a form of presence. As such, differences named within science are the always already encoded forms of mark, in the terms of classical metaphysics, for they appear according to semiosis. We may propose that they are forms of sign. They appear, if at all, as a sign. Or, that is also to say, with reference to modern European critical thought, they are phenomenal. They are always a *phænomenon*. Thus, for science, as Du Bois engages the project and practice of such, no matter the ontological status that may be proposed for these differences, a whole theory of the operation of the sign in its apprehension of "differences of race" must be operated or proposed and elaborated. The idea of "agreement," in reference to the term that Du Bois himself operates here, is the epistemic touchstone of such epistemic necessity and the theorization that arises from it. Thus, for science or knowledge, only as signs can the apparent diversity of bodily form or character be apprehended as of the order of an essence in being or existence that supposedly divides the human into races.

The problematic named under the heading of the sign, it must be said, however, is not only that which remains excessive to a reduction to the order of the traditional idea of the physical, it also distends the determinations of metaphysics and renders the possibility of a remarking of its limits.

Let us turn again to the letter of Du Bois's text as he negotiates this terrain.

We approach here the first and most decisive gesture by which he will attempt to question the whole dominant epistemic determination of the concept of race at the end of the nineteenth century or, better, to question

ON PARAGRAPH FOUR · 33

what is at stake for him in the form of a problem for thought that is situated under its heading. He will propose that there is a radical indetermination between the order of the natural and the conventional:

> Unfortunately for scientists, however, these criteria of race are most exasperatingly intermingled. Color does not agree with texture of hair, for many of the dark races have straight hair; nor does color agree with the breadth of the head, for the yellow Tartar has a broader head than the German; nor, again, has the science of language as yet succeeded in clearing up the relative authority of these various and contradictory criteria. (CR 6, para. 4)

Du Bois herein declares that the theory of agreement operated by the sciences of race is contradicted by the possible articulation of physical characteristics among human kind. The same criteria may show within or among more than one group. Indeed, the distribution of ostensible physical attributes or forms of mark may cross the boundaries between too many of the supposed types of race to function as reliable evidence of the order of difference that is in question. By way of an account of the logical implication of the empirical understood as an order of possibility, Du Bois will declare a theoretical disjunction of the supposed categorical or given structure of reference of physical attribute and a supposed referential object, a certain implied essence of race. In the passage at hand, then, he declares that the concatenation of characteristics or "criteria," the form of mark that science would propose be recognized as an element for knowledge, does not "agree" or coordinate in such a way as to conform to (that is, function as purported physical evidence for) a claim that there are categorical distinctions within humankind as a whole. That is to say, there is no categorical or simple relation of the supposed physical mark apprehended by science and any supposed referent. A given mark may refer to an indefinite number of referents. He disjoins the supposed primordial and determining bond of the physical or natural in the production of the historical appearance of differences among humans. For Du Bois, there is no physical necessity to such a theorized relationship. And, on its deeper registers, the real complication is that such apparently heterogeneous "criteria" could manifest within any given ostensible group. That is to say, a given group is not itself of only one form of bodily organization or concatenation of physical attribute.

This logical critique is the pivotal or first turning moment in Du Bois's discourse on the *concept* of race. We can recognize such a stage of itinerary as decisive in the work of each of several figures among a configuration of thinkers whom I have elsewhere situated as Du Bois's contemporaries from the late 1880s through the turn of the century—Edmund Husserl, Sigmund Freud, Émile Durkheim, Max Weber, and Franz Boas—who were concerned with what was often thought of under the heading, in an epistemological sense, of what they understood (even in diverse ways) as consciousness and the figure of the human, as a problem for science. Here I offer only a reference to Boas's criticism in 1887 of the reductively functionalist evolutionist logic governing the classification and proposed museum presentation of artifacts from diverse human groups from around the globe by Otis T. Mason and John Wesley Powell, which he then elaborated over the next decade (Boas 1989, 57–77, esp. 61–67). However, it must be noted that in his 1894 essay "Human Faculty as Determined by Race," while affirming the critique of biological evolutionism in the understanding of human sociality, Boas nonetheless hesitated profoundly at exactly that juncture of thought in which the concept of race and the idea of the Negro were brought together in a final discussion, in that essay (Boas 1989, 221–70, esp. 268–70). (And, this hesitation was repeated a decade and a half later at the end of Boas's book-length essay *The Mind of Primitive Man* [Boas 1911]). Of an earlier generational florescence, Friedrich Nietzsche's critique in section thirteen of the second essay of *On the Genealogy of Morality*, first published in 1887, with regard to the logic of English penal reformers who proposed to ground a justification of specific practices of punishment on the idea that each technique of punitive sanction in human history was created organically for just such a purpose, should be recalled here as well (Nietzsche 1998, 52–54). This later thought is maintained even as we recall that Nietzsche's relation to a certain biologism is by no means simple, especially in those domains pertaining to the problem of the Negro as a problem for thought.

In the epistemic context of the discourses of race in which Du Bois is operating during the last years of the nineteenth century, this amounts to a nascent counter-theory of the status of physical mark, if you will. It is an opening gesture in the enunciation of a theory of radical "intermingling" on the order of the physical in the making of the human.

This figure, "intermingling," appearing here in the fourth paragraph in a determined locus and with a specific rhetorical and discursive function, should nonetheless be most profoundly understood as the general figure of Du Bois's entire theoretical production in this essay. At least I hope to show that thought of the terms of "intermingling" operates at every decisive stage of the essay. The most fundamental theoretical contribution of the essay is the proposition of "intermingling"—that is to say, in a sense that may be adduced from the discourse of Du Bois in this essay—as the very organization of historicity and historical eventuality.

I note here that this order of thought is developed across the middle paragraphs of "The Conservation of Races," especially in the speculative narrative given in the tenth paragraph. (Part II of the present study proposes an elaboration of this thought.)

While he does not state explicitly his understanding of the way in which the sciences of race current in the 1890s have proposed to resolve the question of "the relative authority of these various and contradictory criteria," he does offer a brief summary account of the outcome of their engagement. First, he simply remarks that they have failed to account for it on their own terms. It might be reasonable here then to propose that, if so, it may well be that such profusion of "intermingling" and variation could not be simply and finally comprehended by science and knowledge. There would be no principle by which this effusion could be determined in its status and regulated for understanding within science. Second, he states that the sciences have been led thus to propose a certain minimal reformulation of the theory: that instead of five races as proposed in the eighteenth century, at the end of the nineteenth century, the "final word of science, so far, is that we have at least two, perhaps three, great families of human beings." Perhaps we can elaborate Du Bois's summary statement of this new theory of the science of his day in a manner that renders his assessment of it continuous with his own new proposition of a thought of "intermingling," a thought we have already begun to adduce.

This "final word so far" of science is the revision of a concept of race that had become traditional during the nineteenth century in Europe and the United States. It was proposed, Du Bois says, by Thomas Henry Huxley and Friedrich Ratzel among others, perhaps in the wake of Charles Darwin's revolutionary proposition of a principle of natural selection as the basis for a theory of evolution (Darwin 1897 [1859]; Huxley 1896c, 1896a, 1896b; Ratzel 1896–1898). It replaced, according to Du Bois, Johann Friedrich Blumenbach's theory that had itself been proposed in the wake of Immanuel Kant's thought—elaborated during the last quarter of the eighteenth century—of teleological principle in understanding organic form (Blumenbach 2001a, 2001b, 1791; Blumenbach et al., 1865; Kant 2007b, 2001c, 2001b).[13]

The conjunction of "final" with "so far" might be understood to name the general form of the historicity of science. In a certain sense, the movement of science in its historical unfolding is such that rather than understanding its itinerary as taking the form of an approach to a simple finality in a banal or vulgar concept of science or even to an *idea* in Kant's more refined, and now traditionalized, critical sense (Kant 1998, A642/B670–A704/B732; 1997, 128–30 [5:161–63]; 2001a; 2007a), it might be more profoundly understood as on the way to another form of problem or a problem for thought, another inhabitation of problematization. The organization of its movement should be understood as the always renewed reformulation of a problematization. The realization of truth is then most fundamentally the realization of another organization of problematization for thought (Foucault 1972, 178–211, esp. 192–95, 207–8; 1997c, 119–33; 1997a; 1997b). It is in this sense that we might say, with Jacques Derrida as he draws upon Edmund Husserl's phenomenological problematization of history, of the historial and historicity in general, that a project of science, even if conceived on the order of a mathesis, is always "on the way toward its origin, instead of proceeding from it" (Derrida 1978c, 131; 1974, 141). Such a thought is quite contrary to ideas of a pure deductive principle that could guarantee the truth of a supposed exact science. Idealization is only possible by way of the change, or difference, that at once makes possible and places at stake all that might be considered articulation, rhythm, or movement for even the most staid sense of an ostensible repetition.

We may be permitted to recognize such a thought in the practices of Cecil Taylor astride the decade from the second half of the 1950s. Indeed, we would not be wont to understand Taylor formulations as addressing the principle of an idealization tendentiously elaborated in the practices among all those understood as African American, at least from the eruption, sifting, and reproduction of the traditions of sense gathered under the heading "the spiritual" across the early modern period of our era, perhaps most especially since the middle of the eighteenth century. Moreover, what Taylor formulated at 1966 with regard to a supposed anacrusis may be recognized in Du Bois's insistence in the penultimate paragraphs of both the opening chapter as well as the closing one, respectively, of *The Souls of Black Folk: Essays and Sketches*—all that he remarks as the gifts "of the spirit" given to America out of the itinerary of the Negro American (Taylor 1966; Du Bois 1903a, 12, chap. 1, para. 13; 1903b, 263, chap. 14, para. 25).

The "word" of science as Du Bois names it here might then be understood as the *truth* given or stated as science—with all of the instability of its historicity at stake within such a claim. Its truth, for Du Bois, then, may well be understood—according to the disposition on matters of historicity just noted above, according to my reading of him—as its form of problematization.

Du Bois is speaking, in the last passages of paragraph four, in the wake of actually existing science, purportedly according to its terms. The rhetorical status of this formulation as a theoretical statement is dynamic and heterogeneous: it is reportage, a constative statement, a representation of a form of epistemic statement, a report of a claim of a certain truth; however, it becomes, or is also, a vocative declaration, a performative statement, a would-be originary epistemological formulation that would announce a truth in its presentation, a claim that is itself a statement of truth. Du Bois's discourse here, thus, has a double register. He will in fact shortly append this "final word of science, so far" to the motif of "intermingling" that he has adduced in the middle stages of the paragraph. In so doing, he will have begun to propose a reformulation of the traditionalized theory of race that stood at the incipit of his discourse.

In this re-theorization, as it is announced here, the concept is reduced to the minimal form of the logic implied in a distinction on the order of essence or being as *of* existence. The claim is about existence: "that we have," as in the statement "there is," one that is on the cusp of the ontic and the ontological. Du Bois, or the theory current at the time of his inscription, begins with the ostensible fact of such, a phenomenal fact, we might say. The statement is that we have "great families of human beings." Certainly the idea of family here participates in a folk theory of kinship that is common in the America of Du Bois's time. Here it provides a theoretical concept-metaphor. Perhaps it can be shown as related to the philosophical idea of a polity as that has developed in European thought since the seventeenth century and in American thought since its inception.

The apparitional logic of the minimal comes here. It is an apparently logical form of a minimal statement of difference. We have "at least two."[14] This would be the logical minimum for a definition of the concept. The "at least" says something like "for sure." In the form of a statement on the epistemological level at which a concept acquires its organization, it joins a logical necessity, almost a hidden form of premise, to a claim about actual existence. The concept of race must—in principle, we might say—operate such a minimal distinction in order to render an objectivity that would be engaged by science.

However, then, a crucial qualification appears: "perhaps three." The "perhaps" of the qualification "perhaps three" suggests that theoretically the nominal determination of races, the number of such, is not and cannot be fixed in any ultimate sense. This "perhaps" should, perhaps, be understood as the theoretical reappearance of the thought of intermingling already announced on the epistemological horizon by Du Bois, for he will declare directly that any further elaboration of difference beyond the minimal difference of the two is by way of "intermingling." What then is the status of this "perhaps" that apparently arrives in the wake of the claim of the "two."

We can now explore the logic of this statement of Du Bois's at the end of paragraph four somewhat more closely. Ostensibly, as Du Bois recalls the theory, it could appear to claim simply that there are two categorically distinct—primordially oppositional—forms of race within the human as an order of being. But the term "perhaps" can be understood to have a dynamic and performative status here. That is to say, this statement of science is in the process of being reinscribed here in Du Bois's own theoretical production. The word "perhaps" marks at the lexical level of the discourse the status of race(s) for Du Bois: it (or they, whatever such would be) is phenomenal, with respect to consciousness in general, thus such it is for science in particular; it (or they, whatever is understood as such) is conventional with regard to practice in general and for the inhabitation of morals as such. This is to say, races—if there are such—are always otherwise than an appearance-in-itself; not only for folk perception but also for the modes of apprehension of the scientist. On the basis of this lexical appearance, the word "perhaps," it can be proposed that a whole discourse is showing forth in a nodal sense and that it can be shown to run—in all truth—throughout the whole of the essay, "The Conservation of Races." The word "perhaps" names an entire dimension of rhetorical practice in the essay that maintains a theoretical caution with regard to the determination of the status of that which is named under the heading of the concept of race. It is properly the unstable discursive register of a critical theoretical point of view. It should lead us, in turn, to hesitate before ascribing to the "two" races named as the first rhetorical claim here near the end of the fourth paragraph the status of supposed pure ontological entities or forms thereof. Or, at the very least, we should not too quickly ascribe the status of the pure—either transcendental or ontological—to the ground of their possibility. Perhaps we might then be led to adduce another order of logic inscribed with the theoretical discourse of Du Bois's subsequent statements.

Thus, while these forms of race might appear as "the two," "the two most extreme," matters might well be more complicated than are given in such an initial apparition. In the course of his assessment Du Bois will disavow the supposed ultimate pertinence of the opposition that would ostensibly organize this schema. If they were in their essence the genetic maintenance of closed, fixed, or primordial, stems, there would in theory and principle be no "perhaps," or such would have standing only according to the ineptitude or mechanical limits of science in actual practice. There is a more deeply sedimented question and paradoxical logic implied in the thought that Du Bois announces here. On what basis could the "intermingling" that Du Bois represents as a declaration of this theory occur at all? Du Bois writes: "perhaps three" and, then, the "other races have arisen from the intermingling of the blood of these two." A certain logic of the reciprocal, but asymmetrical, organization of necessity and freedom in the promulgation of sameness and difference is implied therein.

Perhaps the problematization that is here given rhetorical form as a production of Du Bois's discourse can sustain greater interest and elaboration within critical thought in our own time. How might its radicality be rendered?

If there is manifestly a concatenation of differences among humans, yet originally there were only two great physical groups of humans, then the current plethora of physical types means that there must have been a process of intermingling and intermixing of physical character in the evolution of such groups. Could the thought of this possibility, "intermingling," have led Du Bois to question the idea of the pure, of the simple, of pure being, implied in this statement of the new truth of science as given in his summary of it? Perhaps. If so, one could think with Du Bois that if there is not some absolute or absolutely given ground and categorical determination of the physical as an apparition of being, then, as the possibility of this difference, there will always have been an essential opening in or as the infrastructure of the order in question, nature (as it issues from "the constitution of the world" or is given as pure being). That is to say, there is an essential opening of the play of chance or freedom in the infrastructural organization of the order and form of being in question, here that which is understood as nature, as an order of necessity, and the human body understood as a form of such. Such an order would be historical, even evolutionary, but otherwise than a simple form of repetition. It implies a concept of nature such that a principle of freedom must be recognized as operating therein, if *principle* as a way of thought retains any status in this radical domain. There must be or will always have been an essential opening within the physical, or nature, itself (if there is such) of that which cannot be simply determined. Nature is understood to maintain within the core of its determinations an essentially open structure. Nature is historical. There is, perhaps, in this thought, an idea of a radical freedom operating within the devolution of natural history. Natural law would then be conceived as simultaneously a name for necessity and as announcing the form of an essentially open structure of possibility. Rather than the thought of a categorical duality exhibiting an inexorable logic of absolute predetermination, it is a thought of this opening and the possibilities that could be understood to unfold according to its movement that begins to emerge into thematic relief, if not full propositional configuration, in this closing stage of the fourth paragraph. As a theoretical proposition, it can be placed under the heading "intermingling." And the logic of this nodal thought will be borne out later in the essay, in the tenth paragraph, when Du Bois adduces a capsule speculative narrative of the historical process by which human difference unfolds: one of the two major motifs of that narrative is a process that Du Bois describes as the "breaking down of physical barriers" between human groups (CR 9, para. 10). (See part II for annotation on this paragraph.) The critical or desedimentative logic of this intervention has already been produced by Du Bois in the middle stages of this paragraph in his questioning of the logic of the traditional theory of race. The logical disjoining of the physical mark, and the scientific attribution of its meaning, opens a conceptual space for a rethinking of the possibility of the physical mark itself. Here, in the last lines of the paragraph, we are in the midst of the affirmative construal of the implication of that negative demonstration. If, with regard to linguistic distinction, some have spoken of the confusion of tongues as a result of the loss of divine ordination, then with regard to the play of that mark of physical difference among the human called racial by nineteenth-century science, Du Bois describes a confusion of marks and the play of differences as its root or essential structure.[15] The possibility of this confusion points us toward the next theoretical implication of Du Bois's thought of "intermingling."

That is to say, if such question, the possibility of "intermingling" as proposing the thought of a radical freedom in the order of necessity supposed in traditional theories of race, is one track by which Du Bois's discourse shows its theoretical perspicacity, that very same possibility points to another dimension of the logic of sameness and difference, by which those traditional theories are undone here. For the effusion and confusion of differences yielded by way of intermingling also suggests, paradoxically perhaps, the thought of a dimension of the common or the same that would stand as an unconditional condition of the different, indeed of difference, on the order of human being. And yet that common may well be the radical order of possibility that is here named "intermingling" in Du Bois's discourse. Thus, having adduced a root possibility of the effusion of the difference of the phenomenal mark, of "criteria," that would be the apparition of race within the order of the physical, Du Bois will now begin to adduce from the same order of radical possibility a dimension of the common among humankind.

Du Bois, then, in these last sentences of paragraph four, construes the general epistemological implication of this new formulation of a theory of race. It is, indeed, an "acknowledgement" within the current mainstream theories of race that difference in the physical appearance of humans does not explain the historical apparition of human groups. Du Bois recognizes it as naming a distanciation of the supposed link of an order of unconditional necessity and an order of institution, the latter comprising the historical as conventional. It affirms a thought of the disjunction of the physical and the metaphysical on the plane of the historial—as the appearances of "the differences of their history" among humans—*for* science. And, it "declares"—although we might say in our critical reinscription that in all actuality it only implies, while for Du Bois in the midst of his theoretical performance it is a declaration—that the "purely" physical "likenesses" of men are greater than their physical "unlikeness." This is to say that, even at the level of the physical—here in the context of a theory of the genetic possibility of the noumenon by way of the logic of the appearance of the phenomenon—the order of the common "is" the more fundamental order in a conception of the human in general in the domain of the nineteenth-century discourses of race. Without this essential infrastructure of the same or the common on the order of the "purely physical," the differentiation that would be supposed as among or within the so-called human and called by the name race would have no status for science, could not appear as such. An order of the common would be essential on the level of the "purely physical" in order for "intermingling" in Du Bois's terms to be possible. Yet this essence of the common, here, can only be, perhaps paradoxically, the general possibility of "intermingling" (interbreeding or the production of fertile offspring in the languages of eighteenth-century sciences of race in Europe and the Americas). Which is to say, if there would be a common on the order of the human as a form of being, of the natural order of such, then a movement of "intermingling" will always have been its general condition of possibility. This thought of the common structure of differential articulation can thus be understood as a premise of the logic that guides Du Bois's twofold theoretical statement here: first, that physical difference among humans are intermingled such that they cannot be coherently understood by science to explain historical difference and, second, that physical sameness across supposed race differences is greater than physical difference across that same order of differences.

It must be underscored here that it is the rhetorically secondary formulation that is indeed the affirmative one of this twofold statement. And, in an epistemic sense, the whole enunciation proposes an ontological statement and not simply a logical or statistical one. Despite Darwin's own ambivalent statements in this domain (Darwin 1896), that of a debate about the "origins and destinies of races" among humans, Du Bois invokes his authority: "It declares, as Darwin himself said, that great as is the physical unlikeness of the various races of men their likenesses are greater" (CR 6, para. 4, [but note for context the full paragraph quotation at the head of this section of part I]). Du Bois proclaims the unity of the human on a basis that would be different than the kind typically claimed by the African American intelligentsia at the end of the nineteenth century. Epistemically his basis is philosophical (and scientific and secular) instead of theological (and religious and sacred).

This would be a distinction, for example, that would mark the epistemic space defining the relation of Du Bois's discourse to that of Alexander Crummell, perhaps the most respected of the auditors of this address on the occasion of its delivery. Alfred Moss attributes to Alexander Crummell, in part—the notation by Moss's text appears to represent it as a stenographic transcription—the following statement, or at least its sense, at the founding meeting of the American Negro Academy in discussion of Du Bois's paper: that "race was a divinely ordained category of human existence" (Moss 1981, 51). Moss indicates that this position was put forward by Crummel, with Matthew Anderson indicating the same, in a challenge to William S. Scarborough's worry in reply to Du Bois's paper that he could not "'conceive of two races ... equal in every particular, living side by side, without intermingling'" (Moss 1981, 50). And Moss's account shows how Crummell's status in the moment of the founding of the Academy, as the elderly father figure, was recognized throughout the process of its organization and especially in his election as its first president at this founding meeting (Moss 1981 24, 33, 38, 44–45, 48–51, 54–55). Wilson J. Moses confounds this difference between Crummell's theological premise and Du Bois's explicit theoretical displacement of such (Moses 1989, 264–65; 1993, 284ff.).[16] (In this sense, in his relation to Crummell, Du Bois's intervention should be understood as a paleonymic practice in which a new thought in its incipit must be announced under the heading of the old.

Theoretically, the idea here is a certain thought of "intermingling," the differential concatenation of sameness and difference within the order of the "purely physical" in which a certain sameness is announced paradoxically only as the yield of an order in which a radical disarticulation of the pure will always have been its mark. Or, alternatively stated, the thought of a certain sameness among the order of being called the human is, in turn, rooted in the general possibility of "intermingling." It is the appearance of the common in the form of the order of being called human as an organization of the radical possibility of difference. Upon this possibility of intermingling, perhaps paradoxically, science can name likeness. Du Bois then summarizes this thought as an ideological or truthful presentation of science: "upon this," this paradoxical thought of sameness, "rests the whole scientific doctrine of Human Brotherhood" (CR 6, para. 4).[17]

IV. ANOTHER PROBLEMATIZATION

If the ultimate theoretical concern, as announced on an epistemic level, is to adduce an answer to the question of what constitutes the apparent historical differences among humans, then under the impress of the critique of its logic that Du Bois gives in the fourth paragraph, the traditional concept of race has been exposed as incoherent and incapable of naming a constitutive order of determination. Du Bois has proposed that if there is such as that which has been called race in the traditional sense of the science of his day, it would be otherwise than physical. Or, perhaps it can be put in more general theoretical and epistemological terms: that which is named under the concept of race in the traditional sense, in the sense given by science, specifically the science of nature, is nothing in itself. That which is asked about in this question, in a certain sense, thus escapes the pertinence of the traditional sense of the question of essence, "what is . . . ?" What is at issue under the heading of the concept of race cannot give an answer to that question with a full, final, certain or ultimate judgment—at least not in any immediate sense, not with an already given, or pre-comprehended, determination. This is perhaps the most sedimented dimension of the epistemic horizon in which the problem that Du Bois is addressing is situated.

Yet Du Bois proposes that there is nonetheless an order of organization of difference among humans that can and should be recognized by science. For him, such an order can still be understood (at least in the register of his formulation that is first apparent) as constitutive of historical differences among humans. And, it still should be placed under the conceptual heading of race.

Yet the status of the presumption of essence within the concept as proposed by Du Bois has begun to shift from a presupposed stable theoretical position, from a constitutive premise, to take on another organization, as a form of question, the form of another problematization for thought. If in the traditional conceptualization race is a thing in itself that can be apprehended by the senses and understood by science, then after Du Bois's critique in the fourth paragraph, if that which has been understood under the heading race is anything at all, it should certainly be understood as nothing *in itself.* If one would be able to recognize an order of being that would constitute historical differences among humans, then its status would yet be that of something that can be apprehended as an existent only in its appearance according to the forms of historicity that can be adduced within the norms of a performative practice of knowledge—that is, a science that is a practice of interpretation, in its inception and in its ultimate implication. In the language of critical philosophy, if there is race, it is at best a phenomenon. The problematization then acquires another theoretical articulation. How does one recognize such difference within science? How does one conceptualize it? According to what "criteria" might a certain kind of knowledge still demarcate and recognize a specific form of historical entity among humans that one might call race?

In the epistemic space opened by his critical account of that which was called race in the science of his time, Du Bois will propose a different ground for understanding the supposed historical differences among humans. That is to say, even as he continues to use the term and concept of race, in his construal Du Bois begins to attempt a shift of the articulation of such difference onto a different order of epistemological distinction—and, indeed, in its eventuality, to announce a different theoretical organization of this epistemic terrain. The thought of this other organization of epistemic ground in the understanding of "historical differences" among "men" is the most deeply sedimented theoretical movement in Du Bois's essay. And, the organization, that is the distribution of thetic force and metaphoric emplacement in its promulgation, is the most unstable and the least decisive of the theoretical productions across the whole of the essay. And yet, it remains a contribution on a fundamental level within the discourses of the Negro and the sciences of the human at the turn of the twentieth century. And, further, it remains of the greatest import for understanding the implication of Du Bois's thought in this essay for our contemporary situation and perhaps for thought beyond its horizon. For, as I have already remarked, it can be shown that the dilemmas and paradoxes negotiated in Du Bois's discourse at this conjuncture are of a fundamental sort in general, confounding modern thought from the era of the Enlightenment right down to the opening decades of the twenty-first century and perhaps beyond.

Let us turn, then, to the letter of the fifth paragraph of this essay and attempt to outline its course of problematization.

> Although the wonderful developments of human history teach that the grosser physical differences of color, hair and bone go but a short way toward explaining the different roles which groups of men have played in Human Progress, yet there are differences—subtle, delicate and elusive, though they may be—which have silently but definitely separated men into groups. While these subtle forces have generally followed the natural cleavage of common blood, descent and physical peculiarities, they have at other times swept across and ignored these. At all times, however, they have divided human beings into races, which, while they perhaps transcend scientific definition, nevertheless, are clearly defined to the eye of the Historian and Sociologist. (CR 6–7, para. 5)

The guiding theoretical question of the essay as a whole has been restated here, in the subordinate clause of the opening sentence. The problematic is to explain "the different roles which groups of men have played in Human Progress." And here, Du Bois also restates the *truth* that he has adduced in the fourth paragraph: that physical difference cannot explain historical difference in the scientific understanding of differences among humans. But the central theoretical premise of the essay as a whole has also been restated here, in the ordinate clause of this sentence: "yet there are differences... which have silently but definitely separated men into groups." This is a restatement, here as premise, of the thesis of the second paragraph: "that human beings are divided into races." Yet, while the epistemic terrain on which this thesis reappears remains the same in the broadest sense—we are still addressing the problematization named under the heading of race and according to its order of question—the ground in question has been reworked by a certain labor of desedimentation in the course of the fourth paragraph such that it is not and cannot be thought as simply the same. This labor has yielded new soil, so to speak; a shifting in the organization of theoretical mark as given in a traditional concept of race has been set afoot. The character of the premise (or claim, or supposition and judgment) has begun to shift. The organization of its thetic status, distribution, and concatenation have all undergone a certain shifting and sliding such that Du Bois's claim or judgment at this stage of his discourse "that there are differences" which have "definitely separated men into groups" cannot, even rhetorically, be understood in the manner by which one might first apprehend the discursive appearance of such a statement in the second paragraph of the essay (that is, unless one disavows critical reflection itself in the course of this apprehension).

However, this has simply yielded *another form of this problematization*.

If the difference among humans that has been understood under the heading of race cannot be recognized by science according to the apparition of the physical mark, and, yet, if nonetheless one would maintain that *there is* (in the sense of the question noted above as traditions of philosophical questioning, from canonical ancient Greek thought, within modern philosophy as science) such an order of difference, how then can such difference be apprehended and understood within science and knowledge in general?

The question remains one of the determination of ground. Du Bois's restatement of this problematic retains the problem of knowledge given in the tradition, but following upon the desedimentative work of the fourth paragraph, he proposes a slight but nonetheless fundamental (and perhaps decisive) redistribution of theoretical force in his attempt to determine the organization of ground for a new conceptualization of race. There are, he says, "subtle, delicate and elusive" differences that have operated "silently" in history, distinguishing groups among humankind. In these formulations he still maintains a discourse that cannot in all truth be rendered as different in the topographical organization of its semantic statements with regard to traditional discourses of race and, specifically, with regard to the Negro. Yet from the very next sentence he begins to put a certain pressure on the sedimented lines of this continuity, and its elaboration can be shown to stretch and distend the organization of traditional theoretical concatenations. Thus, a certain dynamic spacing begins to form in an epistemological sense, here of the concept of race, which sets afoot an ensemble of discrete disjunctures within the theoretical registers of the epistemic order that would by its own determination of principle seem to decide the limits of his thought.

While "blood, descent and physical peculiarities" "*generally*" mark the lines of such supposed differences, their implication for Du Bois should not be understood as a categorical determination (my emphasis). The letter of Du Bois's text, both the stated and the unstated, leads us to understand "generally" here to mean precisely *not always*, for Du Bois proceeds to declare in this same sentence: "they have at other times swept across and ignored these." Thus, the ostensibly given of human existence that is of a natural order, what Du Bois described herein as "the natural cleavage of common blood, descent and physical peculiarities," should not be understood to be the manifest of an order of absolute determination. We can propose that while they might well be a condition of another order of differences among humans, historical difference, according to Du Bois's discourse here, while they might well be a necessary condition (even in their indetermination), they are not a sufficient condition, for they can be "swept across and ignored" by the movements of history. A certain exorbitance to condition begins to show its affirmative theoretical face here. The natural order of things, we can now say, would itself be one composed of objectivities whose bearing would be determined according to a more radical order of historicity. This critical delimitation maintains the same register of conceptual and theoretical hesitation that we saw Du Bois announce in the fourth paragraph, but here it begins to take on an affirmative and assertorial form.

Yet the "subtle forces" of history, the "subtle, delicate and elusive" differences "which have silently but definitely separated men into groups," while *not always* following a pattern of physical differences among humans, has indeed for Du Bois, nonetheless, *always*, "at all times," "divided human beings into races."

Might not this conjunction of indeterminate determination and determinate indetermination exhibit the asymmetrical reciprocity of sameness and difference that we began to adduce in our reading of the last stages of the fourth paragraph?

This whole thought then allows us to pose a twofold question. First, what is the status in an ontological sense of the "subtle forces" or "differences" that produce the differences among humans that Du Bois still wishes to place under the heading of the concept of race? And, second, how is knowledge of such an order of "subtle forces" and "differences" possible: this is to ask, in the discursive context at hand, what are the forms of "criteria" by which it can be apprehended by science?

With regard to the status of these "forces" or "differences," Du Bois answers almost immediately that "they perhaps transcend scientific definition." According to his statement, they are not a simply given form of existent. If these "forces" or "differences" have phenomenal status, it is not that of a simple, or simply given, object for thought. Indeed, that which he calls "forces" and "differences" in the opening sentence of the fifth paragraph he immediately describes as "silently" rendering their effects; they would remain almost nonsensible, almost beyond objectivity, almost beyond representation. They are not themselves an existent or an order of being whose being would be simply and directly questionable. They are not a simple thing in general in any sense. In the philosophical sense of the term, ancient or modern, they are not an essence as such. They do not arise from or arrive at an order of pure essential being. In the terms of the questions of science, in the modern sense, they should not be conceived as a simple predetermined structure of necessity under the heading of nature. They are not simple or a one in any sense. For all appearances, the movement of "subtle forces" and "differences" that he proposes for thought—in all its thetic brevity—in the fifth paragraph cannot be made to answer simply and directly to the question "what is? . . . , " even as Du Bois will attempt in the next paragraph to give a summary answer to the question "what . . . is a race?"

If his thetic insistence upon a certain appearance, or better apparitional effects, of difference—as "differences"—is apt to lead us to think that Du Bois is attempting in the fifth paragraph to name an order of existence that is simply present and available for thought, we must nonetheless recognize that not only does he describe even such appearance as "subtle, delicate and elusive," the theoretical register of his discourse (beyond the semantic) suggests that the status of what is at issue would be something other than a present form of being.

We might then remark the respective orders of a movement of "differences" or "subtle forces," on the one hand, and the definite announcement of historical separation or division within the form of being understood as human, on the other.

The former pertaining to the thought of paragraph five will be given its theoretical elaboration presently. The latter will be addressed below as the thought of paragraph six, where it is formulated in positive terms by Du Bois; for in the fifth, in all truth, only a declaration of its possibility is made.

Yet a critical recognition of these two different levels of theoretical reference in Du Bois's discourse of the fifth and sixth paragraphs is decisive for any approach to a reading of the essay as a whole. This critical judgment, which I propose here in a thetic manner, can only be shown and justified in the work of an elaboration—by the possibilities in thought bequeathed by the path that is thereby opened.

At this juncture let us attempt to proceed a step further in our reception of Du Bois's thought amidst the middle passage of the fifth paragraph.

Du Bois proposes here the thought of a process, a movement, a dynamic infrastructure organizing an ensemblic relation of forces. The dynamic and relative character of the movement that Du Bois proposes in this theoretical statement is the most difficult and unstable determination within his intervention in this essay on the terrain of the problematic of the concept of race. At the semantic level of the word, Du Bois operates an ambiguous use of the terms "differences" and "forces." He uses them as synonyms. As a word, the former can be understood to declare a nominal referent: *differences*, with an *s*. If so, then the thought of this word would presume what it needs to explain—whence "differences" as objectivity emerge, unfold, and function. But, the rhetorical deployment of these two terms can be understood as a form of synonymia in which each gesture of thought must in turn be taken up as a stage within a discourse, an open-ended and always relative sense of whole. If that is so, then the term "differences" can be read as a figure in the operation of Du Bois's theoretical discourse. We might then be led to propose that Du Bois's formulation yields a thought of the irreducible asymmetrical reciprocity of difference(s). In this sense, there will always already have been the force of differences or differences of force. There will always have been a movement of differential forces—all the way down—so to speak. It would be a movement in which differences unfold in a manner that is always already otherwise than any possible predetermination or pre-comprehended necessity. As such, there will always have been a certain freedom or chance in the movement of differences according to the conceptualization of what is at stake that Du Bois's thought in discourse implies here, although he does not proffer a proper name for it. And, its irruptive freedom would be such that the crossing of boundaries of any kind, especially those that science has understood as natural—of nature—is an essential possibility. In this sense, "intermingling" and intermixture would be the general structure or infrastructure of this movement. Such a movement of "subtle forces" and "differences" would be almost, or perhaps essentially, beyond given forms of objectivity. As such they will have been essentially *otherwise* than a simple essence and *of* the movement of the historial determination of being (as existence, as historical being), a movement which might yet well remain nothing in itself. It will always have been such that "silently but definitely separated men into groups."

Approximately seven and a half years later, in the essay "Sociology Hesitant," a text that remained unpublished during his lifetime, Du Bois wrote again across this order of fundamental problematic. As the matter of the discourse of this essay poses its own exceedingly rich internal horizon of problematization, I recollect the text at length, for the thought in the passage at hand, the closing stage of that essay, must be apprehended as a kind of whole.

> What then is the future path open before Sociology? It must seek a working hypothesis which will include Sociology and physics. To do this it must be provisionally assumed that this is a world of Law and Chance. That in time and space, Law covers the major part of the universe but that in significance the area left in that world to Chance is of tremendous import. In the last analysis Chance is as explicable as law: just as the Voice of God may sound behind physical law so behind Chance we place free human wills capable of undetermined choices, frankly acknowledging that in both these cases we front the humanly inexplicable. This assumption does not in the least hinder the search of natural law, it merely suspends as unproved and improbable its wilder hypotheses. . . . Finally it remains to point out that such a restatement of hypothesis involves a restatement of the bases of Sociology. Suppose now we frankly assume a realm of Chance. . . . The duty of science then is to measure carefully the limits of Chance in human conduct. That there are limits is shown by the r[h]ythm in birth and death rates and the distribution of sex; it is found further in human customs and laws, the form of government, the laws of trade and even in charity and ethics. As however we rise in the realm of conduct we note a primary and a secondary r[h]ythm. A primary r[h]ythm depending as we have indicated on physical forces and physical law; but within this appears again and again a secondary r[h]yrhm which while presenting nearly the same uniformity as the first, differs from it in its more or less sudden rise at a given time, in accordance with prearranged plan and prediction and in being liable to stoppage and change according to similar plan. . . . We must assume Law and Chance working in conjunction—Chance being the scientific side of inexplicable Will. Sociology then, is the Science that seeks the limits of Chance in human conduct. (Du Bois 2015g 277–78, paras. 22, 25–28, brackets mine; 1980b)

We can mark the intimate theoretical apposition of "Sociology Hesitant" to "The Conservation of Races." That is to say, first, that in the unpublished text of 1904–1905, Du Bois affirmed precisely the dynamic and inextricably interwoven orders of a certain necessity and liberty or freedom in the production of human being as existence that we have begun to recognize in his earliest formulations of this problematic, as we have begun to find it in the early paragraphs of the early 1897 essay.

Yet, more in a more fundamental sense, we might elaborate the thought we have formulated by way of this conjoined reference on the terms of our contemporary horizon as a radical thought of difference and relation.

From, or within, the open structure, or better dynamic infrastructure, to construe Du Bois's statements, as to the existence of the human, as we have recognized such locution in "The Conservation of Races," arises an asymmetrical reciprocity of sameness and difference, indeed a complex concatenation of sameness and difference. On the one hand, we can speak of the double(d) (infra)structure of *a general order of the same*, a physical structure in the ontological sense (shall we say an organized entity), in which all humans are understood as more alike than different, and *a specific level of difference*, a physical structure in the morphological sense, in which humans are always marked by patterns of a peculiar concatenation of "intermingled" attribute. On the other hand, continuing to follow the logic implied by Du Bois's formulations, we can speak of the double(d) (infra) structure of *a general order of difference*, a general historical structure, that which Du Bois will construe under the heading "differences" of history (my emphasis), which he will describe as "spiritual, psychical differences," differences that in his terms give the general demarcation of human forms of being as disposed into groups, and *a specific organization of the same*, a specific historical structure, a particular and peculiar promulgation of an ensemble of "ideals" announced on the level of a collectivity.

Along this pathway, we shall later be able to propose that, for Du Bois, race, the historical form of actual differences among groups of humans announced by way of this movement of differences and "subtle forces," in the sense that he is adducing it here, is an essentially open infrastructure in which "intermingling" and intermixture is not a derivative possibility, but its most radical and definitive character.

The movement of "differences" and "forces" if there is such, *is*, perhaps, insensible. The metaphor "silent" might then be well taken as a titular figure of Du Bois's theoretical description of this process. In itself, in a manner that confounds the thought of an in-itself in the traditional modern philosophical sense of the term, this level of "the constitution of the world" (CR 5, para. 3) is not susceptible to objectivity and remains in its dynamic performativity inaccessible to representation as a form of presence.

Yet, formal or theoretical language, and perhaps language in general, must always proceed by way of the pre-comprehension of the copula. To the extent that thought, here, in particular, as philosophy and science, as knowledge, must always begin with the constituted, theoretical discourse that would not presume the status of the supposed real or reality, the noumenon, the thing in itself, or being as a present form, might declare its most fundamental thought only in the active passivity of form such as the order of language that is coded as the temporality of the future anterior. And, indeed, such active passivity names the conjoined stakes and performativity of the discourse of Du Bois and that of our own projection in a critical re-inhabitation of the terms of his practice. This labor of critical theoretical desedimentation shall remain always unfinished, open, at stake, in each instance of its promulgation. Thought addressing the status of such a movement as we have begun to adduce within and by way of Du Bois's theoretical discourse—which perhaps is something other than just one order of movement among others—is also addressing the status of limit and possibility as the configuration of its own discourse.

This whole question of the operation of possibility, here as the devolution of "differences" and "subtle forces" in the making of historicity, is one of the most deep-seated and general concerns of Du Bois's thought, certainly at the end of the nineteenth century but, in truth, throughout his entire itinerary.

The other question posed above, how knowledge of such an order of "subtle forces" and "differences"—more precisely their bearing in history—is possible, likewise raises a fundamental dimension of Du Bois's thought in general. The answer given by Du Bois *assumes the critique of the status of mark* by which the differences among the human might be understood that he carried out over the course of the fourth paragraph. How, then, can the differential movement theorized in a nascent manner in the first two sentences of paragraph five be recognized and known by science or some other practice of knowledge? As something other than a punctually present form or existent, the movement in question cannot be grasped by natural science, at least not traditional natural science, not a science that would assume the practical accessibility of the natural as a given order of objectivity. And it must be recalled that it was such a science, proposed in the sciences of race of the eighteenth and nineteenth centuries, that Du Bois confronted in these opening paragraphs of "The Conservation of Races."

If one supposes that there is a manifestation of such a movement of forces and differences, then its objectivity for knowledge would be both indirect and partial. Its apparition will always have been on the order of a "secondary rhythm." (See the 1905 essay "Sociology Hesitant," quoted above, for the full passage in question [Du Bois 2015g].) This is to say, that it can be named, if at all, only by way of an epistemological judgment that would be always *both* retrospective *and* productive on the level of a theoretical claim. It would never arrive on the mark—its mark. The theoretical action must performatively gather the differential terms of reference by which a relation could be remarked announcing a whole that cannot be assumed as simply constatively given. And, paradoxically, its truth would show forth, if at all, not as the final promulgation of a statement about an ostensible given, but a theoretical form of understanding of an order of name for historical limit and possibility. In this sense a name would always be already historical. There would be only name*s*, no name in the absolute singular, no so-called proper names. It would be a theory of the sense of the historicity of a mark or of differences within the field of the historically given.

Such an order of difference, showing forth as differences in the devolution of historicity among humans, would manifest, if at all, another order of "criteria"—criteria that would appear otherwise than the naturally given—and would require another form of knowledge. Du Bois will call the latter "the eye of the Historian and the Sociologist." While these "subtle forces" or differences escape the sciences of nature, their non-absolute yet determinate historical effects, "races" in Du Bois's ambivalent reformulation of the term, only critically defined so far in his essay (up to paragraph five), "they . . . are clearly defined to the eye of the Historian and Sociologist." This is to say that Du Bois's proposition of a certain status and form of knowledge maintains the epistemological shift he has already proposed in his critical account of the objectivity in question. If the objectivity must be understood as other than a thing in itself, then it must be apprehended according to a mode of knowledge in which the act of knowing is an activity of a distinct kind: a theoretical judgment that would arise in the course of an interpretation. Such an act might well amount to a kind of understanding (otherwise than a sensory perception). In speaking of the "eye" by which such an activity would be carried out, Du Bois has made thematic that the objectivity is an appearance that can be recognized only according to certain forms and norms of knowledge. While it remains that Du Bois will insist "there is" such as race, that it, we might say, is not simply reducible to the status of a phantom or a spectre, it is an appearance that acquires its objectivity *for* a certain mode of knowledge. The practice of knowledge in this domain would be active, productive, and even performative. To engage it one must practice a mode of knowing that would make understanding, interpretation, and judgment its sine qua non. These are, in all truth, touchstone concepts in Du Bois's work of the turn of the century. And they register here the unstable line of the scientist and the advocate, even as Du Bois will thematize a certain objectivity (sometimes as impartiality) and a notion of rigour as theoretical ideals almost everywhere in his work at this stage of his itinerary.

The general status of interpretation in Du Bois's approach to the study of the human, even if only given under the heading of an approach to the Negro as a figure of the human, should be remarked, even if only in brief. While committed to an ensemble of empirical methodologies (from the archival to the statistical, from the photographic to the anthropological [notably as the study of human anatomy and physiology], from the historiographical to the ethnographic), Du Bois theoretically announced and practiced as his preeminent commitment an approach to the scientific study of the social that can properly be understood as an interpretive one. He explicitly placed it as the capstone of the approach that he outlined in his first programmatic text, "The Study of the Negro Problems," which was initially presented as a public lecture in November 1897, nine months after the essay we are considering here, "The Conservation of Races." Sketching the nodal points of the general program for the study of the Negro that he is proposing to the American Academy of Political and Social Science, Du Bois wrote:

> The study of the Negro as a social group may be, for convenience, divided into four not exactly logical but seemingly most practicable divisions, viz: 1. Historical study, 2. Statistical investigation, 3. Anthropological measurement, 4. Sociological interpretation." (Du Bois 1898, 18, para. 38; 2015i, 90, para. 38)

And then, several paragraphs later, in his description of "the fourth division," he indicates—even as he does not declare it—that its position in his outline is the result of a theoretical decision and is not as epistemologically arbitrary as his initial announcement could perhaps lead one to surmise.

> The fourth division of this investigation is sociological interpretation; it should include the arrangement and interpretation of historical and statistical matter in the light of the experience of other nations and other ages; it should aim to study those finer manifestations of social life which history can but mention and which statistics can not count, such as the expression of Negro life as found in their hundred newspapers, their considerable literature, their music and folklore and their germ of aesthetic life—in fine, in all the movements and customs among them that manifest the existence of a distinct social mind. (Du Bois 1898, 20, para. 42; 2015i, 92, para. 42)[18]

Interpretation certainly should (a) make possible theoretical judgments of the given, as in Du Bois's statement that it would undertake the "arrangement and interpretation of historical and statistical matter" pertaining to the American Negro in a global and comparative frame of reference. But, it should (b) also proceed beyond a reference to the apparently given, by way of a certain work of understanding that would at its limit of demand and possibility organize itself as a performative practice: "to study those finer manifestations of social life which history can but mention and statistics can not count." The status of the problem of interpretation in this sense within Du Bois's own practice is shown by the fact that its primary exemplification is given as the whole of his justly most famous text, *The Souls of Black Folk: Essays and Sketches* of 1903, which sought to show "the strange *meaning*" (my emphasis) of being an African American in the United States at the turn of the last century (Du Bois 1903c, vii, "Forethought," para. 1).

In this sense, if his work of the two decades surrounding the turn of the twentieth century is understood in the integral sense of its project, Du Bois should thereby be properly placed among the configuration of thinkers—Max Weber, Émile Durkheim, Franz Boas, Edmund Husserl, Sigmund Freud—who were so definitive at the turn of the twentieth century in problematizing the status of objectivity in the study of the human and thus in announcing an interpretive problematic within the founding moments of the disciplinization of the human sciences.

And the early theoretical position given to the problem of judgment and interpretation is sustained across Du Bois's itinerary even as he is drawn to think and act beyond its original frame as a project in the human sciences and his concerns are recast on a more explicit global historical level in both *Darkwater: Voices from Within the Veil* (Du Bois

1975a, 1920), published in 1920 in the immediate aftermath of the First World War, and *Black Reconstruction: An Essay toward a History of the Part Which Black Folk Played in the Attempt to Reconstruct Democracy in America, 1860–1880*, the magisterial rethinking of the project of "America" first published in 1935 during the difficult closing half-decade of the interwar years (Du Bois 1976a, 1935). And it remains, to take an example that is not one among others, in the study *The World and Africa: An Inquiry into the Part Which Africa has Played in World History*, published in 1947 in the aftermath of the Second World War (Du Bois 1976b, 1947).

This is a figuration of Du Bois that remains, at best, in ambiguous profile for critical thought in our time even as the question of the status of the ostensible objectivity he announces in the formulation "those finer manifestations of social life which history can but mention and which statistics can not count" returns anew and a fortiori, perhaps in a perennial manner, and runs across the whole of our contemporary scene. However, I can affirm, here, a felicitous formulation by Hortense Spillers in a signal essay, "The Idea of Black Culture," as a parallel reference to how I understand Du Bois's thought here. In a discussion of the ways in which the problematization as given in the title of her essay might be set aside under the aegis of contemporary critiques of identification, she writes of a certain exorbitance that remains at issue. It pertains to "the everyday requirements of a fictitious subject, to the unrecordable and indeterminate excesses of the social fabric, and to the memorial structure that writes itself into human activity from language acquisition to the conscious pursuit and expression of the arts" (Spillers 2006, 10).

So, what is the implication for a concept and theory of race of this thought of a movement of differential forces whose effects must be recognized and understood by way of a productive labor of interpretation of the mark (the sign, the phenomenon, or the social fact)?

If the general theoretical task that Du Bois has posed for himself, as in the opening sentence of paragraph five, is to find or develop an explanation of "the different roles which groups of men have played in Human Progress," then in the opening sentence of paragraph six, Du Bois proffers his response to that question, a theory of historical eventuality in the devolution of human groups. It is, properly speaking, a speculative proposition. It is a theory of historicity that is built upon his revision of the concept of race in paragraphs four and five.

If this be true, then the history of the world is the history, not of individuals, but of groups, not of nations, but of races, and he who ignores or seeks to override the race idea in human history ignores and overrides the central thought of all history. What, then, is a race? It is a vast family of human beings, generally of common blood and language, always of common history, traditions and impulses, who are both voluntarily and involuntarily striving together for the accomplishment of certain more or less vividly conceived ideals of life. (CR 7, para. 6)

Historical differences unfold as the playing out of a dynamic movement of "differences" and "subtle forces," an order of indeterminate determinations that makes possible the concatenation of humans into groups. And, Du Bois still calls such groups by the old name "races."

While in other passages of this essay and other texts Du Bois will on occasion operate the terms "race" and "nation" as synonyms (as I noted above), here in paragraph six he gives them distinct theoretical determinations. The subject of history must be distinguished from two different orders—that of the "individual," as in person, and that of the "nation," as in a geopolitical entity within a worldwide horizon. The "true" subject of history within the horizon of "world history" is here for Du Bois on the level "not of individuals, but groups, not of nations, but of races." The polemical horizon is of import. It is the "American" horizon of the United States. Du Bois is theoretically rejecting *both* its individualism *and* the idea that the Negro American is already circumscribed entirely within its horizon as given. Du Bois's concern is not so much to insist upon the discrete reduction of the Negro in America to a subnational horizon, even as it specifies a theory of the terms of relations on the level of the group itself and on the level of the national, as it is to posit the possibility of an inscription of such a group into an international, global, and comparative horizon of history.

And the problem of theoretical language that we have annotated according to the terms of the fifth paragraph is rearticulated on the terms of the sixth, but here a more profound dimension of the difficulty can be brought into relief. In the fifth, the problematic was whether and how a theoretical discourse might be able to speak of that which is perhaps otherwise than an order of the form of the present by yet proceeding in all necessity from the constituted and, thus, whether and how it could be commensurate in its thetic gestures with the difficulty most radically afoot in the problematization that is its own specific irruption. In the sixth, the problem can be understood as arising at the same conjuncture of ontological complication but pivoted according to another theoretical orientation. There the theoretical orientation was to a movement that would be infrastructural and sub-individual in all senses (a movement of "differences" and "forces"). Here the theoretical disposition is toward a sense of whole ("individuals," "nations," "races," humankind, "the world," "the history of the world," "all history," etc.).

It can be said that any thought of the whole, that is, any concept or theory that comprehends the objectivity in question in terms of *idea* (*eidos*, form, whole, or *telos*) must necessarily pre-comprehend its determination of essence. And such would be the problematic far beyond the discourse of Du Bois. It can be theoretically understood in the terms of post–eighteenth-century philosophical thought on the order of a certain "transcendental illusion" remarked above.

The thought as given in this phrase as indicated above is from Immanuel Kant's discussion of the unavoidable illusions of reason in the section on the "transcendental dialectic," especially its appendix, in the first critique, the response to which is given in his thought of a distinction of the "constitutive" and "regulative" use of "ideas" (Kant 1998, A643/B671–A704/B732). However, Nietzsche formulated this problematic in another register when, in *On the Genealogy of Morality* (essay 2), he proposed that any concept that would propose to summarize an entire semiotic sedimentation cannot be defined and that "only that which has no history can be defined" (Nietzsche 1998, 52–54; 1991, 37–40). Also, the matter of the language that would open the possibility of the "transcendental" *epoché* as it took shape in the discourse of Edmund Husserl is apposite (Husserl 1999, cf. secs. 49 and 59; 1969, cf. sec. 2). In this sense, Heidegger's thought of the necessary pre-comprehension of being in language and the distinction of the ontico-ontological difference opens as a reposition of this problem (Heidegger 1962, 21–64; 2000). Further, the thinking through of the constative and performative operations of the speech act in ordinary language in the work of J. L. Austin would remain apposite in a fundamental manner (Austin 1975). And yet, most extensively perhaps, it is at stake in the work of Jacques Derrida, in his formulation of the necessary production of an "ultra transcendental" thought, as he first proposed it in the early to mid-1960s, but then performatively elaborated it across the whole of his itinerary (Derrida 1978a, 66–76; 1976a). All of these problematizations from the tradition of philosophy in Europe since the late eighteenth century would be apposite to index here. And the difficulty is not at all divorced from everyday so-called natural languages.

The problematic and the risks in question do not belong only to the discourse of Du Bois. On the contrary, his negotiation is a powerful and complex example that demands another, further and ongoing, engagement in contemporary thought.

How should we understand the thought of a whole here in Du Bois's formulation of a concept of race in the sixth paragraph? If races are groups whose status—in origin and destiny—is exorbitant to a natural determination, then how can they be *defined* as such? If they are not a given in any simple sense, how then should we understand Du Bois's conceptualization of them here? On the one hand, Du Bois proposes an account of races in terms of a conceptualization of the ground of their possibility: he theorizes an essential indetermination in the movement by which they are constituted. On the other hand, he proposes a theory of the determination of their devolution, the historical order of their existence, in which he presumptively states, almost in the form of a peremptory declaration, that the eventuality of races is *telic*, organized in terms of an *idea* (even if the conditions and possibility of their realization would always remain at stake), and to that extent his discourse on history here is inscribed within a philosophical horizon: the historical is that which can be rendered meaningful. There is thus a dynamic interplay between these two theoretical gestures that remains unresolved, and perhaps unresolvable, within "The Conservation of Races." And this interplay provides the text with its most pronounced theoretical syntax—a contrapuntal rhythm of rhetorical registers—in which a persisting gesture of the scholar's humility in submitting his apparent knowledge or truth to an open and perhaps ceaseless inquiry is conjoined to the theoretician-philosopher's high-minded declaration of ultimate truths.

The central paradox that we have found in Du Bois's text can be stated here: that while Du Bois proposes his discourse in "The Conservation of Races" according to a declared principle of "conservation," what he describes or theoretically produces therein is an alogical logic (a logic that goes beyond traditional logic or a logic of noncontradiction) of "intermingling" and intermixture that would always have implied an irruptive movement of chance, of play, of freedom, of possibility—that remains, or that moves beyond, any given form of limit.

Perhaps it is here, then, that one should note that across the whole of his itinerary, despite the difficulties of its maintenance, Du Bois resolutely sustained the motif of a double or redoubled gesture—of double identification in subjectivity, of the reciprocity of doubled "ideals," of horizon as a name of the structured possibility of the illimitable. It can be understood as the thematic thought of the constituted name of a radical order—which might well be beyond order in any simple sense—of freedom and chance. Here such is named by the motific figures of difference—of the always at least and thus never only double. This is a tremendous question, running across the entirety of Du Bois's itinerary and through all the strata of his discourses.

We must, in our own discourse, if it seeks to become critical (that is, to try to give some useful, hopefully fundamental, consideration of the conditions of its own possibility), attempt to recognize both gestures of Du Bois's theoretical production here. This means understanding in what way his thought of limit is rooted in his thought of possibility and, in turn, in what way his thought of possibility is rooted in his sense of limit. If on the level that might be metaphorized as of *ground*—a movement of "differences" and "subtle forces"—Du Bois theorized an essential indetermination, that (nonetheless) yields the possibility of determination, as always different forms of such, as differences, here, on the level that can be thought by the concept-metaphor of *horizon*, he theorizes a form of determination that is in its essence indeterminate—a "striving"—always in the process of becoming, never fully given as such. These two theoretical formulations—indeterminate determination and determinate indetermination—should be understood then to remark two sides of Du Bois's thought of "the whole question of race in human philosophy" (CR 5, para. 3).

This sense of a thinking of the "whole" will be borne out later in the essay "The Conservation of Races," at the end of paragraph nine, at its conjunction with paragraph ten, marking thereby the linkage of Du Bois's account of "real" history to his production of a speculative narrative of the history of human groups in relation to "ideals of life," the phrase "this whole process" appears to account for the movement of race in history in his sense (CR 8–9, paras. 9–10).

The question of this status of the whole is the horizon of theoretical question that is elaborated as part II of this study.

For the subject of history as Du Bois would propose such here, that is to say, so-called races in the sense that he is seeking to give that term in this essay, there is an essential opening of play that remains within the horizon of its determination. It is the structure of a movement of intentionality and self-reflexivity that Du Bois calls "striving." While necessarily inscribed within the orders that give the "involuntary" of human action as determination, even as necessity perhaps, the movement that arises therein can also reinscribe such determination, perhaps of another order of necessity, within the movement of the "voluntary."

Let us examine this difficulty by considering more closely his sense of group. Du Bois uses an old and overdetermined metaphor as his title term: a "family," "a vast family." Du Bois's use of this term should not be understood as a theoretical lapse or accident, for it is itself a deeply sedimented layer within the discourses of race in general. It is of that layer of the discourses of race that comprises a concept of the body as an organized entity and the theory that places it within a genealogy. It would be the social face of a theory in which the body is understood as a figure of history. Du Bois's mobilization of this chain of concepts and the manner in which he does so threatens to subsume and overwhelm all of the desedimentative work that has been accomplished so far in his discourse in this essay. For the idea of a family as a supposed naturally determined form of relation, both vertically and horizontally, is the quintessence of the traditional theory of race that Du Bois is engaging. It threatens to redeploy all of the determinations of the naive and reductive naturalism that had guided the traditional theorization of race from the last quarter of the eighteenth century through to the end of the nineteenth.

However, the unstable sites of disjunction that I have proposed can be remarked between the thought of Du Bois and the tradition by way of a tarrying with his discourse might well be brought into some dimensional relief here—in the specific context of his operation of the concept-metaphor "family."

The idea of family for Du Bois in "The Conservation of Races" is *not* an entity whose origin would be of a simple essence, or whose substance would be a pure form of being, or whose destiny would be given by a fixed or closed order of determination. The motif of indeterminate determination that we have already adduced on the order of a movement of differential force or force of differences can be notated here as one of determinate indetermination: the interrelation of family is conceived by Du Bois here as always short of absolute or final. *Their relation is determined as an itinerary of "striving."* (This concept-metaphor, "striving," and the motif it outlines in Du Bois's thought of the 1890s and the first decade of the twentieth century is of such depth and multiplicity that it can sustain an entire engagement on its own. In that sense, the discussion in part II on the question of the illimitable is simply an opening meditation on the infrastructure of its deployment in "The Conservation of Races.") Their "striving," in his formulation, is *both* voluntary and involuntary. The ostensibly given that is named in the metaphors of "blood and language" would be only "generally" determinative, that is *not always*. The instability of the determinations and the limits of metaphor, which are given their bearing within the ensemblic movement of discourse, must be recognized here. But it can be proposed that an interpretation of the play of such effects must be construed in this context *as or in light of* the theoretical level of Du Bois's claim. Such is my proposition at this juncture of my own discourse. And, this is so no matter the radical incoherence of the metaphor of blood. And so, likewise, the idea of the latter, that is language, regardless of whether we would in another context affirm or deny its placement adjacent to the figure of the natural that is the image of "blood," thus apparently susceptible to any tendentious insistence that it operates implicitly within the latter's determinations. The theoretical pertinence of these metaphors here is that for Du Bois (first, but not only), the effectivity named by these terms remains indeterminate and limited within the historical devolution of the groups involved.[19] And thus, it can be proposed most precisely, that in Du Bois's sense the concept of "family" as the figure of "race," as a name for the order of that which will have "always" been "common," is *an order of practice*, which in all of the heterogeneity of its determinations is itself a constituted: "history, traditions and impulses."[20] In addition to a remark of their necessary polysemic structure of reference, the effects of which no theoretical discourse can control absolutely, or with which no practice could maintain a commensuration, these terms should in all propriety to Du Bois's discourse in this essay and at this stage of his itinerary be understood as names of the instituted forms of practice. Although relative in the ontological sense, such forms of institution, would have their own levels of effective, and even irreversible, determination. They are each in their own distinctive manner terms that name a self-reflexive practice. The "common" dimension of such "family" in the sixth paragraph of "The Conservation of Races," then, if anything, would be that of a certain self-reflexivity. Self-reflexivity here is then in every sense only announced in relation. Not before. Or after. In this sense then *a* race, as a kind of group, metaphorized according to an idea of family, is a constituted proposition of entity, organized as such, by its active and dynamic relation to "ideals of life," by its "striving." It would be produced in history as an always particular form of historicity and would be maintained, if at all, only as a self-reflexive practice. The negative form of the infinitesimal gap between the "voluntary" and the "involuntary" remarked above can here be given a positive formulation: self-reflexivity on the order of the group would be a critical performative inhabitation of the historical relation of determination and freedom.

Thus, in paragraph nine, once he has moved to a plane of discussion that for him is an address of "real history" as he will describe it at the beginning of paragraph seven, Du Bois will recapitulate the terms of his reconceptualization of race as we have followed it across paragraphs four through six here. Insisting, once again, that "no mere physical distinctions would really define or explain the deeper differences—the cohesiveness and continuity of these groups," and claiming that the "deeper differences are spiritual, psychical, differences—undoubtedly based on the physical, but infinitely transcending them," Du Bois proceeds to nominalize the kind of mark that could serve as the "criteria" by which to recognize and distinguish the groups he would call races in his new sense of the concept. All of those terms are figures of self-reflexivity, of intentional activity (even if not realized as in a simple arrival at a telos or final end), of instituted forms of practical activity: "a common history, common laws and religion, similar habits of thought and a conscious striving together for certain ideals of life."

At this stage of the discourse of "The Conservation of Races," it can be summarily said, Du Bois has certainly displaced the traditional understanding of the concept of race as ontological, that is, as an essence given on the order of a simple or absolute necessity within nature. It is no longer conceptualized as a closed and pre-comprehended structure of determination. Within his discourse, it has been rethought as a historical determination that arises according to a dynamic and essentially open infrastructure of becoming. The effusive dynamics of such infrastructure would in an essential sense remain, perhaps, illimitable.

Yet here is the scene of deepest difficulty for Du Bois's thought. (But, in all truth, it perhaps remains so for our own considerations, leaving open the question of the limit of the "we" inscribed here.) He would propose to practically submit the effusive possibility of such self-reflexivity in the instance—any given instance in which an actual determinate outcome is at stake—to the figure of the *one*, to the determination of the singular as a form of the absolute.

For example, citing the closing lines of Alfred, Lord Tennyson's *In Memoriam*, at the end of his speculative narrative in paragraph ten of "the whole process" that can account for the history of races in his sense, Du Bois will speak of "that 'one far off Divine event'" that would orient historical eventuality (CR 9, para. 10).[21] In "Strivings of the Negro People," in a phrase that appears only in the original essay from 1897 (and not in the revision of the essay that appears as the opening chapter in *The Souls of Black Folk: Essays and Sketches*), at the penultimate paragraph of that version of the essay, Du Bois writes of "the hope of a higher synthesis of civilization and humanity, a true progress, with which the chorus of 'Peace, good will to men,' 'May make one music as before, / But vaster,'" quoting the same poem from Tennyson at the end of his sentence (Du Bois 1897b, 197, para. 11; 2015h; also note 1903a, 10, para. 11).

Understood in its broadest reference, thus, Du Bois's epistemic situation may be formulated as one organized in terms of the most profound difficulties for thought in general in our time: this is the ensemble of paradoxes that attend the question of essence; when it pertains to the concept of the human in general; when it is a question of the respective and reciprocal status of the concept of race and the problem of the Negro as a problem for thought, the latter in all of its misapprehended apparent particularity. In a word, the gesture of a sovereign refusal of the naive presumption of essence, in all of its senses and registers, paradoxically, restitutes that presumption in its very enunciation and proclaimed theoretical statement. And such restitution is all the more profound for its appearance under the force of denegation. In the situation of Du Bois, announcing his discourse and proposed theoretical intervention on the plane of the epistemic horizon that set afoot the discourse of the Negro, one in which the presumption of a pure or absolute form of being on the order of the human and the historical was maintained in the midst of the critical promulgation of the eighteenth century in Europe and the Americas, a maintenance that has persisted in its aftermath, by way of the hidden or obscured idea of the singular transcendental status of the historicity of "Europe" and the European "man" and of "America" and the ("white" or "Euro") American, a theoretical gesture—by a figure such as Du Bois—that would declare its authority as sovereign (a peremptory judgment and decision), that of an affirmation *or* denial of an essence with regard to the (so-called) Negro, would have the apparently paradoxical effect in either case of evacuating the historial status of any form of existence named under such a heading. Thus, all the more does a thinker-practitioner such as Du Bois in "The Conservation of Races" declare the unity and project of the Negro, even or especially only as a form of "psychical, spiritual" difference among others, on a global historical horizon, all the more does he reproduce within his gesture the premises of the naive forms of essentialism that he would combat in the practices of distinction and hierarchy in terms of the idea and concept of race of his day. Yet, to refuse such a projection, even in the ultimate figure of unity, the "one," would just as assuredly leave the existing and declared projections of violent and destructive hierarchy of a persisting *status quo* (before, then, and now) unremarked or unchallenged in theoretical practice, as well as institutional organization, if not leave it intact (Chandler 2014: 42–50).

In the specific contour of his discourse in this essay, Du Bois could no more reject the thought of the "one" on the level that I have elsewhere metaphorized as *horizon* than he could accept it on the level that I have earlier in this part of the present study metaphorized as *ground*. Du Bois, that is to say, in the discourse of "The Conservation of Races" could no more refuse the figure of the *one* than he could accept it. He was obliged to undertake both and neither gesture at the same time.

As the problematization that Du Bois confronted, that of thinking the so-called problem of the Negro (in the ninth paragraph of the first chapter of *The Souls of Black Fok: Essays and Sketches* remarks this problematic as "half-named" (Du Bois 1903a: 8, para 9)) has too often been taken as a parochial and derivative one in a naive or simple sense, it may be apposite to index this difficulty as it announces itself in the respective itineraries of two of the most influential philosophical thinkers of the twentieth century, Martin Heidegger and Jacques Derrida. We mark the latter's magisterial engagement astride the middle years of the 1980s with the problematics of "spirit" in the discourse of the former. In *Heidegger et la question: De l'esprit / Of Spirit: Heidegger and the Question*, discussing Heidegger's invocation of a "spiritual" destiny for Germany and Europe, and national socialism in particular, during the 1930s, which Derrida is subjecting to a powerful *Destruktion* or desedimentation, the latter yet cautioned:

> One cannot demarcate oneself from biologism, from naturalism, from racism in its genetic form, one cannot be *opposed* [punctuation of translation modified; emphasis in the original French] to them except by reinscribing spirit in an oppositional determination, by once again making it a unilaterality of subjectity [en en faisant de nouveau une unilatéralité de la *subjectité*], even if in its voluntarist form. The constraint of this program remains very strong, it reigns over the majority of discourses which today and for a long time to come, state their opposition to racism, to totalitarianism, to nazism, to fascism, etc., and do this in the name of spirit, and even of the freedom of (the) spirit, in the name of an axiomatic—for example, that of democracy or "human rights"—which

directly or not, comes back to this metaphysics of subjectity [revient à cette métaphysique de la subjectité (*no* emphasis in the original French)]. All the pitfalls of the strategy of establishing demarcations belong to this program, whatever place one occupies in it. The only choice is the choice between the terrifying contaminations it assigns. Even if all the forms are not equivalent, they are *irreducible*. The question of knowing which is the least grave of these forms of complicity is always there—its urgency and its seriousness could not be overstressed—but it will never dissolve the irreducibility of this fact. This "fact" [ce fait], of course is not simply a fact [un fait]. First, and at least, because it is not yet *done,* not altogether [n'est pas encore *fait*, pas tout à fait (emphasis in the original French)]: it calls more than ever, for what in it remains to come after the disasters that have happened, for absolutely unprecedented responsibilities of "thought" and "action." (Derrida 1989, 39–40, emphases in translation modified to accord with the original French text; 1990b, 53)[22]

How, in our own time, must one understand the terms of discussion in a contemporary discourse that would brush past these enigmatic difficulties in order to proclaim another and ostensibly new order of problematic, under the heading of a supposed idea of the neutral and still under the authority of an old thought of the transcendental? One cannot accede to such discourse or accept it all in one gesture. The contemporary critique of sovereignty replicates the limit that it would denounce in that very gesture. This intractable confounding of all gestures that would propose to simply reach the outside of the question of essence as it has been thought within metaphysics cannot be displaced on the order of a theoretical decision. Only a practical theoretical engagement in the form of an always renewed and redoubled effort can propose such a displacement—by way of its inhabitation, if you will, of the limits of thought. In the hollow or opacity marked out by the limit of a practice—its unthought or its exorbitance to a theoretical decision—remains the yet impossible possible form of possibility. Such is the mark of the itinerary and practice of W. E. B. Du Bois. His theoretical production in "The Conservation of Races" unfolded within the vortex of an epistemic horizon that would propose to foreclose the pertinence of his thought—as if he could be simply for or against the proposition of essence, as if he could simply avow or disavow an already comprehended idea of the "Negro" or "American Negro" (that there is such or there is not such)—reducing it to a figure of the simple same. Yet there remains in the discourse of this text a persistent affirmation of limit as also the announcement of the other side of possibility rather than as the ground of distinction that would enable a sovereign judgment. Du Bois remains open to that which would remain beyond absolute determination. His practice submits the thought of limit to the question of possibility. This I would propose is the discursive form of a practical theoretical inhabitation—sustained across the whole of Du Bois's itinerary—that remains instructive for our time. For it remains that even as I would insist on affirming the inimitable disposition and practice of the late Derrida on these matters as given, for example, in the passage quoted above from *De l'esprit / Of Spirit* as a fundamental and distinctive one, a certain tarrying with the practical-theoretical discourse of Du Bois of just over a century ago may reveal that his thoughtful practice should be understood to have already proposed for us the necessity to formulate a profound and sober theoretical caution in this domain of thought and action. This is simply to say that despite the proclamations otherwise in our time, we are not free of the epistemic and political horizon that took shape as the problematization of the Negro as a problem for thought for Du Bois at the turn to the twentieth century. Our question necessarily becomes: what are the limits and possibilities for thought and action that remain for us in this enigmatic and difficult domain? In this sense, *we*, all, remain more Du Boisian than we might be yet wont to admit.[23]

V. A PRACTICAL THEORETICAL PROJECTION

It can now be said, then, in a return to the letter of the text at hand, that a concern with the historical possibility rendered available for the Negro American at the end of the nineteenth century, by way of an essential opening, of chance and freedom, in the structure of historicity was the abiding and preeminent practical concern of Du Bois across the entire essay that is "The Conservation of Races." If such availability could be reflexively and critically announced within thought, it would mark out the scene of an "American Negro" "striving." Race, then, as Du Bois conceptualizes it in these opening paragraphs of the essay, is the theoretical name of a project in the realization of historical possibility.

Certainly this will be the titular thought of the seventh paragraph of "The Conservation of Races"—as well as that of his immediate auditors and interlocutors, the thirteen assembled men in attendance at the founding meeting of the American Negro Academy—and it will mark thereby all the key junctures that follow over the course of the remainder of the essay, especially at the turning points of the eleventh and twelfth paragraphs on the one hand and the seventeenth and eighteenth on the other, as he turns from this critical account of the idea and concept of race to propose an interpretation of his historical present, the global scenography of human groups in the closing decade of the nineteenth century.

Yet this sense of race for Du Bois as I have adduced it in the reception of his essay given in this part of the present study is borne out in the next major text he will prepare after his production of the theoretical discourse of "The Conservation of Races," after the labor of composition of this essay, which had taken place from the end of the month of February through the first days of March 1897. The first major subsequent text is "Strivings of the Negro People," which he completed just over three months later, perhaps proximate to mid-June of that same year, and published that August. At the penultimate moment of statement in the latter essay, a conjunction occurs in which Du Bois invokes precisely the term "race" in the sense that he had proposed that it might be understood in "The Conservation of Races"—as a titular name of a project of collective "striving."

> Thus the second decade of the American Negro's freedom was a period of conflict, of inspiration and doubt, of faith and vain questionings, of *Sturm und Drang*. The ideals of physical freedom, of political power, of school training, as separate all-sufficient panaceas for social ills, became in the third decade dim and overcast. They were the vain dreams of credulous race childhood; not wrong, but incomplete and over-simple. The training of the schools we need to-day more than ever,—the training of deft hands, quick eyes and ears, and the broader, deeper, higher culture of gifted minds. The power of the ballot we need in sheer self-defense, and as a guarantee of good faith. We may misuse it, but we can scarce do worse in this respect than our whilom masters. Freedom, too, the long sought we still seek,—the freedom of life and limb, the freedom to work and think. Work, culture, and liberty,—all these we need, not singly, but together; for to-day these ideals among the Negro people are gradually coalescing, and finding a higher meaning in *the unifying ideal of race*,—the ideal of fostering the traits and talents of the Negro, not in opposition to, but in conformity with, the greater ideals of the American republic, in order that some day, on American soil, two world races may give each to each those characteristics which both so sadly lack. (Du Bois 1897b, 197, para. 12; 2015h, 72–73, para. 12, my emphasis)

In the publication of a revised version of this essay as the opening chapter of *The Souls of Black Folk*, the periodization shifts somewhat. Whereas in the formulation of mid-1897 the present appears as a moment in the midst of the "third decade" since "emancipation," in the revision of late 1902 and early 1903 it is defined as the difficult time for "the American Negro" that "dawns" after "forty years of national life, forty years of renewal and development" to the extent that "the swarthy spectre" still "sits in its accustomed seat at the Nation's feast" (Du Bois 1903a, 6, para. 7).[24]

Indeed, one could staple or append "The Conservation of Races" as a long footnote to this entire paragraph at the juncture of this phrase, the statement of "the unifying ideal of race," in "Strivings of the Negro People." Or, alternatively, one could append or attach the whole of the essay "Strivings of the Negro People" as a long footnote precisely at the conjunction of the sixth and seventh paragraphs of "The Conservation of Races." They are part and parcel of the same theoretical statement.

It is with this thought of race in the sense that he has begun to propose in the opening stages of the latter essay as the heading of a problematization for thought—both practical and theoretical, the relation of which will always have been determined in the modalities of practice—that one can turn to notate here the implication that Du Bois will draw from the labor of thought we have been following.

First, I can underscore the epistemic horizon on which this work of conceptual and theoretical desedimentation should be situated in our reception of it as epochal on a global scale—the terms of Du Bois's thought of a global "problem of the color line"—by reference to the decisive question of the closing chapter, "The Sorrow Songs," of the *book* that would become *The Souls of Black Folk: Essays and Sketches*. The chapter is an essay that Du Bois drafted over the course of the two months from the second half of January to the first half of March 1903, standing thus as the most general and profound *coda* of that text, written almost exactly seven years after "The Conservation of Races" (see letters of Francis Fisher Browne to W. E. B. Du Bois, January 21 to 11 March, 1903 [Du Bois 1980a, reel 2, frames 433–518]).

> The silently growing assumption of this age is that the probation of races is past, and that the backward races of to-day are of proven inefficiency and not worth the saving. Such an assumption is the arrogance of peoples irreverent toward Time and ignorant of the deeds of men. A thousand years ago such an assumption, easily possible, would have made it difficult for the Teuton to prove his right to life. Two thousand years ago such dogmatism, readily welcome,

would have scouted the idea of blond races ever leading civilization. So woefully unorganized is sociological knowledge that the meaning of progress, the meaning of "swift" and "slow" in human doing, and the limits of human perfectibility, are veiled, unanswered sphinxes on the shores of science. Why should Æschylus have sung two thousand years before Shakespeare was born? Why has civilization flourished in Europe, and flickered, flamed, and died in Africa? So long as the world stands meekly dumb before such questions, shall this nation proclaim its ignorance and unhallowed prejudices by denying freedom of opportunity to those who brought the Sorrow Songs to the Seats of the Mighty? (Du Bois 1903b, 262, chap. 14, para. 24)

In the few paragraphs of "The Conservation of Races" that we have been examining, simply its opening stage of discourse, we have found Du Bois already proposing his own theoretical response to this question, *before* the letter of *the book* of *The Souls of Black Folk: Essays and Sketches*, by way of a critique and reformulation of the concept and theory given by the sciences of race of his day, to these "sphinxes on the shores of science."

Second, we can note the orientation for practical organization that he will proceed to develop, over the course of the remaining two sections, in a theoretical sense, of the "The Conservation of Races," those sections that in Du Bois's words deal respectively with "what has, in the past, been the law of race development" and "what lessons [for the future] has the past history of race development to teach the rising Negro people," which he develops on the basis of the reformulation of the concept of race that he has produced across the fourth to the sixth paragraphs of the essay. He gives a summary statement of the principle of this orientation across the eleventh and twelfth paragraphs, one of the turning passages of the essay. At the head of the eleventh paragraph he declares, that "the fact still remains that the full, complete Negro message of the whole Negro race has not as yet been given to the world" (CR 10, para. 11). He declares his response in the concluding sentence of the twelfth paragraph.

> The . . . people of Negro blood in the United States of America—must soon come to realize that if they are to take their just place in the van of Pan-Negroism, then their destiny is *not* absorption by the white Americans. That if in America it is to be proven for the first time in the modern world that not only Negroes are capable of evolving individual men like Toussaint, the Saviour, but are a nation stored with wonderful possibilities of culture, then their destiny is not a servile imitation of Anglo-Saxon culture, but a stalwart originality which shall unswervingly follow Negro ideals. (CR 10, para. 12)

The itinerary of practical work prescribed by this orientation is then given its first outline across the conjunction of the seventeenth and eighteenth paragraphs. For Du Bois, it calls for the development of a certain form of collective organization.

> As such, it is our duty to conserve our physical powers, our intellectual endowments, our spiritual ideals; as a race we must strive by race organization, by race solidarity, by race unity to the realization of that broader humanity which freely recognizes differences in men, but sternly deprecates inequality in their opportunities of development.
>
> For the accomplishment of these ends we need race organizations: Negro colleges, Negro newspapers, Negro business organizations, a Negro school of literature and art, and an intellectual clearing house, for all these products of the Negro mind, which we may call a Negro Academy. (CR 12, paras. 17–18)

The question of the practical work of "self" organization returns us to the incipit of Du Bois's discourse. For, although he has felt the need to "rise above the pressing, but smaller questions of separate schools and cars, wage-discrimination and lynch law, to survey the whole question of race in human philosophy" in order to address the so-called Negro problem, these apparently "smaller questions" are the epistemic apparition or form of the historical condition that indeed has set in motion his practice of critical reflection and discourse. Although they were through and through philosophical in their form of attention and pertinence, the guiding questions of his inquiry in "The Conservation of Races" were not in the first instance, nor the last the order of solicitation given by the respective imperatives of a scholarly treatise or a critique of knowledge. Nor is his essay a work of imaginative contemplation. Rather, the critical and theoretical labor of the opening paragraphs we have here examined—distributed around the nodal paragraph four—were concerned to do the preliminary epistemological work necessary to orient oneself, as individual and group, in a practical political projection (and here the term political should be understood in the broad sense, that is, in every sense),[25] the work of an organization that would then, in the words of Du Bois to the assembled members of the American Negro Academy, "lay, on [this] basis of broad knowledge and careful insight, those large lines of policy and higher ideals which may form our guiding lines and boundaries in the practical difficulties of every day" (CR 5, para. 3).

This then will have always been a thought on the bias. That bias, the path of our own work of desedimentation, according to its general implication, should be remarked. It is my closing gesture for part I of the present study.

In a letter addressed to the late Herbert Aptheker dated January 10, 1956, in the context of a receptive commentary on a text by him, Du Bois wrote in the first person of his own initial stage of intellectual maturation during the last decade of the nineteenth century, in contradistinction to its characterization by the younger scholar (Aptheker 1955).[26] Writing of the opening chapter of Aptheker's text, in this letter Du Bois slightly chides his interlocutor, declaring in a rhetorically turning gesture, "Perhaps you do not remember that it was in search of answers to the fundamental problems which you discuss, that I went to Harvard." He continues by recalling that after his study with William James, Josiah Royce, and George Santayana at that institution, "I found and adopted a philosophy which has served me since; there after I turned to the study of History and what has become Sociology." Du Bois, thus, writes of his own philosophical disposition:

> I would express my philosophy more simply. Several times in the past I have started to formulate it, but met such puzzled looks that it remains only partially set down in scraps of manuscript. I gave up the search for "Absolute" Truth; not from doubt of the existence of reality, but because I believe that our limited knowledge and clumsy methods of research made it impossible now completely to apprehend Truth. I nevertheless firmly believed that gradually the human mind and absolute and provable truth would approach each other and like the "Asymptotes of the Hyperbola" (I learned the phrase in high school and was ever fascinated by it) would approach each other nearer and nearer and yet never in all eternity meet. I therefore turned to Assumption, scientific Hypothesis. I assumed the existence of Truth, since to assume anything else or not to assume was unthinkable. I assumed that Truth was only partially known but that it was ultimately largely knowable, although perhaps in part forever Unknowable. Science adopted the hypothesis of a Knower and something Known. The Jamesian Pragmatism as I understood it from his lips was not based on the—"usefulness of a hypothesis," as you put it, but on its workable logic if its truth was assumed. Also, of necessity I assumed Cause and Change. With these admittedly unprovable assumptions, I proposed to make a scientific study of human action, based on the hypothesis of the reality of such actions, of their causal connections and of their continued occurrence and change because of Law and Chance. I called Sociology the measurement of the element of Chance in Human Action. (Du Bois 1973, 394–96)

To be precise, as noted above, Du Bois in his 1905 essay "Sociology Hesitant" formulates it thus: "Sociology then, is the Science that seeks the *limits* of Chance in human conduct" (my emphasis). Continuing, with our reference to the 1956 letter, therein he specifies his approach to these general fundamental questions as proceeding by way of a problematization of the so-called Negro question, situating his project in the engagement of the Negro as a problem for thought in the context of his philosophical reflection.

> For myself I set out in 1896 on the task of studying human action in exhaustive detail by taking up the Negro Problem. I set forth my thesis at a convocation of the University of Pennsylvania in 1897 and then for fifteen years at Atlanta University. I began to recount and classify the facts concerning the American Negro and the way to his betterment through human action. I assumed that human beings could alter and re-direct the course of events so as to better human conditions. I knew that this power was limited by environment, inheritance and natural law, and that from the point of view of science these occurrences must be a matter of Chance and not of Law. I did not rule out the possibility of some God also influencing and directing human action and natural law. However, I saw no evidence of such divine guidance. I did see evidence of the decisive action of human beings. Here most persons who understood what I was saying left me quite alone and reverted to firm belief in unalterable Law, thus to my mind changing Man to an automaton and making Ethics unmeaning and Reform a contradiction in terms. (Du Bois 1973, 394–96)

As the problematization that is retrospectively gathered in the form of this profoundly rich and vibrant late octogenarian reflection remains vastly excessive to any reception I can offer in the present context, I simply attach it here (reserving for another and proper occasion the necessity of a sustained engagement); then, further, I would yet only turn and fold the entire previous discourse of this part of the present study across the frame of this late reflective formulation of problem by Du Bois, acknowledging the latter thereby as the palimpsest for the annotations I have adduced herein. In that sense, part I of this study is an opening stage of an attempt to reinscribe the locutions of the 1956 letter for our time, now somewhat more than six and a half decades later, perhaps offering some passage toward a way of sounding its lower registers.

In a more delimited and partial sense, the single theme I wish to draw from this epistolary record is that of the forms of audition of the thought of Du Bois. Thus, it is the response of his auditors, the "puzzled looks," with which Du Bois was met (according to his own account) whenever he addressed this domain of thought, that I wish to remark. In so doing, I propose that we accept the "The Conservation of Races" as a published fragment of a "fundamental" reflexive and critical discourse coursing its way throughout the entire itinerary of Du Bois—one to which those "scraps of manuscript" of which he speaks above would also belong. (And, it should almost go without saying that the essay "Sociology Hesitant," written circa 1904–1905, which remained unpublished at the time of Du Bois's 1956 letter, would be another.)

How, then, has the most fundamental thought of "The Conservation of Races" been heard? Rather than recount the rich and complex history of this reception—a project that demands an essay in its own right—I will offer nodal examples from two moments: the immediate reception on the occasion of its delivery and publication in 1897 and the engagement with it announced across the 1980s and 1990s in the context of a generalized critique of essentialism in contemporary thought.

The immediate discussion that followed Du Bois's address as recounted by Alfred Moss registers a certain confusion of apprehension across the spectrum of statements of response from his auditors—specifically with regard to Du Bois's thought of "intermingling" as I have adduced it here. Opposing positions, those who were affirmative and those who were negative with regard to his thesis of "conservation," each bypassed the possibility that Du Bois had offered a discourse which proposed a theory of *both* "intermingling" and "conservation" (in which the latter as a guiding project would necessarily be rooted in the general possibility of the former). Du Bois was essentially understood as proposing a *categorical* preservation of something understood according a dominant traditional and variously distributed popular idea of race and the conceptualization developed according to those commitments. Yet, as some auditors averred, such as W. H. Ferris, Richard Robert Wright, and William S. Scarborough, such might be practically impossible or actually against the desires of a putative Negro leadership (from among the "educated" and well-to-do classes, etc.), and thus "intermixture" should, or would-in-fact, happen. Alternatively, the address was defended across the statements of Kelly Miller, A. P. Miller, John L. Love, and Alexander Crummell as rightly declaring that the Negro in America should maintain an integrity, understood as rooted in and expressive of its apparition as forms of body and corporeal existence—avoiding "race destruction" and affirming a certain "race enthusiasm"—because (in words Moss attributes to Crummell and Kelly Miller, respectively) "race was a divinely ordained category" and "Providence" placed Negroes in America for a purpose (Moss 1981, 48–51). This latter hearing was proposed despite Du Bois's explicit attempt in the locutions of his lecture (such as we have it in the subsequently published text) to displace any theological premise as a governing axis in a consideration of the problematic named by the idea and concept of race.

But this "puzzled" reception was extended in the secondary hearing of the time as given by T. Thomas Fortune's response to the idea of the American Negro Academy in general and to Du Bois's address in particular in the form of a newspaper article that prompted the most public discussion on the occasion of the founding event and the first issuance of the Academy's occasional papers (Du Bois's text was second in the series) (Moss 1981, 54–57). On the one hand, as the "foremost proponent of the term 'Afro-American' as the appropriate designation for all blacks," Fortune "attacked the society for its use of the word 'Negro,' a term that he considered applicable only to persons of unmixed Negro descent" (54). Along this track, Fortune thematized the question of an intra-group complexional color line (the phrase is my own adaptation of Fortune's), affirming the idea of a leadership among "Afro-Americans" by the "lighter skinned" among them (even rendering a personal dimension to his claim by reference to the putative phenotypical features of members of the new Academy and their respective wives, Du Bois in particular). Resolving all of these registers into one, Fortune declared the disposition of the Academy as resolutely "anti-mulatto." On the other hand, he specifically adjudged against Du Bois's proposition of the cultivation of a specifically Negro "spirit" or "genius" in America, for "Anglo-Saxon ideals" would "predominate . . . to the end of the chapter, absorbing to themselves all that makes for national beauty and strength" (55–56).

Even beyond its confounded polemic along a proposed intra-group color line, in the context of our discussion of "The Conservation of Races," Fortune's apprehension of Du Bois's argument in the address is almost precisely the opposite of the annotation we have proposed: where Fortune thought he recognized a discourse against the mulatto, we recognize a complex philosophical formulation of the general possibility of "intermingling" among humankind; where he saw an a priori assumption of determination according to an already accomplished whole, we recognize in Du Bois's thought an effort to formulate a dynamic concept of horizon.

If such was the exemplary form of the critical discussion at the end of the nineteenth century, what was its character at the end of the twentieth?

While the philosophical horizon of our contemporary debate generally presumes the reduction of a theological premise with regard to the problematic of the idea and concept of race, on a conceptual and theoretical level, the confusion of a century ago with regard to the radical thought of *the general possibility of "intermingling"* that we have been able to bring into relief in Du Bois's address, and perhaps his discourse in general, has been maintained right into the time of our own discourse. That is to say, the thought of "intermingling" within this text has gone unrecognized. Let us say, then, that the fundamentally irruptive character of Du Bois's discourse in paragraph four of "The Conservation of Races" has thus far remained obscure in the contemporary debate, of which I refer here only to an exemplary pathway of engaging its discourse.

As noted above, approximately two generations ago, K. Anthony Appiah proposed that Du Bois's engagement with the "problem of race" in "The Conservation of Races" amounted to not much more than a form of "racist anti-racism" (Appiah 1985). The provocation of Appiah's challenge to Du Bois helped to set afoot a small cottage industry within philosophical circles. His singularly notable interlocutor was Lucius T. Outlaw, whose fundamental engagement with Du Bois should be understood to have long preceded Appiah's intervention. And Outlaw can be said to have rightly affirmed the necessity of Du Bois's vindication of the differential capacity of the Negro in the American scene and its general implication for contemporary thought (Outlaw 1996a, 1996b). And then further, while bringing a heightened attention to the form of explanation with regard to the question of the concept of race proposed by Du Bois, in perhaps the most patient (and brilliantly astute) address of the letter of the text of the essay "The Conservation of Races" up to that time, the radical order of a thought of "intermingling" in this essay remained even apart from the guiding concern of Robert Gooding-Williams in a mid-decade reassessment of the debate during the 1990s (Gooding-Williams 1996). This to say, astride the discourse of the last decade of the twentieth century, scholarship had yet found no approach to adduce even the very question of a thought of "intermingling" for Du Bois in this essay and thus its pertinence for his thesis of "conservation." Certainly, then, it does not surprise, on sober reflection, that the logic of the concept of race proposed in Du Bois's essay would appear "contradictory" on the terms of that debate.

Why has the discourse of paragraph four remained so unreadable in contemporary thought—in our own time? The answer to this question must truly remain yet to come. However, my principal line of thought in response is that we have obscured for ourselves the extent to which Du Bois's problematization in "The Conservation of Races" remains our own most unthought presumption in our claims of identification, historicity, and dispositions toward social order. Indeed, in just this manner, he remains our contemporary, in thought and practice. (In lieu of a further elaboration of this conundrum for thought in our time within the present study, perhaps I may be permitted to indicate that such problematization is indeed the guiding question of the opening and thus the heading chapter of an entire study that I have devoted to several considerations of this question (Chandler 2014, esp. 11–20).

However, it can be said that in general a fundamental critical engagement with the status of the Negro as a problem for thought—which necessarily entails root-level desedimentative work on the problem of the concept of race—with regard to the relation of the thought within philosophy since the middle of the eighteenth century in Europe and America of the possibility of a pure form of being within the order of the human to any thought of historicity (no matter its level of generality, that of nation, culture, or civilization, for example) remains in abeyance—astride the second decade of the twenty-first century. Hence, the pertinence of this question for our understanding of the most "fundamental problems" of thought in general as such shows in the problem at stake under the heading of the Negro and the heading of the term race, respectively and reciprocally, remains obscure in contemporary criticism. And, it is perhaps likewise that the implication for fundamental thought in general of any discourse, such as that of Du Bois or our own, that takes seriously the implication of the idea of "intermingling" and the problem of a supposed "intermixture" as the general possibility of the order of being called the human would remain at best obscure within the itinerary of such thought.

And, further still, the address that is "The Conservation of Races" should thus also be simultaneously understood as something other than a philosophical treatise on the idea and concept of race, even as it proposes a philosophical meditation whose profundity can be desedimented to yield the exorbitance of its resource for any interpretive gesture that would reduce its implication to that of a political tract beholden only to the time of its enunciation.

It is both and neither.

It is the discourse of a thought that moves otherwise than the simple and beyond the given. It is a theoretical practical discourse that is simultaneously irruptive—even within its necessarily confounded moments of theoretical declaration—in its political vision and in its epistemic implication on this horizon of the centuries from the eighteenth to the twenty-first, our historical present.

This recognition of the fundamental reciprocity of practice and theory as only respective norms of a theoretical practice, maintaining an unfungible oscillating emphasis on both terms of such—the practical work of an "intellectual clearing-house," for example—would then constitute nothing other than an engagement with the way in which the so-called problem of the Negro in its broadest sense is always as such also a problem for thought. Or, alternatively put, the problem of the Negro as a problem for thought is itself a fundamental path of the historical devolution of the so-called Negro problem.

The premise that one may responsibly turn aside from this condition of thought can be declared only if one could imagine that the thought of the neutral, the transcendental, or the universal in our time could be thought apart from such—specific historicity (which is specific only in appearance, as an apparition). In all truth, this specific historicity of the so-called Negro question is of the warp and woof of modern thought in general—in particular in a pronounced philosophical form from the second half of the eighteenth century to the present, if not already at stake across the preceding three centuries at least, even if such was then and still now remains unbeknownst to the dominant practitioners of thought within modern Europe and contemporary inheritors of the legacies of ancient Greek thought in pursuit of a realization of a commitment to truth under the heading of the concept in general. This is a historicity in which the problem of the "American Negro," even in its transpositions under the nominalized headings "African–Negro–Colored–Afro–Black-African" or "American," across the past centuries has remained and yet still announces—despite its apparent partiality—an exemplary general fundamental difficulty for contemporary thought.

The most difficult of questions had already acquired a certain tractable coherence of organization—despite the unavoidable intractability of the problem named therein—in the productions of Du Bois's theoretical labor that is the opening of "The Conservation of Races" as well as in the text as a whole and in the work he elaborated in its aftermath. How might we—whoever is such—think beyond the horizon of the idea of the one, the supposed utter singularity, by way of, rather than despite, our inscription within historical forms of limit. In the course of this elaboration upon the question of a paragraph, within Du Bois's discourse, I have proposed that we must continue to traverse again *yet always in a different way* the difficult paths so laboriously worked by Du Bois, precisely because we have not exceeded the horizon of its problematization. This problematic remains exorbitant within our own thought and thus also it remains exorbitant to our thought. In this sense, it might be necessary to understand thought as a form of problematization that takes shape along a path whose appearance announces itself in the course of our step. This, then, perhaps, will have been the legacy of one W. E. B. Du Bois in the project of a certain desedimentation of the figure of another possible Africa and another possible America in the so-called problem of the Negro in the United States at the turn of one century of change to another—a century and a quarter past.

PART II
....

*For Cecil Taylor, in
the time of writing*

On the Question of the Illimitable in the Thought of W. E. B. Du Bois

I. INCIPIT

Along with the radical status that might be justly granted to a protocol that would insist on passage to the absolute or to a concept of the whole in general, it remains that thought must also affirm that being announces itself or is at issue only in and through an asymmetry of limit and passage.

In this sense it might be said that the epistemic demand of our time calls for a dilation of imagination by way of a certain labor of contraction. And in the domain of this order of thought, particular figures of being and historicity acquire their general pertinence by way of their partiality and their limited emergence in the field of existence.

Perhaps, then, it is not too much to propose that this thought belongs to Cecil Taylor, when he wrote, of the anacrustic incipit of the musical group, or "unit" in terms of his stated poetics at the mid-1960s, articulating itself, to itself, in an essential movement within its constitution, as such, in its heterogeneity, according to a principle of freedom as well as a principle of necessity as it undertakes the making of music, in a fashion that guides us here: "form is possibility" (Taylor 1966).

Such a thought might well formulate the question of the status of a paleonymic practice for any project of a general desedimentation in thought and discourse. In the strict sense of a dialectical premise, we might translate such a formulation here, in proximity to certain contemporary discourses, as an unceasing movement of asymmetrical reciprocity in the unfolding of what Taylor called the atopic "area" configuring "anacrusis" and "plain" as relation. The orientation (and here no such descriptor can maintain or sustain an unmotivated pertinence), on the level of the discourse that I offer here, is toward the sense of the illimitable, an immanent concatenation of the possible and the impossible, the impossible possible world or, even, another world, as the imperative that solicits thought as practice or practice as thought.

Yet thought is not understood here as a finality or idea, but as a *problem* of existence.

If we formulate this ensemble of question on the terrain of the discourse of W. E. B. Du Bois the question is: what is the character of *the example* in Du Bois's itinerary, of life and work?

I have proposed elsewhere that one can approach this question of example in the itinerary of Du Bois along two principal thematic or topical tracks, the autobiographical and the historiographical (Chandler 2022).

Here I propose to further follow the trail of the historiographical example in Du Bois's discourse by examining his engagement with one situation, that of the Negro or African American in the United States. Even more precisely, I seek to annotate the way that the question of the historial genesis of matters African American may be understood to articulate within the earliest gestures of his efforts in thought. More precisely, I take up one ensemble of movements in his consideration, his first attempt to engage the so-called Negro question in its philosophical announcement for him at the very inception of his maturation as an independent thinker.

The text is a certain middle stage, a handful of paragraphs, of the discourse of "The Conservation of Races," from the early spring of 1897. Our inquiry in this second part of this study follows from the itinerary of questioning that we began to elaborate by way of a certain tarrying with the practice in thought that we can recognize in the fourth paragraph of Du Bois's essay. There our elaboration was desedimentative, seeking to break up encrusted bedrock within contemporary thought as it articulates in the reading and thinking of the early work of Du Bois. Here our elaboration is affirmative seeking to adduce a certain order of attention to the sense of possibility that may be announced under and by way of all that we may remark according to the heading African American, if there is such.

What Du Bois sought to expose for thought in these textual passages that constitute the middle stage of his essay is the possibility of an African

American contribution to the sense of world. From such possibility, he proposed, could arise *an* originary way for *the* world in general.

A. PROBLEMATIZATION I

Three internally complicated epistemic conditions, as theoretical axes, may be outlined at the outset.

First, during the time of his writing, in order to even formulate the question of the originary possibility of a group that might be called the Negro or the Negro American, in particular, Du Bois must confront the epistemological paradoxes produced for practice as thought (in this case reason as logic that moves from principle) by the general historical phenomenon he calls "the problem of the color line." That is to say: he must address this problem as it appears in the general project of philosophy as science. The epistemological nexus at issue is the concept-metaphor *race*. And, it should be underscored here that this is an index of the discourse of Immanuel Kant first of all.[1] However, it would later entail much practice of the philosophical in the work of the canonical figures of European and American thought of the late eighteenth century and of the nineteenth and twentieth centuries: such figures as Thomas Jefferson, G. W. F. Hegel, Friedrich Nietzsche, Edmund Husserl, Sigmund Freud, Max Weber, and Martin Heidegger. That is to say, it entails philosophy, or the philosophical in post-Enlightenment discourses in general, the lead formal discourses of Europe and America of the past two and a half centuries.

Second, the paradoxes are such that Du Bois must simultaneously avow and disavow this concept-metaphor. He explicitly disavows its naturalism (a register of the eighteenth century) or its biologism (a register of the nineteenth and twentieth centuries), that is, its physical determinism. Yet he avows it as a titular concept-metaphor by which to name historical subjects or to specify a historial order of the structures of subjectivity. (In this sense alone, he is negotiating the terrain of discourses of the spirit in European thought from Kant to Heidegger.) One can then note Du Bois's own account of what he calls "race" in his sense in history. He places it under the heading of distinct singular ideals. This heading, singular ideals, is understood to name as a whole the order of the highest form of values for living, for individuals, but above all for any collective of such individuals. However, despite such supposed singularity, the process of emergence and duration that he describes is one of fundamental intermixture and "intermingling." This thought of the conundrum of the articulation of such singularity only from and by way of heterogeneity was the concern of part I of this study.

And third, the organizing question that Du Bois then confronts within the premises, problematization, and itinerary of his thought is the articulation of historicity that may be gathered under the heading of the African American, which also articulates in other words the question of an African American subject of history. Yet, too, the fundamental order of the the question is about the future. He would propose to expose an origin of world or sense of world. However, he does not wish to ground the exposition upon any determination that would issue from an already fixed origin. To do so, for example, would directly replicate at the root of his own discourse the premise of a proscription carried out under the heading—however indirect—of the concept of race (which I index here in the traditional sense). Du Bois, it can be said, engages this problem in terms of three interwoven dimensions: that of the reciprocal character of the performative and constative gestures by which a titular authority might be proposed that would then serve as a heading in the search for ideals; the temporal character of the search and, therein, the status of freedom, assumed as if as a principle, as the basis for an affirmation of the future, or the futural form, as the privileged temporality of historicity (the ontological mode—shall we name it here, with reference to a conventional sense of the traditions of thought at stake—of "ideals" for Du Bois is that they are not simply given); and issues of duty and responsibility wherein the historical subject is only possible by way of a certain affirmation or maintenance. I would propose, thus, that for Du Bois, the concept-metaphor "ideals" might be understood as the name for an order of problem: it is the order by which the historicity of the collective is rendered an issue for it. Therefore, the structure of the inaugural organization of this historicity—the structure of its originarity—is complex. Its genesis does not take root in a primordial essence. Nor is its revelation an absolute as simple, a telos as end, a finality, or ultimate fulfillment.

Its organization might, perhaps, be best characterized as the complicated *alogical logic of the second time or the movement of the secondary rhythm*.[2] That is to say: the appearance of a specific form can take place only according to a genetic movement in which the supposed origin can appear as such only by way of its emergence in the shadowed blind of repetition, the ostensible realization of which is essentially otherwise than given as the same.

Or, as Taylor, astride the first maturation of his practice, formulates the matter in the making of music, if you will: form can only announce its possibility according to an infrastructural organization in which "the root of rhythm is its central unit of change." Indeed, to extend the metaphor from Taylor's musical practice, the matter of the "unit" remains everywhere and always at stake. This is so even for that which we might take as an incipit (in the medieval sense of the word) or, likewise, in the apparent movement of all that we may consider as an anacrusis (in both the ancient and contemporary senses of that word) (Taylor 1966).

Here, in part II of this study, I will endeavor to approach a theoretical inhabitation of this formulation of problem for practice primarily in the course of my reading or passage through the texts of Du Bois, leaving for another occasion the exploration of some of the strata of this thought of the second time, in a more general sense.[3]

The matter at hand concerns the organization of the problem of the Negro as a problem for thought for Du Bois in the terms of historicity, understood here as pertaining to how we might think about any historical domain as marked by a specific or particular organization of sense and value, as an originary historical domain, as an example of such. The theoretical analogy here is quite simple to declare: so the movement of the production of musical form, as we take it from Taylor's formulations of the mid-1960s, so we understand the general organization of value and meaning in its historical devolution. An apparently secondary order nonetheless always places at stake and in some essential sense determines at once not only the futural articulation of the given but also the determinations of the past, of what counts as past, in both fact and idea, in its apparitions, for the past also remains at stake. Not only is the future yet to come, but so is the past, or better, the pasts, plural.

In all truth, beyond such a claim, such a declaration, that is, as a matter for thought in general, it broaches the question of our most far-reaching considerations about the very opening of historical possibility.

To my own understanding the problematization is about the way in which matters African American pose the most fundamental questions for thought in our time for all that we might consider of, or about, matters of human social organization and practice in general.

As I turn to read Du Bois's own inscriptions, in preparation, it seems apposite to acknowledge the academic discussion, however briefly, for the matter of Du Bois's 1897 essay as an object of thought in the contemporary scene is itself quite complex. It became the focus of renewed attention in the mid-1980s and has sustained a more or less ongoing discussion for the better part of the past two generations. One lead position in the earlier forms of this contemporary debate approached Du Bois's thought as operating with the limits of the term *race* in a manner that *in its end game* would not be much different in a theoretical sense from the historically pejorative, that is racist, deployment of the term (Appiah 1985, 1986, 1989,1992a; Moses 1993, esp. 289). The other major position of that earlier interlocution, which was only in part a response to the lead position just named, for in fact it has had a very long-standing enunciation, rightly venerable, within African American discourses, which means that in a sense the persistent enunciation of its claim predates the leading formulation of the other 1980s claim. This other major position argued for the essential integrity of Du Bois's affirmation of the Negro as a social and historical figure, as a certain vindication of that figure and its historical devolution (Outlaw 1996a, 1996b).[4] In a sense, other statements in this discussion sought to effect additional clarification of Du Bois's statements, often affirming him but offering essentially different forms of *external* contextualization as the *ultimate* basis to adjudicate the bearing of this essay for contemporary thought (Kirkland 1992–1993, 164, n. 66; Lott 1992–1993, 2001; Moses 1993; Holt 1998). Even in the singular lucid touchstone critical accounting of the terms of that contemporary debate, the dual order of the discussion just described had already determined the order of question that was most present and at stake at that juncture in discourse (Gooding-Williams 1996, esp. 50–51 and 54 n. 5). A certain limit in an approach to Du Bois's text seems to me to have remained despite the rich contribution of thought occasionally contained therein, a richness notable in the contributions of Frank M. Kirkland and Robert Gooding-Williams.[5]

The specific line of intervention offered in the present discourse should be understood as one stage in a larger theoretical reengagement with the thought of Du Bois. In this sense, in conjunction with part I, this part of the study forms simply one side of a hinged or folded discourse on "The Conservation of Races." There, part I, we were concerned with the concept of race. Here, part II, the attention is to the essay's proposition of a theoretical understanding of African American historicity.

The protocol followed throughout my approach to Du Bois, as I also attempt elsewhere yet perhaps even more astringently here, is to take his locution, the declaration of his concerns and dispositions as the guide or line of attention that first solicits our own inquiry into his discourse. That is to say, I understand our first interpretive and theoretical task as an address of the question of recognizing (here in my own manner; others may have theirs) *the way of* Du Bois's thinking in discourse, to follow at an infrastructural level a passage in his thinking. Among other virtues, this way may offer a kind of illustration of Du Bois's step, or manner of movement, along his path in thought—in particular, at the outset of his itinerary.

Herein, this means to read and remark Du Bois's practice at the level of the sentence and the lexemes that arise therein, that is to say on the order of the paragraph, in thought.

B. PROBLEMATIZATION II

The initial methodological premise here, as in the part I, is to produce an understanding of Du Bois's essay that is first internal to his stated declarations. This need be said because two generations after passage of an efflorescence in a "structuralist" project as such in the approach to African American literature (one can note R. A. Judy's postmortem from the early 1990s [Judy 1993, cf. 1–32]) and yet in a somewhat perverse approach to the problem of theoretical labor, a generation ago the resolute privilege of putative contextualization with regard to matters of African American thought returned a fortiori in the midst of an academy-wide, generalized anti-theoretical historicism. There is thus a need, at once historical and epistemological, for a renewed insistence upon the fundamental pertinence of the most elementary modes of engagement in terms of the matter of reading Du Bois *in text*, that is to say, a necessary tarrying with *the letter or grapheme* of the text, as the un-fungible passage in any address of its modes of emplacement within any delimitable texture in general and in the most general sense.

A further aspect of our disposition here is to formulate a judgment with regard to the status of this essay in the context of Du Bois's thought—beyond or in addition to its actual or literal presentation—to read it in the context of Du Bois's other texts.

And, then, it is from epistemic space of a turn toward and into the text, if you will, that the most ambitious modes of an additional contextualization, a re-contextualization (or textualization), might most rigorously and demandingly be undertaken.

Proceeding in such a manner, a certain form of repetition, that is to say, a re-narration, given with a certain practice of irony, or hyperbolic interpretation, taking Du Bois's own indefatigable and exacting thoughtful labor as a provocative example with all of its risks, may yet make possible a rethinking of our most general concepts, theories, and positions with regard to the understanding of the "futural form" of the historicity of our time.[6] In this way, a theoretically adventurous gesture, one that remains a careful, scholastically grounded consideration of the most precise character of Du Bois's understanding of the African American situation in modernity, a form of engagement with his thought that must privilege his writing, may help at once contemporary discussion of Du Bois and contemporary theoretical discourses (social thought and the humanities) *in general*, assist these practices to move through, and thus beyond, some of their own most intractable impasses.

The central thetic disposition that I offer, as hypothesis or theoretical formulation of problem, if you will, is that Du Bois's essay proffers a still viable formulation of *the problem* of thinking the question of African American historicity. It stands to reason that the implication is also that it proposes in its apparent simplicity formulations that may be of contemporary interest in its engagement of some of the most fundamental questions of our time pertaining to the social and the historical with regard to the human in general.

C. RE-PROBLEMATIZATION

The matter here may be clarified somewhat by specifying the question with regard to the order of problematization that the dominant philosophical traditions of Europe would consider as ontological, that is to say in the most general sense of this lexeme (concerned with being, and form as being, in its sense and possibility). Yet to formulate the matter this way is not at all to privilege the projection of an ontology or the supposed privilege that is often thought to attend to the status of inquiry that proceeds under that heading. The attention I affirm here ought not be thought of as oriented by or toward the recognition of an ontology. Whereas, of necessity we think toward and beyond the problematizations articulated from the advent of critical philosophy in the European traditions afoot in the eighteenth century or the paths of the reformulation of traditional ontology since that time, but stemming from the early modern period, or even thinking otherwise than an ontology as proposed in the mainstream of the phenomenological traditions of thought referenced to an idea of Europe since the 1890s and the 1930s, respectively, our attention can be more radically or precisely understood as *para*ontological. Its concern is to call into question indeed all that has been understood as the ontological, in a certain manner, that is in a precise and necessary manner, with regard to the problem of the Negro as a problem for thought and matters of thought in general.

If ontology were to propose an account of the status of being (and such an account would be concerned with two orders of existence, the predication of supposed ground of being and the organization, or telos, of being—with the latter given according to many different modes of inquiry), then I propose that we may give the operational name of paraontology to the project of a desedimentation (at once genealogical and deconstructive, if you will, yet also neither) of the status of distinction among supposed beings or forms of being.

Notably, the matter at stake here most certainly entails considerations of all that is understood as pertaining to the human, to all forms of an anthropology, pragmatic or philosophical, or the derivative or ancillary sciences of such. The practice of a paraontology as I have sought to indicate such in my own practice is a critical thought. It is not an affirmative concept, that is to say it is not the proposition of an essence or essential referent for thought or practice, nor any existent that is the underside, alternative, or otherwise supposedly hidden dimension of an existent or order of existence. Rather, I have sought to propose it in my own practice and as I understand it here, the lexeme is a critical theoretical term that nominalizes the practice of a fundamental questioning of any claims of an ontology or of ontological sort, any such claim, or disposition, with regard to all that has been understood under the heading of the human.

The practice of a paraontology is a critical account of the ostensible ground, or predication, of such. Likewise, it is a critical reconsideration of the hierarchies and orientations by which they are articulated, or understood as, in relation. For such distinctions operate not only as a kind of transcendental illusion (a solipsism, fooling oneself, or a paralogism, fooling others) as given to us in the European philosophical tradition by Immanuel Kant, in the critical dimensions of his discourse, but as practices that operate as if to maintain as its ultimate resource (as ostensible origin or end) the disposition or presumption of an absolute mark or determination, with regard to existence and all objectivity, in general. In such a thought the distinction would be given a theoretical elaboration that would determine it as categorical, absolute, or pure—*of* God, or *of* nature, in an eighteenth-century or early nineteenth-century European sense (or modern classical sense), as given in the work of Kant or Thomas Jefferson or G. W. F. Hegel. The problematic may be thought as a general question of the relation of supposed necessity and supposed freedom. For matters of the Negro or African American, of the African in general, it is understood with regard to the supposed devolution of the forms of being for the human (Chandler 2014, 11–30).

Too, as the matter at hand is the specific topos of the question of the relation of differences and the common amongst, or within, the so-called human, it is always otherwise than neutral with regard to historicity and specific forms of existence.

The being of existence as life, is everywhere, through and through, and always, at stake.

While, on the one hand, one can never be commensurate with what is at stake under the problematization that goes under the heading of ontology, nor headings such as the order of distinction that I have just remarked, on the other hand, were one to attempt to retreat from engaging such a heading, the force or claim of such an order of distinction, in its supposed generality, would remain, without measure or effective displacement.

It is truly a matter of the living *and* death.

It is thus that one must practice a kind of *para*ontology.

While I have just offered in one breath, as it were, a schema of comprehension, and elsewhere (as just noted above) I offer additional considerations, in what follows here I propose that as an example of what I understand as at stake in such a practice, we can take as our guiding theme the question of the example, with regard to the so-called question of the Negro, in the early thought of W. E. B. Du Bois. Indeed, in a certain sense, one that is not ultimate or absolute, for contemporary intellectual generations operating in this dimension of problem, it seems to me that the necessity of going by way of Du Bois remains un-fungible. The question placed him at stake. In just this way both the question and the thought of Du Bois is at stake for us. To try to think without engaging either is to presume one or the other or both. It is to be uncertain, imprecise, and most likely of limited capacity in our ways to practice all that we do beyond the limits of contemporary presumptions in thought. It would be to foreclose an essential opening for our futural capacities in addressing the matter of human differences on a global scale of reference. For it has to do with our very idea of the human, not as the same, but as the incessant articulation of difference.

I propose that we take up a passage in Du Bois's discourse that might seem like *the* most singular locus that would be the least promising of an affirmation for a critical reengagement of the questions of example, subject or subject position, identity, or historicity that would respect the salutary cautions of critical thought in the aftermath of the Second World War in a global context. Or, indeed, the presumption might be that others have already done what work can be accomplished in this domain. Yet the premise here is not that we should simply restitute the terms of Du Bois's discourse. Nor is the suggestion that we can translate directly and seamlessly from Du Bois's discourse into our own. Instead, the proposition is that in that dimension of modern historicity that shows forth as the complicated forms of inhabitation, and which entails a necessary production of ensemblic domains of subjectivation (no matter what nominalization *we* offer, for *we* cannot avoid so doing), we are not free or outside of the vortex that formed the warp and woof of the fabric in which Du Bois was enmeshed. Thus, it can be understood that the fundamental problematic of Du Bois's thought remains *our* own—and here it should be underscored that the pertinence of the pronominal shifter cannot be restricted. It is thus instructive to think with him.

This claim is made not only despite or beyond contemporary critiques of a supposedly naive essentialism in discourses that would name a subject. I propose something even further: that Du Bois's thought in practice offers a necessary riposte to the simple and categorical declarations of some aspects of contemporary theory. Neither the thought of the transcendental nor the thought of immanence proposed in its wake are radical in the domain of the problem of the Negro as a problem for thought. Such theoretical position tends to presume the possibility of a neutral or quasi-transcendental ground, whether such be thought under the authority of philosophy as science or philosophy as moral theory, or the premise of the ultimate (for all purposes of theoretical decision) truth of a materialist or post-philosophical intervention on the same terrain. The limitation of the terms of much contemporary discourse in this domain can be named. In essence such discourse remains confounded in its theoretical determination, thus in its practice, as it approaches the problem of genesis or the possible irruption of an originary difference within historical process, historical becoming, within any specific historical context.

It may be shown and will be shown here that such apparent origination is always complex. (The term *genesis* is my own preference in theoretical discourse and thought.) There is no simple. There is always and everywhere an originary complication. Certainly, for thought, one always begins with the constituted (rather than, say, concept or pure idea). Yet if the constituted is always already given, it can become such (originary) only according to the movement by which it is at stake in its very emergent articulation it its would-be and yet-to-come apparent repetition.

Hence, any gesture in thought that would accede to an apparent origination that is understood as simple, pure, replete, would both belie its own foremost or primary possibility and presume its supposed accomplishment as already given, precisely otherwise than historial in its very being.

Such limit shows forth most dramatically at the discursive seam where the question for thought is the relation of the enunciative position of discourse to the terms of its own articulation.

Hence, for example, it can be shown that, on the one hand, an uncritical premise of "Europe" as a transcendental subject remains as ground of the most ambitious projects of a general desedimentation of thought and practice of our era, perhaps since the eighteenth century (cf. part I notations on Europe).

Too, in terms of our example here, on the other hand, too often in discourse that would engage what Du Bois has elaborated as the "problem of the color line" in modern historicity, contemporary thought presumes it is possible for it to speak *as if* from a horizon that would not be partial, *as if* a putative position of the supraordinate could be inhabited as *the* horizon of power and thus as presumptively the most general or radical in elucidating the structures as stake. In both of these ways the complication for any vocative enunciation of the general or the whole is introduced by its emergence only in the recoil of historicity—that it can announce itself only in the form of the reflexive gesture of a generalized movement of the double—is too easily set aside when it arrives in the domain of *the general problem* of the Negro as a problem for thought.

It must be said, then, that to the extent that an organization of the question of the terms by which the inaugural form of the historicity that poses the African American as a problem most precisely but not only as a problem for thought, remains open to this difficulty for thought, in just *such a way* it takes one not only to the roots of modern projects of knowledge and understanding but also to their most contemporary projections and beyond. In this sense it is part of the opening instances of the question of thought in the modern era, not its simple derivative. And it demands that the history of contemporary thought be reconsidered all along the seams of these stress points. It is part of their foremost possibilities and not the scene of their belated application. Or, better, one cannot think the African American problematic starting from such limited and foreshortened perspectives as they remain within the *presumptive* aspects of the legacies, past and contemporary, of critical thought.

Thus, it is that I propose a certain reinhabitation of the thought of Du Bois.

II. INDENTATION

A. TRANSLATION

Let us take a first iterative translation of our discourse, of questions, by way of Du Bois's text from 1897, "The Conservation of Races"—recalling perhaps our path of reading earlier, in part I, notably our attention to paragraph four of that essay—such that we can begin again, this time attempting to think with his discourse.

He first proposes that there are "races." And, for now, here, I leave all of the qualifications to the context of the discussion at hand.

Further, he proposes that there is a group, a "race," called "*the Negro*"(my emphasis). Properly said, at the level of a critical discourse that must account for its formulation of an objectivity for thought, this is a performative operation that is presented *as if* it were constative. It is at the cusp of an invention. Holding reference to a solicitation from almost two generations past, we may call it a "theoretical fiction" (Spivak 1988b). It operates on the same terrain as the phrase "we the people . . ." of the American "Declaration of Independence" (Jefferson 1999 [1776]; Derrida 2002a). And, the thought given in Du Bois's discourse may be understood to propose a profound critical relation to that earlier declaration (Chandler 2022, cf. 137; note also Derrida 2007). What is powerful and remains instructive for us is that, if we assume here the formulations of speech act theory, the constative-performative presentation is turned inside out, as it were (Austin 1975, lectures 11 and 12; Derrida 1982c, 326–27; Butler 1997, 157–63). We have a problematic that not only demands a performative engagement, but issues as a theoretical imperative that such engagement be *reflexively at issue* for thought as practice and *in the most general sense*. Du Bois for example will speak of the relevant context of his discourse as "the whole" question of race as it is at stake in "human philosophy." In this case the operation cannot be produced without an explicit register of auto-critique. And, in such an utterance a resource has not only been named—it is also always in its iteration an act that generates and produces effects in a manner commensurate with all that it receives.

Understood with Du Bois's thoughtful practice as informative, then it is no surprise for this practitioner that by the end of the century so well named by him (the one we commonly describe as the twentieth) that such a difficulty was fundamentally acknowledged in the *theoretical discourse* centered in the academy as a problem of general global pertinence. Yet it remains, a full generation after the turn to a new century, that the same discourses have continually stumbled as the object of address has been the work of Du Bois. They have been wont to be patient enough with his discourse such that its complications might stand within its own declared terms *and thus* might solicit theirs and our thought, that is, assist us (all) in asking critical questions of our own ground and standpoint such that we can better recognize, and perhaps inhabit, a way that allows our thought to be drawn beyond its own pronounced and given limits.

How might we proceed otherwise?

We must rest, remain, with the problem as problematization for us. In the situation at hand, for example, if one wishes to move beyond the limits encoded in the term or concept of race such that one could then *forget* it as an effective epistemic structure, then one must practice an active remembering of the past theoretical labor that has been undertaken to prepare for the possibility of its dismemberment or dismantling. For that is the implication, in a manner that seems paradoxical only from within the limits of standard existing discourse, that Du Bois's text, as the legible trace of a practice, documents and renders available for paleonymic reinscription within our own practices. The word race, *as well as* the concept of race, while susceptible to a certain limited desedimentation in our time, are at once, each and together, distributed across too many layers of our operative discourses at all levels of the social to sustain any decisive delimitation of their effects. In addition, and more fundamentally, they remain too constitutive of the thought, in our time, that would seek to carry out such displacement for any reinscription to be sustainable in general, whether in practice or in theory or in the inhabitation of each and both together. Thus, I will *not* avow the *theoretical decision* of the young Du Bois in the "The Conservation of Races" to reinscribe this term, "race," as appropriate, commensurate, or sustainable in the contemporary moment, our own time. This judgment is so even as I must inscribe this term and the concept that is iterative thereof within the citational structure of my critical or desedimentative practice. Nor do I have any wish for it to be tenable; on the contrary. However, two qualifications must be remarked here, one about Du Bois and one about *us*. Du Bois would have been hard pressed to sustain any conceptual and theoretical invention in this domain that would be free of the limits for thought that are exposed in the concept of race—whatever one might call it or however it might be formulated; and yet, the historical imperative to remark the terms of social and historical acknowledgment were no less un-fungible. Thus, I will affirm the *theoretical labor* that Du Bois undertook on both the concept of race and the general problem of essence that inscribes it in the history of thought. As for us, *all* of those terms with which *we* might seek to operate in order to displace either this ensemble in particular or the general limits pertaining to the question of essence are also radically compromised and still far too limited, if not terminally so. This would include the conceptual systems attendant to both of the terms *culture* and *historia* or, on another but related epistemic plane, the concept of "man" and its epistemological derivative "the human." But this seems to me also to remain the case for such interventions, to take the liberty of exemplary reference to a French horizon of discourse, as "situation," "problématique," and even "bio-power" or "différance" (Sartre 1956; Althusser 1970; Foucault 1980a, Derrida 1982a). If I have come to maintain and to iterate the somewhat traditional term historia, it is the result of a strategic calculation, which yet always remains a circumscribed and limited one. There are two orientations involved in this calculation. The first judgment is that this term maintains enough variegation among the chains of mark distributed throughout its strata such that it remains susceptible to multiple desedimentations and reinscriptions. It can be placed at stake in potentially generative and effective, if not entirely new, practices, procedures, and engagements that can affirm the possibilities of futural liberty of inhabitations and practices of existential freedom. This will always remain a relative and open judgment. It is *always* at stake. The second is that it maintains an explicit—however complex and unstable—question of the relation of the specific (or particular) and the general as the very threshold of its articulation. Indeed, it is the problem of example, in my own case the African American example, that guides us here. One practices, then, a theoretically reflexive committed inhabitation wherever possible, for one cannot escape this difficulty of term or concept simply by mentioning it. Thus, it is the case that this seam is what sustains our attention in this domain.

 Let us now mark a passage through the text, entering on the letter of this thinking, reembarking *en medias res*. We are at the eighth and ninth paragraphs of the essay "The Conservation of Races." We will include, as inextricable, consideration of paragraphs ten and eleven. However, it is always necessary in the practice of thought that we proceed by way of the example, as such. My practice here is simply the rhetorical form of that necessity.

B. THREE ANNOTATIONS

I must place three annotations as orientation for our passage.

First, at the level of the propositional logic and rhetorical organization of his discourse, Du Bois has already in the opening stages of the essay, especially in its fourth paragraph, declared the logical and empirical incoherence of the thesis that the *physical* characteristics of humans indicate what I wish to nominalize here as a *historial* character that would be nameable under the heading of race. Fundamentally, at the most infra-referential level he has proposed that there can be no consistent correspondence of a discreet physical characteristic, or ensemble of such, and a putative entity or group called a race or, that is, a group of human beings named under such a concept. The operative term by which he adduced this disjunction was "intermingling." The characteristics were all intermingled across the lines of the putative races that had so far been proposed by natural science: it thus precluded, according to Du Bois's statement, any coherent formulation of race in the traditional sense as an object of knowledge. I elaborated this thought in part I of this study.

Second, Du Bois yet has sought to produce a concept of a distinct order of differences among humans that would articulate them as groups. According to the terms he proposes in this 1897 text, the putative distinction would be "spiritual, psychical, differences." On my reading, the one adduced herein, this is an attempt to formulate a concept of the sense of historicity of specific groups of humans—we might say their subjective sense of world.

Third, then we might say that Du Bois's essay has three components. The first part is an engagement with a traditional concept of race, and this engagement itself constitutes a critique of the old concept and the attempt to formulate a new one in its place. The second is an account, in the register of a speculative, or philosophical, anthropology, of the history of the production of races, including the situation of Du Bois's present, the end of the nineteenth century. Then, finally, the third part offers a proposition about the historical course that such groups might follow in the future, attempting on its basis to elucidate the present and to determine a specific course of action for the future as commensurate with such an understanding.

At the present stage of this study we are entering the text of Du Bois then at the juncture where he begins to turn from an account of the past, across a reckoning of his present, to an account of the future—of races in his sense. Thus, we enter as Du Bois describes his present as a global horizon composed of race groups. From here my own discourse will assume the rhythm of the paragraph structure of Du Bois's text as its essential rhetorical reference but in this practice I propose to announce as my own reflexive mode a pattern of interlaced discursive gestures, of Du Bois's and mine, of the problematics of an African American discourse and that of contemporary thought in general. It is my hope that the attentive reader can always decide where one is located, if you will, according to a sense of the breath, or paragraphic enunciations, of the text "The Conservation of Races."

III. ELABORATION

A. PARAGRAPH EIGHT

Du Bois gives, in the eighth paragraph, a synoptic classification or description of the configuration of racial differences and the groups marked thereby that he understands to exist in his historical present, at the turn from the nineteenth century to the twentieth century. He gives a profile of groups defined by "race." He gives a broad division between major and minor groups. He uses here, alternately, the terms "races" and "nations" to describe the character of these groups. This alternation seems to articulate Du Bois's conception of the double character of the reference, the social groups, he is ostensibly talking about: at one and the same time they are given entities that one can describe and yet also structures of being whose essential destiny and forms of historical becoming remain always open and yet to come. As given entities they would be understood as more like "races" in the traditional sense, which can be described. As "nations" they would be more like Du Bois's reformulated conception of races in that they are descriptively accessible primarily under the heading of an ideal, a heading which refers to something that is not fully or simply given.

> We find upon the world's stage today eight distinctly differentiated races, in the sense in which history tells us the word must be used. They are the Slavs

of eastern Europe, the Teutons of middle Europe, the English of Great Britain and America, the Romance nations of Southern and Western Europe, the Negroes of Africa and America, the Semitic people of Western Asia and Northern Africa, the Hindoos of Central Asia and the Mongolians of Eastern Asia. There are, of course, other minor race groups, as the American Indians, the Esquimaux, and the South Sea Islanders; these larger races, too, are far from homogeneous; the Slav includes the Czech, the Magyar, the Pole, and the Russian; the Teuton includes the German, the Scandinavian and the Dutch; the English include the Scotch, the Irish, and the conglomerate American. Under Romance nations the widely-differing Frenchman, Italian, Sicilian, and Spaniard are comprehended. The term Negro is, perhaps, the most indefinite of all, combining the Mulattoes and Zamboes of America and the Egyptians, Bantus and Bushmen of Africa. Among the Hindoos are traces of widely differing nations, while the great Chinese, Tartar, Corean and Japanese families fall under the one designation—Mongolian. (CR 7–8, para. 9)

Du Bois produces in this passage both a stated and elaborated qualification of his classification and an implied thetic premise.

1. A persistent and remarked qualification is introduced by Du Bois as applicable to every term of his classification. Each group or difference is marked by in-definition and ambiguity. There is no pure term. There is in this description no pure "race." Du Bois's description of the "races" of his historical present are all marked by a fundamental internal heterogeneity. They are all essentially heterogeneous. As seen here in his description of what he represents as actually existing races, intermingling and intermixture are at the core of Du Bois's understanding of racial difference. The "American," perhaps especially the "white" or "European" American, which Du Bois places under the heading of the group he calls "English," is described by him in a decisive phrase as the "conglomerate American." Moreover, addressing the precipitant focus of this essay, Du Bois states that "the term Negro is, perhaps, the most indefinite of all," a phrase whose radicality is echoed in every aspect of the essay and sounds its conceptual depth structure. The term "perhaps" in this last phrase carries all the rhetorical weight of the indication or representation of the undecidability and instability in question. This theme of the essential heterogeneity of racial groups is restaged in the opening chapters of his 1915 text *The Negro* (Du Bois 1915, 1975c).

2. Further, an implied thetic premise, which remains unstated until the end of the ninth paragraph, organizes this entire account of actual racial groups

here in the eighth: that "races" are historical entities, that is, that they have an emergence, that they must come into being, and, thus, are always in the midst of transformation. As such, they would in principle, be capable or susceptible of becoming something else altogether—disappearing in the received form of their essence. And it will be possible to confirm this thought by following the movement of Du Bois's capsule narrative of the unfolding of racial difference in human history in the tenth paragraph of the essay.

3. This general theme of the non-simple then announces the central epistemological difficulty posed for knowledge by Du Bois's conception of race as other than some "thing" determined by the physical order of being or as issuing only according to a naturally given order out of which character is understood to issue, to make manifest or to be given in manifestation. For if the movement of thought summarized above in three orienting annotations stands, it remains that Du Bois is left with a conundrum. If "race" as he proposes it has no ultimately determinate physical sign, how might one recognize it? His answer, in brief, is that it may and must be by way of a practice of interpretation, for the object is a certain organization of "ideal." Let us read the text to see how he negotiates this conundrum. In the opening sentence of this paragraph, the eighth of the essay, as he begins to speak of so-called actual history, negotiating this deep conundrum in his premises, Du Bois specifies that race, the object of reference, that is to say the status and functionability of the object of thought he seeks to trace, is defined in a specific sense: this is "the sense in which History tells us the word must be used." That sense refers to the critical reformulation of the concept of race he has adduced in the immediately preceding paragraphs, especially the fourth (which, of course, we are *not* considering directly or in detail here, for it was already the immediate concern of our assay in part I of this study). This reformulation, suggests, above all, that if there are such things as races, they are not correlated (or explained) by reference to physical differences. Indeed, as he has already put it in the fifth paragraph, they "transcend scientific definition." They are not announced in a punctual present; nor do they persist in the fullness of a presence. That is, they are not simply given. They must be produced. And they remain always at issue or at stake. As an object of a knowledge, and this is the complication, race can be recognized only according to the epistemological protocol that understands that its objectivity must come into being: such is its most essential apparent ontological character. Or, that is to say, the apparent mode of being of races in Du Bois's sense is irreducibly temporal;

its ostensible expression is only according to temporization. Thus, if for him, they can be nominalized according to a certain order of distinction, as is his guiding hypothesis, it is only because their mode of appearance is according to a profound asymmetrical reciprocity of each instance of their unfolding. While they are not simply given in a final instance, they are yet tractable according to the apparition of form as *of* passage. They are "always" marked, as in conditioned, by shared or common "history, traditions, impulses." Such idioms of supposed commonness are always at stake, always at issue. The root concept-metaphor in my own discourse might be movement. In this text and others of the two decades adjacent to turn to the twenty century Du Bois will use the concept-metaphor "strife," which is a basic term of his thought at this time, to describe the character of their persistence or maintenance. This object of inquiry, in Du Bois's sense, is not an already given objectivity or simply a discrete entity. It is a form of the movement of becoming or possibility. It is the specific organization of such possibility that is announced as historicity. Such would be the object for thought that Du Bois has here, at this juncture in this essay, called "race."

From this juncture, Du Bois's discussion of the actual function of "race" in history takes up two questions successively in the next two paragraphs. First, he re-poses the question of the ground of the race groups, the racial "distinction[s]" or "differences," of race, that he has just described. Second, he proposes a narrative description of the development and function of these groups in history, offering a capsule narrative of this process.

B. PARAGRAPH NINE

As if to recall and reaffirm the critical displacement of a traditional conception of supposed race that he has already adduced at the opening stages of his essay (which I have only summarized above in this chapter, as it was taken up in part I), now that he is on the stage of "real" history, Du Bois once again poses the question that serves as the immediately pertinent form of the general question about the "origins and destinies of races," which was the threshold form of his problematic in this essay (as it was given in the essay's first paragraph): "The question now is: what is the real distinction between these nations?" That question concerns the relative ground of the differences he has described as racial. Are these differences grounded in the physical as an order of nature or something otherwise than a natural order of being in the traditional sense? Du Bois maintains quite directly that nature in such a traditional sense or the differences supposedly given as a natural order, physical differences, provide some basis for the differences he describes here as *of* race (my emphasis) but that such a basis is limited. They are *not* ultimate. Rather, for Du Bois, something other than nature as the physical is the deeper or more fundamental ground or basis. He calls them "spiritual, psychical, differences."

> The question now is: What is the real distinction between these nations? Is it the physical differences of blood, color, and cranial measurements? Certainly we must all acknowledge that physical differences play a great part, and that, with wide exceptions and qualifications, these eight great races of to-day follow the cleavage of physical race distinctions; the English and Teuton represent the white variety of mankind; the Mongolian, the yellow; the Negroes, the black. Between these are many crosses and mixtures, where Mongolian and Teuton have blended into the Slav, and other mixtures have produced the Romance nations and the Semites. But while race differences have followed mainly physical race lines, yet no mere physical distinctions would really define or explain the deeper differences—the cohesiveness and continuity of these groups. The deeper differences are spiritual, psychical, differences—undoubtedly based on the physical, but infinitely transcending them. The forces that bind together the Teuton nations are, then, first, their race identity and common blood; secondly, and more important, a common history, common laws and religion, similar habits of thought and a conscious striving together for certain ideals of life. The whole process which has brought about these race differentiations has been a growth, and the great characteristic of this growth has been the differentiation of spiritual and mental differences between great races of mankind and the integration of physical differences. (CR 8–9, para. 9)

We must continually recall that the formulations here draw on Du Bois's conceptual labor in the opening stages of this essay, "The Conservation of Races," namely, paragraph four. This is an accomplishment that I am assuming here. Let us gather up and emphasize, as a transitional summary and preparation for a further elaboration, four propositional motifs of the logic in the formulation adduced here, so far, by Du Bois: first, that there are manifest differences among human beings (physical differences, for example, those privileged by science, the sciences of differences of supposed race); second, yet, that there is no necessary correlation of a traditionally supposed or given difference and a given sign or attribute that would ostensibly signify that difference; third, further, thus, the actual historical differences among humans cannot be reduced to physical difference; and, fourth, yet, there are differences among humans, differences that Du Bois persists in calling in their apparition according to the nomination "race," which can be conceptualized and understood.

In the ninth paragraph, thus, it is the last of these four propositional motifs that is at issue.

1. The question is, what is the respective status of the "spiritual, psychical" and the "physical" orders of race as Du Bois describes it? According to Du Bois's description throughout this essay (but especially in paragraphs four, nine, and ten), nature, as the name of necessity, gives legible indication that it should not be understood as an essentially closed structure. At the level of statement, in this paragraph, Du Bois proposes a specific organization of the relation of the two aspects that in his understanding constitute the character of race in the "sense in which History tells us the word must be used."

2. And, of course, it is precisely at this level that the question I have remarked above as a conundrum shows forth: it is the question of the possibility of representation at all. Du Bois, however, will persist in the attempt to describe or name. What is at stake is the possibility of articulating a historial profile in a historical situation in which such an articulation pertains to the very terms of existence: to survivance in both fact and concept. The philosophical maintenance or destruction of a historial profile is in its most fundamental dimension interwoven with the maintenance or destruction of such in all the other dimensions (political, legal, moral, economic, social, cultural, etc.) by which we may recognize historicity, or existence, as an issue.

3. Let us then restate Du Bois's formulation. My restatement is translative, here, in an initial gesture, still oriented toward Du Bois's own declaration of terms. First, we must remark the general *titular* question and its organization according to Du Bois's own text in this paragraph: what accounts for the "cohesiveness and continuity" of the race groups he described in the eighth paragraph as existing in his present? Let us note two key features of Du Bois's statement as we pass through this staging of the text. Du Bois again emphasizes the ambiguity of physical character: "mixture" and "crossing," "wide exceptions and qualifications." And, the operative presumption throughout, even though it remains undeclared until the end of the paragraph, is of temporization as the existential mode of appearance (the apparition that has been too easily thought under the heading of, or as, ontological) of what he calls "race differences." Second, we must remark the specific *interlocution*, as a question: what is the relation, or relative status, with regard to ground, of the two broad principal aspects of race as Du Bois proposes to conceptualize it? Third, then we

can say directly that, for Du Bois, their relation is complex: on the one hand, a necessary "basis," for existence we might say, is the "physical" (here called "race identity and common blood"); on the other hand, "infinitely transcending" this "basis" is the "spiritual, psychical" (enumerated in this instance as "common history, common laws and religion, similar habits of thought and a conscious striving together for certain ideals of life").

4. Can the character of this "transcending" process or movement be further clarified? This is *our* question, given to us by our own time, place, and issue.

a. At this juncture my translative gesture or movement is to pull Du Bois's textual inscriptions into my own discursive vortex more explicitly. My position, as an interlocutor within this vortex (even if understood within a rhetoric), is double voiced. I am certainly following Du Bois's terms and declared statements. However, an order of thought operating in those very terms points beyond the context(s), in every sense both "internal" or "external," on the basis of which terms can be reflexively elucidated or declarations made (by Du Bois, for instance). Proposing a certain concept metaphor of our own, we can call it the order of sedimentation: of historicity in all dimensions but here as thought, as the sifting movement that forms layers and strata. It would be the actual process of the specific organization of relations, an order of necessity but yet not categorically determinate even in the instance of implication. Such movement also always entails processes of desedimentation. Following such lines or concatenations makes possible the inscriptive recognition of other paths, for example problematizations of supposed sex differences, differences of gender, dispositions toward death (the last nominalization noted here, whether as lexeme or philosopheme, is in part to remark all that is supposed under the term religion) by which an affirmative desedimentation of concept and theoretical position might be carried out.

b. In a formal linguistic sense then, as a word, the word "transcend," most often understood as a verb in its transitive mode, in a motif that runs across all the semantic sheafs historically associated with it, suggests the movement of going beyond, of crossing over boundaries. In the sedimentation of this motif is the essential idea of capacity. Indeed, the *Oxford English Dictionary* (OED) gives us, as the first entry for the transitive verb form, "to pass over or go beyond (a physical obstacle or limit), to climb or get over the top of (a wall, mountain, etc.)." And, in its second entry with regard to the same form, it gives us "to pass or extend beyond or above (a non-physical limit); to go beyond the limits of (something immaterial); to exceed," specifically indexing the theological idea of the independence of "the Deity in relation to the universe." With regard to the adverbial and substantive form of this lexical item, the OED refers to the Aristotelian conceptualization of categories, especially its legacy in medieval and modern philosophies, and refers to a "transcendent" as "a predicate that transcends, or cannot be classed under any of the Aristotelian categories," those categories being interpreted in the scholastic period as "Being, Thing, Something, One, True, Good." The OED refers to both the *Metaphysics* and the *Nicomachean Ethics* of Aristotle (see Aristotle 1966, 1975). From the moment such lexical genealogy is reinscribed in the problematization of a thought of the transcendental, especially as formulated in the work of Immanuel Kant, the whole problematic begins to pivot, to turn and fold, thus proposing a movement exorbitant to any transitive horizon, and the question becomes in its eventuality one of the status of the critical relation to "the interests of reason."[7]

In a philosophical register in our own time there is no simple or direct outside to this game. Along this track, the lexical alone, we are noticing how Du Bois is inscribed in the most fundamental movements of thought in modern philosophy. For our concerns in this study the primary bearing of this formal aspect is simply that Du Bois does not and cannot be commensurate with all that he indexes by his deployment of this term. Nor can we (whomever is such) be or become commensurate with its reinscription by us in our consideration of his text. (One might note my consideration of this problematic in part I by way of my references to the work and itinerary given to us by Jacques Derrida. Yet too, such is the bearing as I understand it of the opening discourse of my efforts to reflect upon the problem of the Negro as a general problem for fundamental thought [cf. Chandler 2014, 11–67].) It is the line of a whole other subsequent reading: a further complication in the processes of elaboration. Here, in this study, we simply remark this exorbitance even at the formal level as a palimpsest by which we can remark the ideal objectivities in the logical and conceptual orders that Du Bois seems to adduce in this paragraph.

c. In a logical or conceptual sense, perhaps not so much an *onto*-logical one, as a transitive figure, as Du Bois describes it here, in the terms of his own textual utterance, the movement of "transcending" can be understood as a figure of the double, or the non-simple, par excellence. The term and concept of the idea of transcendence here is that of a structure of relation that precisely disrupts the idea of the one, the pure, or the simple. Moreover, it always implies a heterodox relation to that which is traditionally called origin or ground, in contemporary thought indexed to discourses issuing from Europe since the seventeenth century.

Let us take Du Bois's term "infinitely." We can propose that such "transcending" might well be minute, infinitesimal, but at the strictly logical level then it would yet still announce a passage to the infinite. In this relation of freedom and necessity (where the concept of the absolute is implied), the most infinitesimal difference can propose the thought of an infinite difference. It would mark an irreducible freedom, here metaphorizable, nameable by reference to a mathesis as chance, perhaps, in the devolution of necessity. I can formulate this implicit logic thus: if that which transcends some supposedly anterior structure is indeed possible, it certainly implies that this possibility was already, perhaps always, at stake in this anterior order; thus, the transcending movement would mark an original and essential character or aspect of this supposedly anterior domain, which would in all truth remain nothing otherwise than this possibility, which is at once possibility and limit. Further, that is to say as such possibility, it would not be secondary or simply derivative in any genetic or architectonic sense of its logic or concept.

In the general infrastructure of history, the idea of a historicity, that Du Bois may be understood to propose or operate in the ninth paragraph, that which supposedly comes on the scene late or after the fact, in this case, "spiritual, psychical, differences," such would already be open in its essential possibility in that from which it is ostensibly derived, in this case the order of necessity supposedly shown by "physical race lines," "mere physical distinctions," "the physical." This poses the question of exactly what is the essential character of "the physical," or the natural in general, that emerges from Du Bois's description. Perhaps in an analytical sense we can say that its essence is always displaced within it. There is no pure punctual presence of its matter. (And this accords with the thought of an infrastructural level movement of the asymmetrical reciprocity of sameness and difference in the production of historical differences that we adduced earlier, in part I, in our engagement with Du Bois's discourse in the fifth paragraph of "The Conservation of Races.") It can then be understood as only apparently paradoxical, or a truly profound irony, that Du Bois formulates his conception with physical difference, what he calls "race identity and common blood," occupying the rhetorical position of priority as the apparent "first" ground of the distinction that he wishes to understand and that he *only then* describes (in the rhetorical practice of his locution in this essay) the differences, apparently as second, that he calls "spiritual, psychical, differences" or, in another register, "a common history, common laws and religion, similar habits of thought and a conscious striving together for certain ideals of life." This sentential syntax can be understood to propose a thesis. He names the "spiritual, psychical" as both a "second" basis "and more important" than the supposed or apparent first. In this utterance the conjunction "and" carries all the grammatical and rhetorical weight of the relative analytical status that Du Bois explicitly proposes for these terms. On this order of theoretical elucidation Du Bois's explicit statements might be understood to propose here, even in their rhetorical form, then, a certain *alogical logic* by which to think the question of the ground of that which is called race in his sense of the term in this essay. For if the first order is understood, perhaps, as one of necessity and as that which has the status of ground, yet the second order could operate within or on its basis as more important, then ground should perhaps be understood as anything but a fixed point or a closed structure of reference. According to this *alogic*, ground in any traditional ontological sense, or rather according to the dispositions of a paraontology (a critical practice that would call into question all that has been understood as ontology), can be understood as a primary opening of the historial (unconditioned condition) within the structure called "physical" or natural. And one is led to annotate here, in the company of Du Bois's thought of the end of the nineteenth century, the conception of historicity adduced in the last great study of the paleontologist Stephen Jay Gould on "the structure of evolutionary theory" (Gould 2002, cf. 1179–1295). And, thus, the principle of ground in its traditional sense as it pertains to the domain Du Bois is seeking to address can be understood to tremble according to the force that this thought which we have been led to develop by way of his practice recognizes as bearing on the line of a sedimented premise. In this moment of his discourse, the realm of necessity under the heading of the physical as an order of nature, then, is certainly understood as always otherwise than simply coeval with "itself." We might assume some affirmation in this understanding to the extent that Du Bois never uses the term *transcendence* to speak of a past as in final accomplishment. He proposes a movement of transcend*ing*—in the temporal mode of the present and future—a process that would always be at work and at stake.

We can reasonably propose that it can be described as a certain order of a general movement of the double in which origin is always complicated; genesis is never pure; and temporality is always distended across the abyss of duration. Among other terms of thought, I have begun to propose the nominalization of this movement under the heading of the alogical logic of the second time.

5. However, two other dimensions of this problematic can be remarked. One about how for Du Bois such unnameable might be represented. Another for our own implication in this same difficulty.

a. For Du Bois, the means by which this object, race in his sense, is brought to coherence for a description is *also* double. Thought, shall we say, with regard to his formulation of race, both presumes a given objectivity and, yet to some extent, must produce the object of its representation. Certainly Du Bois is involved in this game by way of the conceptual and theoretical labor of this essay in which he is trying to adduce an order of distinction among humans called race that would serve as an object of understanding. Earlier in "The Conservation of Races," in the fifth paragraph, he gives a name and epistemological position to such an act or the labor of thought that would be required to recognize race in his historiographical sense. It is a practice he attributes to the "eye of the Historian and Sociologist," as distinct (for example) from the eye of the natural scientist, a biologist perhaps. He writes there that while races in his sense would "perhaps transcend scientific definition, nevertheless, [they] are clearly defined to the eye of the Historian and Sociologist."[8] The practice of this "eye" is, following the register of Du Bois's position of this phrase in the fifth paragraph of the essay, a kind of reading of signs that does not assume a necessary or simple relation between a sign and a referent. Such a relation must be construed according to a context. Reference, as context, here is thus always relative. The value or character of such relation is thus always relative. That is, it is always at stake in the labor of its own action. It does not accede to a preestablished truth. In the essay "The Study of the Negro Problems," written in late summer or early autumn of 1897, eight or nine months after he wrote "The Conservation of Races," in February and March of that year, Du Bois specifically placed a practice he called "sociological interpretation" as the ultimate method of any practice of social study with regard to matters of what he called there "the Negro problems" (Du Bois 1898). He specifically understood such "interpretation" as a practice excessive to science, with the latter practice itself understood as a project of understanding and knowledge which the protocol of truth was grounded in a strict commitment to represent (measure and describe) or formalize only on the basis of that which had an actual and given phenomenal presence. Interpretation, practiced according to the "eye" of the "historian" and the "sociologist," shares the grounding reference of science, yet it is also oriented toward a reference, if you will, that does not exist as such. It must, to some extent, produce or call into epistemic objectivity that which would serve as its object of analysis or understanding. This is certainly what Du Bois is attempting to do here.

b. Yet my practice (our practice, whomever is such) is also implicated in this problematic. I am proposing Du Bois's formulation of an alogical logic by which nature or the supposed natural is an essentially open structure, a conceptualization that is gathered and unfolded from within a specific ensemble of questions, or problematic, concerning the status of the Negro, whose pathway of formulation and bearing would be nonetheless general. It would bear conceptual force for any radical thought of difference as such and in general. The elaboration of this generality would remain nonetheless a problem for reading and thought. This general bearing is not simply given. Rather, it is itself the product of discourse and the historical unfolding of difference in general. This is the discursive moment and register of my own intervention. Thus, the originality of Du Bois thought must be adduced, produced, through a reading, an interpretive act, a performative gesture, that brings to this reading almost as much as it takes away. As such, the integrity or rigor of the elucidation of this motif of Du Bois's thought, in this essay, is given affirmation not only (1) by the presence of an apparently literal semantic sheaf in his work that ostensibly explicitly represents such a thought but also, perhaps paradoxically, (2) by a certain remainder or excessiveness of Du Bois's thought to the interpretive act of gathering it up within the frame of this motif. That is, Du Bois's thought can be richly illuminated in certain of its interior depths by following this motif of the paradoxical structure of "race" in history as a guide. Yet his discourse in this essay retains a certain opacity if seen strictly from the standpoint of the (apparent) conclusion or destination reached along this pathway, for it is also certain that Du Bois had not, indeed could not, produce an absolute displacement of the inherited concept of race inhabiting his discourse. Such remainder, excessiveness, or opacity of Du Bois's discourse to the reading proposed here is a marker at least of the fact that his discourse cannot be reduced to my own. More profoundly though, it is a legible remainder of the path of irruption of Du Bois's own thought, its working-through as the production, not simply inhabitation, of its own theoretical path. And, thus, such resistance marks the very terms of the possibility of a transformative dimension of Du Bois's discourse just as much as it inscribes a mark of its limits. For the juncture of this resistance as produced in the texture of Du Bois's discourse here, at its stitched seams, remain precisely as marks that inscribe sites of possible, and implicitly solicited, epistemological production (theoretical, conceptual, poetic, tropic) that could, perhaps, provide the terms of epistemic-political habitation, both in actuality and in potentiality. This pensive and suspensive opacity that remains in Du Bois's discourse for us should not be discarded or disregarded in any fashion, but rather affirmed as the solicitation to a labor of desedimentation. This opacity is connected to our being affected by the work of Du Bois—as in the experience of art. It can be taken not as the solicitation first of all or ultimately to a given or specific meaning of the work, but to the vocation and task of a specific labor in thinking—that of a practical theoretical production. Yet neither can I effect a decisive or final displacement. In part, such is a fundamental law in the operation of a critical discourse: there is no discourse that can absolutely displace in thought the limit(s) inscribed in the terms of its own critical enunciation. This is the situation no matter how negative the terms. Thus the opacity or limits of Du Bois's texts for me (only one trace of the limits confronted by the thought of Du Bois) is not only a negative. It also has an affirmative character, to the extent that this resistance of Du Bois's discourse to my own is a fundamental aspect of its rendering tractable for me a given problematization for thought. Within the integrity of this double reference, an affirmative tension (or a kind of interlacing), between the stated aspect of Du Bois's discourse and the sedimented remains of his discourse and text (that is to say, both the originality of his enunciation and a reading that would sound or resound its resonances) one can remark and elaborate a certain desedimentative orientation that could extend to all conceptual topographies of contemporary thought pertaining to the historial.

6. Du Bois himself affirms this remarking of the general bearing of his discourse in the closing sentence of the ninth paragraph of the essay, a paragraph we have been following here under the heading of the question of ground. Du Bois writes of a quite general conception in a deceptively simple fashion.

> The whole process which has brought about these race differentiations has been a growth, and the great characteristic of this growth has been the differentiation of spiritual and mental differences between great races of mankind and the integration of physical differences. (CR 8–9, para. 9)

According to Du Bois's formulation in this passage, the respective conceptual orientation of the two aspects of historial movement that he describes configure a complex pattern of crossing: a kind of inversion. Du Bois's formulation places this movement at the infrastructural level of the historial devolution of race in his sense. It is, if you will, at the conceptual and propositional center of the essay. In the strictly graphic or iconic sense it would perhaps be representable by the figure of an "X" or a figure yielded by a movement of crossing as interlacing. This is, in fact, also one of double-crossing. (Although not simply the same as "intermingling" directly from the legible locutions of Du Bois's essay that I adduced in part I of the present study, it registers the theme of the crossing of boundaries as well and marks thereby a motif that is quite general and persistent in Du Bois's thought. The theme is registered in both the earlier and the later movements of Du Bois's thought and itinerary.) There is no pure term in this configuration. Du Bois's formulation positions a process of intermingling and intermixture at the root of this conception. We can thus trace or outline in linguistic terms this figure of the "whole process," adumbrated by Du Bois as a complex movement of the simultaneous production of sameness and difference. This production opens and remains, however, as a figure of what we might call the general movement of difference or the general possibility of "intermingling," indexing in this latter phrase the theoretical accomplishments by Du Bois in the fourth paragraph that we has sought to remark it above. First, what Du Bois calls "spiritual and mental differences" have proliferated. Such proliferation alone would raise logical difficulties for any premise that such differences are grounded in a structure of a priori determination or limitation. The liberty of a difference that would be excessive to any supposed structure of absolute or primordial unity is suggested thereby, a unity such as that usually presumed as the ground of any traditional concept of race. What is common is this differential mode of appearance. And, if differences are recognizable as such, it would be only according to having such status in common. Second, what Du Bois calls "physical differences" have always undergone a process of mutual "integration." A certain double play or movement is implied here. Such integration or sameness comes on the stage of a scene already marked by an originary differentiation. Yet the movement of integration, the production of sameness, would raise logical problems for any theoretical premise that would propose to maintain an understanding that such originary differentiation could ever have been or become absolute—that is oppositional or categorical—between different physical types of humans. Thus, the sameness implied by the movement of physical integration posed here by Du Bois affirms the primordial, radical, order of a movement of difference (that is, difference as the heterogeneous structure of sameness and difference), the general possibility of "intermingling" as the inaugural figure of this whole process. Such inauguration will always have been as an originary complication. It is also the case that the integration in question does not result in a final moment of simple or absolute sameness of physical type; in the logical sense such would not only most certainly contradict the movement of difference that I have suggested is at the core of Du Bois's conception; it would also contradict the "manifest" or obvious evidence of physical heterogeneity posed in the contemporary actual global scenography of the existence of humans as he describes it here. The general process that Du Bois conceptualizes here is a movement of difference in which both sameness and difference are infrastructural, posed in or at every juncture of this movement. Ground, the ground of differences of race, is anything but the play of fixed or given primordial identities in this formulation by Du Bois. Rather, ground, if there is such, is the complex movement of the production and reproduction of crossing, that is to say of intermixture and "intermingling."

In this domain of Du Bois's discourse, then, we might say we are on the track of the illimitable as a movement of existence. Historicity is the itinerary of this process.

Historiography, then, in general, is a narrative of this process. Such is the thought that Du Bois may be understood to have proposed here astride the middle stages of this essay.

The alogical form of a movement of "transcending" that we have just been able to recognize in Du Bois's theorization of race (built on the critical logical work on the concept in the earlier paragraphs of the essay, in particular the fourth through the sixth) describes the organization of a general possibility that Du Bois will place as both the inception and the fullness of devolution, up to his historical present, of race groups. It is a structured, irreducible opening within the order of necessity. This whole reconceptualization makes possible a certain narrative of historical process. It is given in Du Bois's account according to the two commonly understood historial senses of temporality, in terms of an idea of duration, that is oriented on the terms of a supposed present, thus toward a past and a certain understanding of the future.

C. PARAGRAPH TEN

An irruptive and illimitable movement of "intermingling," "intermixture," and "crossing" can be shown to come into relief in Du Bois's speculative or philosophical narrative of race in history.

The age of nomadic tribes of closely related individuals represents the maximum of physical differences. They were practically vast families, and there were as many groups as families. As the families came together to form cities the physical differences lessened, purity of blood was replaced by the requirement of domicile, and all who lived within the city bounds became gradually to be regarded as members of the group; *i.e.*, there was a slight and slow breaking down of physical barriers. This, however, was accompanied by an increase of the spiritual and social differences between cities. This city became husbandmen, this, merchants, another warriors, and so on. The *ideals of life* for which the different cities struggled were different. When at last cities began to coalesce into nations there was another breaking down of barriers which separated groups of men. The larger and broader differences of color, hair and physical proportions were not by any means ignored, but myriads of minor differences disappeared, and the sociological and historical races of men began to approximate the present division of races as indicated by physical researches. At the same time the spiritual and physical differences of race groups which constituted the nations became deep and decisive. The English nation stood for constitutional liberty and commercial freedom; the German nation for science and philosophy; the Romance nations stood for literature and art, and the other race groups are striving, each in its own way, to develop for civilization its particular message, its particular ideal, which shall help to guide the world nearer and nearer that perfection of human life for which we all long, that "one far off Divine event." (CR 9, para. 10)

I will not attempt to address this narrative fully here. Such may not even be possible. Although the epistemological character of Du Bois's narrative can be stated quite simply, that is, it describes the development of races in his sense in history as the simultaneous unfolding of historical sameness and difference among humans, the range and implication of its bearing for what is often traditionally understood as ontological may be understood as excessive to any such reference, to any attempt at a simple retrospective or anticipatory gathering of its logic or motifs. We might do well to propose this excessiveness by way of one line of the continuing political bearing of Du Bois's discourse for thought in our time.

In general, the entire narrative can be understood as a meditation on the general theme of possibility, for a social group, for a people, or, as he nominalizes it, a race. That is to say, it is about chance (in terms of mathesis) or freedom (in terms of the sense or habitation, that is to say, values, morals, or ideals). Understood in the context of this text as an address, an appeal, to the founding session of the American Negro Academy, an organization of the African American intelligentsia of Du Bois's time, this is a discourse on the possibilities of hope. In one entire aspect the question of this essay is: on what basis can there be hope for the world or on what basis can there be hope for the Negro?

This general question of chance and freedom is a deeply sedimented ore-line in Du Bois's work. Perhaps it is the most deep. It should be addressed elsewhere in a manner commensurate with its profound pertinence within his discourse.

Here we simply annotate an approach to the two dominant motifs of this narrative, the status of physical difference and the status of "ideals of life."

In taking "The Conservation of Races" as an illustrative example of Du Bois's thought, perhaps we can remark only, to some limited extent, the question of "ideals."

As demonstrated above, we must retain here the understanding that the order of physical difference to which Du Bois gives a certain decisiveness always arrives only on the basis of an *always* previous movement of what he had earlier in the essay formulated as "intermingling." Perhaps it may also be useful in the context of the whole intervention of this study, to also nominalize what is at stake here under the heading of the term intermixture.

In the context of our own address of Du Bois's idea of the historiographical example, it is more necessary to adduce some clarification, perhaps, of what Du Bois might mean by "ideals" in this essay. While Du Bois will speak in the tenth paragraph of singular ideals attached to a singular "race" or "nation," a logic of the simple or the simply pure is not the most radical movement outlined in the narrative. Let me briefly track this on two levels, general and specific.

1. The premise of the concept of an ideal in general is quite simple. Yet it can be elaborated as rich and complex in structure. It might well be thought of as a constituted name for a general movement of "transcending" differentiation. As such it would be double in its essential structure. It must always operate as an immanent movement within a given structure. It maintains as its mode of being an essential and irreducible articulation in that which exists, however tenuous its apparition. The ideal cannot find its coherence and historical bearing without such. However, it is also always that which is other or beyond any given or nameable limit. Its essence is, in a sense, always to exceed itself.

Along this path of thought, in the formal sense, the movement of idealization can be recognized as the operation in which origin is figured only through the orientation of a goal, purpose, destination, or telos. Such a figuration is a curious structure in which the origin becomes what it is, an inaugural moment, only through the production of a repetition or realization of the orientation of this origin. The repetition is, in this reciprocal rhythm, also the origin of the origin (which is thus also a kind of non-origin).

Such a figuration conceptualizes possibility or an infinite concatenation of the two sides of limit as open within that which is apparently simply given as an origin of some kind. This opening of possibility or a certain movement of infinitization means there cannot be a simply given, or already given, destination as such. Thus, that which is named or called origin must be figured or refigured in the apparent arrival of a destination or fulfillment of a telos of some kind. In this way we might suggest, along with Jacques Derrida, that an ideal is always "on the way to its origin, not proceeding from it."[9] This mutual implication of origin and end is the essential double structure of the ideal.

In one register of twentieth-century philosophy we could say that it is the opening of the infinite as history and the opening of history as the infinite. However, in a manner that more profoundly recognizes Du Bois's own interventions, we can say that the ideal is simply a name for the form in which existence appears as a problem. It is, at best, a form of the coming into relief of a problem for existence. In the form of an ideal, its mode is as a problem for thought.

2. We can confirm this general sense of the ideal for Du Bois by considering the question of the actual or specific ideals to which Du Bois refers in this passage. On the one hand, there are those "ideals of life" that have a certain coherent and constituted existence, which Du Bois describes as examples. These ideals, or ensembles of practiced values, are named as follows: "constitutional liberty," "science and philosophy," and "literature and art." Yet these examples are not just some among many. Nor are they simply or primarily a mark of Du Bois's own inheritance of these traditions, whether one affirms or criticizes that inheritance. They are exemplary in a quite specific and powerful theoretical sense of Du Bois own general thought about historicity, one that poses in relief the essentially double structure of the ideal that we have just formulated. It names the actual terms of his intervention into the discourses that would claim the persisting value of those "ideals" described here by him.

The specific ideals named are all practices that inscribe as their essential character a movement of internal differentiation and heterogeneity. All mark a movement of human practice which is precisely about the crossing of boundaries and going beyond that which is given. They each name the production of a value whose essential orientation would always be or become excessive to any actual or given limit. None in their essential movement (including even the most conservative understanding of science) rest with the given or actual as the limit of their reference or frame of possibility. The thought of "constitutional liberty" would affirm the essentially open structure of right, the necessary illimitability of the extension of liberty. The historical unfolding named under "science and philosophy" would have as its inaugural moment the irruption of a formal thought of the infinite within historicity. "Literature and art" inscribe the excessiveness of the freedom proposed as imagination within practice as experience itself. That Du Bois attributes these ideals to particular race groups is both a limitation and a resource. That Du Bois marks these ideals as produced by particular groups is a limitation to the extent it suggests that this attachment is grounded in some absolute necessity. Yet the entire tenor of his argument in this essay, thus far, suggests that we understand this attachment as itself a product of the movement of difference in which essence is a product of the liberty of this movement as much as it might also be a result of the necessity inscribed therein. That Du Bois describes these ideals as produced, that they must undergo a process of emergence and development, suggests a conception in which ideals are not simply given. Du Bois's conception of ideals, then, is not an idealism *tout court*. Indeed, it is a rather resourceful thought of the structure of actual or material historical process; for it his conception the ideal functions as a movement of transformation open within the real; that is to say, the real is necessarily heterogeneous. It is simultaneously, of course, both real and ideal.

3. As important as the already announced ideals are those that Du Bois describes as not signified as a coherent immanence. Here he positions a key concept-metaphor in his thought in this early moment of his itinerary. That concept-metaphor is "strife" or, in its active form, "striving." It is this concept-metaphor, more than any other that explicitly affirms for us the double, that is, the open sense, of ideal that I have proposed as fundamental for Du Bois in this paragraph. Some "groups are striving, each in its own way, to develop for civilization its particular message, its particular ideal." That Du Bois specifies this "striving" as proceeding within "each"

group "in its *own* way" is a limitation to the extent that it speaks as if the groups whose formation he would describe are already constituted. Yet such a performative problematic is irreducible for any form of speculative thought, and that would include the theoretical gesture in general. For the conjunction of "own way" with "striving" suggests that the "way" in question is anything but already decided a priori. Further, although one could perhaps suggest that Du Bois's conception is one in which these ideals are the realization of a given "perfection," to which the process of their realization would remain extrinsic, and one reading of his quotation of the closing lines of Alfred, Lord Tennyson's *In Memoriam* A. H. H. could find therein an apparent declarative affirmation, it remains that Du Bois's actual narrative of that which organizes this striving for the possibility of a participation in a general "perfection" would resist the thought of the arrival of "that 'one far off Divine event'" as a simple punctuality (see Tennyson 1982). Ambivalent and not simply conclusive, this passage of Du Bois's discourse nonetheless affirms the general concept of the ideal I have adduced in his work, in which the ideal, even as a figure of transcendence, is a movement within historicity in which the end configures the origin as much as vice versa and in which the idea is the scene of a materially produced problem for thought.

This thought is one in which the ideal, then, marks and summarizes this structure of historical becoming as open, even if placed under the heading of race, a process that Du Bois describes in this condensed speculative capsule narrative. The differences manifest among humans, assumed by Du Bois in this essay and whose development he is seeking to narrate in this paragraph, were not understood by him in this early text as categories of being, naturally given, defined by opposition, even if placed under the heading of the concept of "race." For Du Bois, these differences are, in the most fundamental sense of the word, historical. That is, they have to occur in a movement of emergence, are always in the midst of transformation, and are never simply given, as such.

If Du Bois maintains a commitment to a certain primitivist or teleological understanding of human evolution, in this narrative or elsewhere in his discourse, it is nonetheless the case that he conceptualizes a radical liberty of the "spiritual" with regard to any prior determinant sense of the "physical," even as he would not avow an idealism in general. For Du Bois, history is the material expression of a certain fundamental liberty.

D. PARAGRAPH ELEVEN

It is in the space of the liberty of historical possibility that he has opened and named in this account of the emergence and functioning of racial difference in the past that Du Bois will then proceed to formulate a conception of the possible functions of racial difference in the future. It is this question to which Du Bois now turns.

> This has been the function of race differences up to the present time. What shall be its function in the future? Manifestly some of the great races of today—particularly the Negro race—have not as yet given to civilization the full spiritual message which they are capable of giving. I will not say that the Negro race has as yet given no message to the world, for it is still a mooted question among scientists as to just how far Egyptian civilization was Negro in its origin; if it was not wholly Negro, it was certainly very closely allied. Be that as it may, however the fact still remains that the full, complete Negro message of the whole Negro race has not as yet been given to the world; that the messages and ideal of the yellow race have not been completed, and that the striving of the mighty Slavs has but begun. The question is, then: How shall this message be delivered; how shall these various ideals be realized? The answer is plain: By the development of these race groups, not as individuals, but as races. For the development of Japanese genius, Japanese literature and art, Japanese spirit, only Japanese, bound and welded together, Japanese inspired by one vast ideal, can work out in its fullness the wonderful message which Japan has for the nations of the earth. For the development of Negro genius, of Negro literature and art, of Negro spirit, only Negroes bound and welded together, Negroes inspired by one vast ideal, can work out in its fullness that great message we have for humanity. We cannot reverse history; we are subject to the same natural laws as other races, and if the Negro is ever to be a factor in the world's history—if among the gaily-colored banners that deck the broad ramparts of civilizations is to hang one uncompromising black, then it must be placed there by black hands, fashioned by black heads and hallowed by the travail of 200,000,000 black hearts beating in one glad song of jubilee. (CR 9–10, para. 11)

This was Du Bois's thought in this text about the future at the end of the nineteenth century. Yet his future is now part of our past. We are in the midst, if not at the inception, of the centuries that were yet to come for Du Bois at the time of his writing at the end of the nineteenth century: ours is the historicity he proposed as the scene of a necessary intervention.

1. A Future Stake

In what way can we read or must we read these lines today: according to our own thoughts of the centuries, both our past, the century that has formally just concluded, and those of the future, perhaps, to come?

On one mark, given the history of the century that Du Bois so aptly named by his phrase "the problem of the twentieth century is the problem of the color line," a century of the Holocaust, of ongoing wars of colonization on a planetwide dispersal, of globalized war across boundaries that were proclaimed as both categorical and hierarchical, and the continuing suppression and exploitation of one nation or state by another, or ensembles of such, that remain definitive of our contemporary moment, Du Bois's formulation here in the eleventh paragraph of this essay should and does call us up short. It demands a pause that in one sense will be ceaseless. At the level of the register of his enunciation, from our standpoint, in our own historical present, we maintain a fundamental hesitation with regard to the possible destructive appropriation of Du Bois's statements in this passage. This is a hesitation that will be never be relieved.

On another mark, it is also the case, however, that we are not so free of the difficulty organizing Du Bois's thought in this paragraph as might be our wish. More often than not, just when we anticipate that we have escaped its horizon, we are most susceptible to the practice of a discourse that would restitute its limits. There are two implications here: one is that contemporary discourses of de-essentialization are not as radical as they might claim; the other is that a certain form of maintenance of this problem of limit may offer a more radical passage into the as-yet-impossible future of thought. Perhaps, in time, there will be much to be said of the limits of contemporary thought in this domain.

Instead, as the thought guiding us in this study is that of tracking Du Bois's practice with regard to the matter of the example (as it is announced as a problematization within thought), and since my concern is to propose a paleonymic reinscription of the discourse of this practice, I will maintain the restricted track that our elaboration has followed so far in order to bring its implication to conclusion. With regard to his thought, it is our responsibility to re-elaborate that in it which can move beyond its own stated limits as given in the historic past. Here is the problematic restated. If Du Bois's statements in this passage, for instance, are understood as the declaration of a finality, an already revealed or accomplished truth, then such an understanding would restitute the logic and premise of the worst forms of idealism in the material practices of colonialism, nationalism, xenophobia, and in modern racism and anti-Semitism. Elsewhere, in an adjacent theoretical reflection, I have remarked the general difficulty that is named in this passage (Chandler 2014, esp. 11–30; 2022, 145–220). If Du Bois's thought is here recognized as *the formulation of a problem*—with all of its limits of time and place, with the limits of its concrete ideological and discursive historicities—then his discourse remains profoundly at issue for a critical elaboration of the problem of historicity in our time. Let us say here in general terms that according to a protocol that is legible as his own most stated declarations in this essay, including in the eleventh paragraph, Du Bois's discourse resolutely affirms a maintenance of difference, of heterogeneity, in both the spatial and temporal senses.

2. A Performative

The entire paragraph can be understood as the discursive scene of a complex theoretical performative operation concerning the question of the entitlement of the nominalization Negro as a heading for the announcement of ideals for the future.

The most decisive aspect of the movement of Du Bois's thought in this paragraph is its opening premise, or rather the anacrusis, for this passage of his essay, although without articulation as such: that the Negro American contribution historial articulation or historical profile is not yet full or not yet decided. In a sense, this is the most decisive mark of the entire essay. Du Bois could have declared the radicality of a primordial sense as comprising the originality of the Negro and Negro American. Indeed, the reference could even have been to a categorically defined original spirit. If Du Bois had thought of race as an absolute given or as constituting an a priori determination (whether of bios or of the socius), then such a primordial or categorical claim would, perhaps, have been his first statement here. Also, he could have declared an absolutely pure finality as already in sight: a movement on the way toward the realization of an idea. Du Bois's theoretical disposition and rhetorical practice here affirms neither of these declarations. Instead his discourse addresses the complex matter of historiographical entitlement directly and as a problem.[10] At a fundamental level, an address of this problematic is the principal burden of the essay: to establish an entitlement on what has often been supposed as ontological ground, that is to say, that which would be claimed by ontology in a modern European discourse, especially by a modern traditionalized philosophical sense of existence as at stake and as a problem for thought (which here also necessarily implies the political, theological, legal, moral, and economic domains) for the narration of a Negro profile, in the general sense, or a Negro or African American profile, in the specific sense, in the history of the world.

3. A Re-stage

It is appropriate and perhaps necessary, at this juncture, to step back and re-stage the summary of this essay in the form of the three annotations I provided at the outset of our consideration in part II of this study. For those summary remarks were more on the terms of contemporary discussion. Now we can remark the problematic more clearly on the terms of Du Bois's text.

The most general or conceptually global level question guiding the entire movement of thought in "The Conservation of Races" is quite simple and explicitly legible, even if it is not declared in the register of an announced heading. This is the *problem* of "explaining the different roles which groups of men have played in Human Progress" (CR 6–7, para. 5). From this recognition on our part, Du Bois's response can be outlined on the basis of four points. First, he proposed that the place of groups of "men" in "Human Progress" is given by "natural law." Second, he claimed that the particular group called the Negro, the question of its existence as such notwithstanding at this stage of the discussion, must act in accord with such "natural law." These two thoughts were announced by Du Bois in the third paragraph according to what he understood as their inextricable interrelation: "For it is certain that all human striving must recognize the hard limits of natural law, and that any striving, no matter how intense and earnest, which is against the constitution of the world, is vain" (CR 5, para. 3). Third, Du Bois determined that the first step in the production of such an accord is to seek an understanding of just what is the character of such natural law. The relevant concept with regard to *the human in general* that Du Bois understands to issue from natural law is the concept of race. His critical work on this concept is one of the two main discursive scenes of the text. It is my concern in part I of this study. He proposed that the natural science concept of race was confounded. Yet he thought that a different conceptualization of such putative difference among humans could be formulated. In this other conceptualization, what has been understood as at stake under the heading of race passes ineluctably through the physical dimension but remains exorbitant to it. Du Bois understood what is at stake under the traditional heading of race as instead oriented by ideals issuing at the level of the "spiritual, psychical." From this reformulation of premise, a reformulated sense of basis, then, Du Bois proposes that one can produce a certain account of race in history. Fourth, and finally, he takes up the question of just what this group, the Negro, should do to develop and maintain itself in accord with such "natural law." As Du Bois writes in the voice of the first-person plural in the eleventh paragraph: "We cannot reverse history; we are subject to the same natural laws as other races" (CR 10, para. 11). Therefore, he declares that if this group is to determine "the different roles which groups of men have played in Human Progress" (CR 6–7, para. 5) to transpose the question from the fifth paragraph into the one that we are reading, or "if the Negro is ever to be a factor in the world's history," as he puts the question even more directly here, in this eleventh paragraph (CR 10, para. 11), then it must acknowledge this sense of race and organize to cultivate and maintain it. With this succinct formulation of the epistemic terms of the problem confronting this generation of African American intellectuals, Du Bois at this point registers on the surface of the text that such solution only raises another form of problem: what is the relation of such specific organization of group, by whatever name, to any horizon beyond it? The legible track to be cited, here in the first-person singular, is: "Can I be both?" We, in our time, could say "can we be both?" This may be understood as the second major discursive scene of the text. (Doubtless the specific statements that Du Bois makes about the organization of the American Negro Academy at whose founding meeting he is speaking could likely be of equal interest to others concerned with this text by Du Bois.) While we will confirm this on another track shortly, it can be said that the affirmation of specificity here functions not against a recognition of commonness (and this is explicit in the seventeenth paragraph of the essay and in the creed that forms its conclusion);[11] it is against the reduction to a simple idea of the same. Thus, "conservation," even in the midst of all its embedded contradictions, should be understood as an affirmation of possibility. This track is our present concern, in this section, part II, of this study.

With this summary in mind, we can now see that what Du Bois wishes to accomplish, in the eleventh paragraph of his essay, is the affirmation of an *entitlement*, and with it the postulation of a *duty* for the leaders of any organization thereof, for the organization of a putative group called the Negro. Such affirmation engages both any understanding that might traditionally be *supposed* ontological (for which instead I have proposed above that it may be better understood as posing a *para*ontological practical theoretical problem for thought), pertaining to the very possibility of any such entity, as well as a political level of consideration, of debate and judgment. (That is to note, the problematic issues for us as a matter of paraontological consideration and practice.) Du Bois will write as if there is already established the putative terms by which to recognize a historial entity, whether by a historiographical or a philosophical practice, respectively—in this epistemic dimension they are the same—called the Negro even as he is inaugurating (or re-inaugurating) the premises and terms by which such a recognition could be solicited. It is a performative operation that necessarily proceeds as if it were constative.

4. A Double Gesture

At least two aspects of this performative operation can be delineated. One is a reference to the putative past of the Negro American. Another is a reference to what can be called simply the Japanese example.

a. A FIRST GESTURE. Du Bois's *first gesture* in the eleventh paragraph is a recollection of a putative African American past. In proposing that the Negro has yet to deliver its "full" message to the world, Du Bois is not claiming that there is in the abstract no historicity or organization of ideal that could be ascribed to the Negro. And doubtless, the same should be said for his sense of the Japanese. And likewise, by extension for the Slav, which he will also name here. For these are the two other examples that Du Bois will name at this juncture in his essay. For him to claim otherwise would just as surely have affirmed a principal claim of *racist* discourse of his time just as if he had proclaimed a simple biological root of the Negro as a historial being. He does neither.

It is here, and on this bias alone, that one should recognize as salutary Du Bois's affirmation in this paragraph of both an ancient Egypt and ancient civilization in general in relation to a putative "Negro" (Ehret 2016; Bonnet 2019). In his contributions to the report on "the Eleventh Conference for the Study of the Negro Problems" of 1906, which was on African American "health and physique," although he quoted copiously from the leading anthropological scholars (namely physical anthropology) contemporary to the time of his writing, Du Bois directly declared in his own voice that "Egyptian civilization was the result of Negroid Mediterranean culture." He then continued: "While to the south arose the ancient Negro civilization of Ethiopia, and still further south we find ruins of ancient Bantu culture" (Du Bois 1906, 19, and see 16–23).[12] And then further, he proposed that "even the primitive culture of the mass of uncivilized Africans long ago reached a high grade."[13] Why is such a claim salutary? Because a claim against the *historial* profile of a putative Negro (and specifically the African in general) has always already been proposed in the American context of the nineteenth century. Such a mark is an essential term by which the question of historicity is proposed to Du Bois. A simple ignoring of such a mark—by proposing, say, the concatenated claim that race does not exist and, thus, that the distinction in question is impertinent and that even the putative Negro in question does not exist—cannot displace its operative effects. Moreover, a simple claim that the historicity in question followed only a racial line—by proposing the figure of a line of putatively unbroken descent called Negro—would augment a racist premise. What Du Bois does is to place a mark within historicity as generally conceived as recognizably produced by people who might now be called Negro or Negroid. It is this un-fungible insistence that opens and disorients the premise of the racist mark. Du Bois's claim *on this order of its enunciation* is on as firm a ground as any possible other claim (Chandler 2014, 44–55, esp. 48–49). For example: one might ask, what is the relation of a putative Europe to a supposedly replete Greece in terms of a traditional nineteenth-century concept of race? It would not be untoward to say that, according to Du Bois's premise, the Negro, whomever that might be, could make a far more ancient claim of a constitutive relation to the culture and civilization of a certain "Greece."[14] The complications ensuing in the wake of Du Bois's thesis as an interlocution disorients a racist proscriptive judgment of the "Negro past" or "the Negro in the past." The affirmative implication of Du Bois's proposition, however, should not be minimized. With this reference to an ancient Egypt, and to other ancient historical figures on the continent now called Africa, as "Negroid," the ostensibly actualized possibility of an originary movement of historicity is proclaimed. Du Bois is thus deep within the thicket of the nineteenth-century debate on the exemplary example of civilization.[15] His ensemblic example here should thus be understood to affirm historical possibility in general: Egypt and the ancient civilizations and cultures of Africa are as affirmable as any other in human history in general.

We can annotate here the new scholarship on ancient Nubia, especially the civilization of Kush. And, then, such reference indeed suggests a general historiographical rethinking of Egypt's ostensibly or supposed internal organization as well as its relation to those ancient civilizations south of the Upper Nile. Scholarship of the first two decades of the twenty-first century has begun to recover the itinerary of ancient Kush (which the Greeks knew as Nubia, from Kerma to Meroë, and otherwise), a civilization of the southern Nile, of autochthonous development, as part of a radical reorientation of our understanding of the continent in the ancient period (Pope 2006, 2014; Fisher et al. 2012; Bonnet 2019; Emberling and Williams 2020). This order of epistemological intervention proposes to pivot the whole perennial debate of the status of ancient Egypt, and Kush, in the history of civilizations and situate it according to a different axial orientation. This whole thetic disposition, in general afoot for the past half century and more in scholarship, has found its articulation not only with reference to the ancient period, as just noted, also not only within the new projections of scholarship toward a new general history of matters of Africa, as exemplified, for example, in the volumes up to the nineteenth century of the well-known UNESCO scholarly series (Ki-Zerbo 1981; Mokhtar 1981; El Fasi 1988; Niane 1984; Ogot 1992; Ajayi 1989), but now also within an efflorescence of the new documentary media, notably film (McGann 2019), enabling thereby a truly synoptic yet acute and detailed general understanding (rather than primarily a specialist knowledge) of the scale of the implication that a whole other knowledge of matters of Africa (than what were the dominant forms of understanding two generations past) for an understanding of world history, if you will, on a planetary scale of reference. All this is with regard to Du Bois's principal thesis: the originary production of historial formations of the provenance of the continent now understood as Africa from the inception of human civilizational practices.[16]

It is true that such an intervention might well affirm on a global level "the shadow of a mighty Negro past [that] flits through the tale of Ethiopia the Shadowy and of Egypt the Sphinx," confirming indeed that "the Negro" has long been "a co-worker in the kingdom of culture" (Du Bois 1903a, 4). Yet such a claim is at best still off the mark when the claim of historical vacuity or simple derivation is proposed concerning the Negro in America. As such, it gives Du Bois no hold on the account of the historical becoming of America. It is here, thus, on the same order of discourse that Du Bois issued concerning ancient Egypt, that one must also recall the claim about the status of Negro ideals in the making of America. In paragraph seventeen of our text thus, we find that Du Bois writes of the Negro in America: "We are that people whose subtle sense of song has given America its only American music, its only American fairy tales, its only touch of pathos and humor amid its mad money-getting plutocracy"

(CR 11–12, para. 17). (This passage is presented as part of a full quotation of paragraph seventeen in note 11, for part II.) After preparing the "The Conservation of Races" at the beginning of March, a few months later, during the early summer of 1897, in "Strivings of the Negro People," the essay that would later become the first chapter of *The Souls of Black Folk: Essays and Sketches*, Du Bois would write from the same conceptual space and theoretical position (Du Bois 1897a; 1897b; 1903a; see also 2015h). Echoing the epistemological formulation he had first sounded in paragraph eleven of "The Conservation of Races" essay, Du Bois wrote in the later one from 1897 (most likely in late June) of the positivity of a Negro American profile in relation to America: "Already we come now not altogether empty-handed" (Du Bois 1897a, 198, para 12; 2015h, 73, para. 12; see also 1903a, 11, chap. 1, para. 12). And then, five and a half years later, in "Of the Sorrow Songs," the essay that constitutes the closing chapter of *The Souls of Black Folk: Essays and Sketches*, written during the late winter months of early 1903 and prepared especially for that volume, Du Bois elaborated along the same epistemic track and in the same rhetorical register but in a manner that sediments resources for an elaborative theoretical gesture whose reach might distribute its desedimentative implications along a more fundamental strata. We remark that the incipit of his locution is a form of response—perhaps a response to a version of the "unasked question" as he adduced it in the opening paragraph of the opening chapter of *The Souls of Black Folk: Essays and Sketches*. That is to say, by the end of that book of essays, which includes most certainly autobiographical reflection, "sketches" that might at once be understood as both a form of ethnographical account and nascent sociological interpretation, and adroit political analysis, the perspective (which I am wont to remark as profoundly theoretical) has become deeply historiographical, throwing reference back to the very inception of the modern era.

> Your country? How came it yours? Before the Pilgrims landed we were here. Here we have brought our three gifts and mingled them with yours: a gift of story and song—soft, stirring melody in an ill-harmonized and unmelodious land; the gift of sweat and brawn to beat back the wilderness, conquer the soil, and lay the foundations of this vast economic empire two hundred years earlier than your weak hands could have done it; the third, a gift of the Spirit. Around us the history of the land has centered for thrice a hundred years; out of the nation's heart we have called all that was best to throttle and subdue all that was worst; fire and blood, prayer and sacrifice, have billowed over this people,

and they have found peace only in the altars of the God of Right. Nor has our gift of the Spirit been merely passive. Actively we have woven ourselves with the very warp and woof of this nation,—we fought their battles, shared their sorrow, mingled our blood with theirs, and generation after generation have pleaded with a headstrong, careless people to despise not Justice, Mercy, and Truth, lest the nation be smitten with a curse. Our song, our toil, our cheer, and warning have been given to this nation in blood-brotherhood. Are not these gifts worth the giving? Is not this work and striving? Would America have been America without her Negro people? (Du Bois 1903b, 262–63, chap. 14, para. 25)

It would be a mistake to take these statements by Du Bois as sustaining only a restituting orientation, a naively "nationalist" one perhaps, to the past. The passage in question should be understood as a statement of a problematic that pertains to the future. Du Bois's fundamental orientation here is to name the scene of historical possibility: the form of the surpassing of given limit; to propose a historial form that might be announced as exorbitant to existing limit.

We can affirm, perhaps more profoundly, the theoretical sense I propose that we recognize in this whole orientation that we are adducing in Du Bois's discourse at the turn to the twentieth century by annotation of both what Du Bois does not declare and by a notation of what his discourse yet renders legible across these three examples of statement.

In the strict sense, Du Bois's early 1897 text, in paragraph eleven, passes over in silence the place of a presumptive response to the most deeply sedimented form of the fundamental question that matters for him in the essay (CR 9–10, para. 11). Or it should be properly said that the whole of "The Conservation of Races" is a complex theoretical response to this question, as he put it in paragraph three of the essay: "the whole question of race in human philosophy" (CR 5, para. 3). In the life-course of thought and practice, it was seven years later, in his writing of early 1903, that this most fundamental order of question appears in direct locution, explicitly proposed, appearing in fact in the paragraph immediately preceding the one extracted and quoted in extenso immediately above. That question can be indicated with one sentence from that paragraph in the closing chapter of the whole *book* that is *The Souls of Black Folk*: "what is the meaning of progress, the meaning of 'swift' and 'slow' in human doing and the limits of human perfectibility?" (Du Bois 1903b, 262, chap. 14, para. 24).

That paragraph describes the problematization here as encoded in an ensemble of questions that remain "veiled, unanswered sphinxes on the shores of science." Yet too, here, it must be emphasized that instead of starting from simple presumption or declaring an absolute speculation, Du Bois broaches the matter of limit in knowledge as the form of a question. It is a question about the historical form of possibility, that is, in terms of opportunity. Du Bois continues: "So long as the world stands meekly dumb before such questions, shall this nation proclaim its ignorance and unhallowed prejudices by denying freedom of opportunity to those who brought the Sorrow Songs to the Seats of the Mighty?" (Du Bois 1903b, 262, chap. 14, para. 24). In the face of the ignorance of science, then, the socius in general will maintain its prejudgment as the mark or historical form of limit in the recognition of possibility. But then, with respect to science, while Du Bois does not as such proclaim an answer, that is, he does not do so here in his own voice, in an explicit register that we might today call theoretical, and it is certainly not historiographical or sociological or ethnological at the level of a statement from or about a factum, according to conceptions of these forms of knowledge as disciplines in my own time, it is nonetheless the case that Du Bois formulation of question here puts at stake for us a powerful premise concerning the making of all that we consider as America, even in its very idea, and thus can be quite legibly followed not only in the long passage from the penultimate paragraph of *The Souls of Black Folk* quoted at length above, but in our understanding of the itinerary of his thought in general of the turn to the twentieth century.

At the heart of an account of the place of three gifts of the Negro in an American horizon is the theme, which to my reading may now, for us, indeed, be understood as a kind of theoretical perspective. That is the theme of intermingling, of intermixture, of the crossing movements that yield traditions of sense and sensibility, of morals, of values and, indeed of ideals, that constitute the "warp and woof" of an American historicity.

It would not be untoward for contemporary discourses to recognize therein, in this passage of Du Bois from *The Souls of Black Folk*, especially in conjunction with the thought of "intermingling" that we have adduced in our reading of "The Conservation of Races," the formulation of an epistemological intervention, at once conceptual and theoretical.

To the extent he is able to affirm the heterogeneous organization of the historicity most specific to the African American, Du Bois is in turn able to recognize such for an American horizon in general. Or, better, by way of a certain maintenance or affirmation of the heterogeneity operating in the organization of the African American as an example of historicity, simultaneously maintaining that there is such a figure, or the announcement of the possibility of ideals of such, and yet that such a figure and such ideals remain essentially yet to come, Du Bois is able to insist on the constitutive bearing for America as a whole of the movement by which the African American as a historial problem has been rendered.

This affirmation at the level of a theoretical reflection can be described more closely.

It is certainly legible to read the text of "The Conservation of Races," as well as that of the opening chapter of *The Souls of Black Folk: Essays and Sketches*, "Of Our Spiritual Strivings," as a resolute struggle with this situation: the movement of dissociation in the formation of the subject and the heterogeneous organization of its historicity. There is indeed a manifest gesture in Du Bois's discourse to go beyond the negativity of the non-simple as announced in a Negro American inhabitation of world. For indeed this non-simple, by way of its negative and destructive form, that of given legalized limit and prejudice, for example, confounds all attempts at a decisive practice. Thus, how could such a gesture of resolution not manifest itself here—in this domain of the problematic?

It is also legible within his texts that Du Bois does not relinquish this heterogeneity: he postulates neither a pure sense of being American nor a pure sense of being Negro or Black or African American.

Thus it is that this practical theoretical affirmation of the mark of the limit, paradoxically turns the apparent opposition inside out. It thus reconfigures the limit as a form of the concatenation of being as existence. It marks the site of dissociation, then, not only as the stricture on a putative proclamation of the self or subject as the one or a pure singularity but as the very passage to a sense of the beyond that can yet take the form of an inhabitation of the subject as a historical form of reflexivity. It becomes both a descriptive or nominal name for the interlacing movement by which historicity is rendered palpable and the heading for the practice of a certain responsibility in the maintenance of a possible passage beyond the given forms of historical limit. Thus, Du Bois is not concerned simply with the maintenance of the *given* form of these gifts. Rather, this account is a desedimentation of the past that is concerned with an affirmation in the present of the possibilities of the future.

It remains for theoretical remark in our time that the very path of Du Bois's accession to such a characterization of the formation of "American" ideals is by way of his attention to the formation of a Negro or African American inhabitation of this problematic. Thus, it can be said that Du

Bois is open to the future of a possible America on the basis of his sense that what "is" Negro or African American is not yet. The Negro or African American as a historial figure has this character for Du Bois: that it "is" only to the extent that it is at issue; that it remains at stake in the form of the yet to come; that it is the *very scene* of such complication in the devolution of historicity; that it cannot be reflexively apprehended as a punctuality is the very form of its announcement as a historial figure. This is its relation to both its past and its future.

b. A SECOND GESTURE. However, before taking another step in gathering up the implication of this *first gesture*, a summation of what it renders legible for reinscription, let us address the *second gesture* in this turning moment of Du Bois's performative discourse, for the two gestures are interwoven in his locution, and we must eventually try to recognize their implication as operating as if they occur in a single statement.

What is the place of the reference to Japan in the eleventh paragraph of "The Conservation of Races"?

Du Bois posits a relation of commonness of the Japanese and African American historical examples. His claim operates on two levels simultaneously. One we might call topical or thematic. The other is formal or rhetorical. And, indeed, they are essentially inextricable. We operate with them as different analytical strata only in our own gesture of elaborative projection.

In order to establish a dimension of equivalence between the two historial figures within a theoretical perspective of modern historicity, shall we say, Du Bois must establish the basis of commonness beyond an ensemble of apparent differences—manifest or historical differences. And these differences are major. Japan, on the one hand, at the end of the nineteenth century would most likely have been understood by Du Bois as comprising a group of people located within a relatively discrete geographical space; and, for him, perhaps their physical character at the level of phenotype would have been understood as relatively homogeneous. This would be despite deep and profound manifest heterogeneity on all levels of mark, natural or social, historial throughout. And, perhaps worthy of special remark, its language, perhaps would have appeared primarily as homogeneous, despite its internal diversity and complex historicity, marked by profound diversity of both genesis and devolution. And, too, Du Bois took note that Japan, at least since the advent of the Meiji era, and at the time of his writing, had been reorganized under the restoration of the titular head of a sovereign, the Emperor of Japan. Also, at the time of Du Bois's writing Japan would have been most likely accepted among the intelligentsia in America as a "nation" and specifically one that would be understood as coterminous with a modern state. On the other hand, in this essay Du Bois had so far sought to define the Negro as a kind of "vast historical race" of which the Negro *in America, that is the United States of America,* was understood by him as just one part. Yet, if this were so, the geographical spaces in which the Negro might be found were dispersed across two or three continents, at least, with no singular sovereign authority, even in a titular fashion, and a manifest diversity of languages that could hardly be subsumed under even the most ambitious theoretical heading or a supposed homogeneity of "tongue" that could have occurred in the Diaspora of the African continent in general only on the basis of an always prior process of creolization. Then, likewise, such titular diversity would hold a fortiori with regard to the Negro in America, the United States, even if understood as a kind of whole.[17]

Across such fundamental manifest contrasts how does Du Bois's discourse sustain this reference? On this topical and thematic level, the key is that he is operating with the African American problematic in theoretical mind, as theoretical problem and example. On that epistemic basis he can adduce a whole other strata of historial attention than might appear to a traditional historiography, a nascent tradition that might privilege a supposed immediate empirical reference as the arbiter for its judgement of historical truth.

For Du Bois, we can surmise from his text, *the* Japanese, like African Americans and perhaps Americans in general, were in the midst of epochal change: both were in the midst of the first definitive moment of a somewhat new or renewed declaration about their inhabitation of the modern world. In this sense, the Meiji Restoration can be understood in historical parallel to American Reconstruction, not only in the proximity of their temporal inauguration but also and more fundamentally in the relation of each project to each of the two nation-state's efforts, respectively, to address the major obstacles to its future as a matter of democratization. (And Du Bois will link the moment of his birth to both of these moments in his autobiographical writings.[18]) It seems reasonable to understand Du Bois's fundamentally affirmative remarks on Japan leading up to the turn of the century as indicative of his general affirmation of the leadership in Japan by the first generation to find its historical voice during the early stages of the Meiji era, despite its militarization, even though to my knowledge we do not have a direct statement on this point by Du Bois during the 1890s. For Du Bois, the sense of deep commitment to self-transformation that marked leadership of this era for Japan, one might propose, would have been salutary. This would be exemplary perhaps of both the way time and circumstance may deliver a fundamental demand to a group and the way in which a certain kind of leadership could assume the task or duty as given by such a historical situation. (And this would be so even if I might remark in our own time the deep ambivalence and conservatism of the dominant factions of that leadership, summarized not only in its reinstitution of the imperial system but also more fundamentally in its oligarchic organization.) And here it should be noted that most African American intellectuals of Du Bois's generation on the whole affirmed the project of American Reconstruction, despite its failures (and even if, from a certain perspective of our own time we would underline the limits of its project, let alone the failures of its actualization), whereas such a view was not at all dominant among European or White American intellectuals of the time (Du Bois 1935; Aptheker 1989, 211–56). And, further, we know already from the essay "Strivings of the Negro People," which he would write within a matter of months after the composition of the text we are considering, that Du Bois was deeply critical of the way American political leadership resisted at every turn the protocol of change during the American Civil War and its long aftermath and the way in which a general reaction to change defined the postbellum South through to the turn to the twentieth century. Indeed, we might say that much of this leadership, even if not all of it, was in truth in deep and fundamental reaction. We can also recall that Du Bois was of the generation of African Americans that can be considered parallel to that of the Japanese intellectuals who were born during the early Meiji period and who came of age during the 1890s. In Japan, this generation would include, for example, such very different figures as Mori Ōgai or Natsume Sōseki (even, slightly later, in the adjacent generation, Kitarō Nishida ought to be remarked here). Like Ōgai, for Du Bois the educational system was the keystone to the "modernization" or "uplift" of his group (the former term could summarize Ōgai's approach; the latter names Du Bois's time and situation). There would be a difference here similar perhaps to Du Bois's ambivalent early relation, before 1903, to the project of Booker T. Washington and the work of T. Thomas Fortune. Like Sōseki, Du Bois was ambivalent about *both* the values and ideals that were dominant in Europe (and perhaps among Euro-America) *and* the values and ideas he inherited from his own specific background (certain aspects of nineteenth-century Japan for Sōseki and the impact of the institution of slavery on African American practices for Du Bois) and thus maintained a profound and abiding critical reserve about how to resolve the question of an approach to the future. In a manner that was different from Sōseki's profound and fecund hesitation, Du Bois's work of this time maintains a resolute hopefulness in the midst of this fundamental ambivalence. The comparative status of such hesitation and hope, respectively, marks out a whole domain for contemporary reflection. The operative question might be raised as follows. Ought the relation of sympathy be premised on a sense of loss or on a sense of affirmation? We can propose, then, that the structure of attention that organizes Du Bois's reference to Japan in the eleventh paragraph names an entire domain of historical possibility and relation that yet remains for thought to address in our own time.[19]

For Du Bois, thus, the reference was fundamentally an affirmation of the possibility and implication of difference at every level of social and historical order. It is Du Bois's disposition here toward temporality that provides the key for us, to enable us to understand such bearing. It is with this reference that it becomes clear that Du Bois's ultimate concern is with the present and its future rather than the past. For example, Du Bois could have referred to Japan's own sense of its past—to affirm a history declared to reference millennia and defined in centuries or epochs (not mere decades as in the United States)—in order to claim that a distinct "message" for the world had already been well constituted therein. Also, as Japan was in the midst of the Meiji Restoration—which had in the titular sense reestablished the emperor system—Du Bois could have directly claimed or proposed affirmation of a principle of absolute sovereignty, with the monarchial reference implied, as the justification for recognizing Japan as a historial entity in the present and future. Everything would be under this entitlement: issuing from it, ultimately, and returning to it in the final instance. And if he had proposed either of these positions, he would in essence have declared the heading of sameness—of the simple and of the pure—as the most fundamental principle of his thought in this paragraph. He does not propose either one. Rather, by way of his insistence that the "true" and "full" message of Japan is yet to come, Du Bois may be understood to have resolutely affirmed the movement of a heterogeneity at the root—as the root—of Japan's becoming as a historial figure. Du Bois has thus affirmed the differential form of becoming, named here in the difference of the present of Japan and its possible future as other than this present in the future, as operating within the constitution of the figure of Japan as a historial entity. But, further, this differential structure of Japan's historicity announces and governs the terms on which it would be seen or recognizable in any horizon understood to include it, a global or a worldwide or a "cosmopolitan" *one*. It thus announces not so much a replete simplicity in such context as a differential position. This affirmation of the figure of Japan would stand for Du Bois across the entire remainder of his itinerary. What we might notice in the writings by Du Bois in the 1940s and 1950s, instead, is a profound hesitation about the impact of the United States in postwar Japan. While he would affirm an elaboration of constitutional democracy, he would disavow both the character of its actual promulgation in the United States occupation and the reinstallation of an even more powerful form of the principle of capital accumulation as the titular frame of Japanese "ideals," as leading or guiding values, than had existed before the war. And, while he never releases this affirmation of Japan, one senses that Du Bois still imagined another possible horizon of values that the nation known as Japan had yet to be willing to affirm: democracy as the truly fundamental principle for all matters of the collective—including, for him, the economic dimensions of social order (Du Bois 2012; Chandler 2012b). Perhaps in our own time, the matter remains so, a fortiori, under the contemporary name, Okinawa (Shimabuku 2018; Matsumura 2015).

This differential organization of becoming, named here under the heading of temporality, is the very form of any global horizon of historicity. Above all, however, it can be shown that for Du Bois there was no finality, no given totality, to such a horizon. And for this reason, for him such a system of differences ought to be affirmed, maintained, as a global horizon and not disavowed, diminished, or simply subsumed. To do otherwise would be to attempt a disavowal of historicity, of the modern epoch certainly, if not of historicity in general.

At this juncture, we can now give some depth to a recognition that Du Bois is also operating certain rhetorical forms to adduce the reference to Japan as an affirmation of a nominalization of the African American as a titular heading for a narration. The issue is the proposition of an entitlement for recognizing a historial and historiographical subject. As Du Bois turns from an account of race (in his sense) in history toward an account of the present and future, that is, as he seeks to turn his discussion from one that presents itself as knowledgeable and informative to one that would offer an appeal and a solicitation to action, he elevates the formal tone of his address. At that precise juncture, in a gesture that might be usefully understood as metaleptic, Du Bois steps aside from the scene of common ground he has sought to establish with his immediate auditors at this founding meeting of the American Negro Academy, even as that dramatic scene would continue to unfold as the immediate theatrical background, so to speak. And here he interposes another dramatic historical scenography—that of Japan at the end of the nineteenth century—by speaking as if he could represent, or speak for, a putative point of view that might find its standpoint within that situation. And, then, just as abruptly, Du Bois steps back into this situation of presumptive commonness and continues his address.

This whole contrapuntal rhythm of Du Bois's locution can then be described as a set of formal operations. The discourse operates two primary figures of repetition: synonymia and anaphora. It uses anaphora within a larger synonymic repetition:

> For the development of Japanese genius, Japanese literature and art, Japanese spirit, only Japanese, bound and welded together, Japanese inspired by one vast ideal, can work out in its fullness the wonderful message which Japan has for the nations of the earth. For the development of Negro genius, of Negro literature and art, of Negro spirit, only Negroes bound and welded together, Negroes inspired by one vast ideal, can work out in its fullness that great message we have for humanity. (CR 10, para. 11)

Synonymia is produced by the placement of these two examples in contiguous relation in the context of the syntax of the entire paragraph. Although the example of the Negro is the putative titular preoccupation of this reflection, it is positioned as the second example, producing the overall structure the articulation of synonymia. Then the use of anaphora serves as a formal pattern that joins the two examples across the difference of the appearance here as nominal entities. This anaphoric organization bears within its form the implication of a substantive thesis of a commonness of status of the Japanese and the Negro with regard to the historicity of the present at a global level. It thus implies a speculative dimension that would exceed and encompass their nominal difference. It is this general dimension of possible relation that is then recapitulated by the overall synonymic organization of the presentation of the two main nominal figures in this paragraph.

Du Bois's procedure here, in the eleventh paragraph of "The Conservation of Races," operates in a rhetorical manner that is similar to the form of his reference to a certain "Europe" in his autobiographical discourse—in a text that would become the first chapter of *The Souls of Black Folk: Essays and Sketches* and which was written within months of the reference to Japan that we are considering—in which he understood Europe as a domain that proposed the imaginal horizon of an illimitable association among humans. (And almost parenthetically he references the Slav, in which group he will include Russia, Slovenia, Poland, the Baltic states, and essentially all of the "eastern" countries of "Europe." Indeed these countries remained a "group" of fundamental interest for him throughout his life.) In light of the formulations that we were able to develop in the opening sections of part I, perhaps we can adduce this gesture as a metaleptic formulation of illimitable (external) association by way of an affirmation of (internal) dissociation. It may be understood as a general problematic in Du Bois's thought (Chandler 2022). Here we can say that the formal practice of repetition just outlined above—hyperbolic in character and metaleptic in implication—names an order or dimension of historicity in which two specific and concrete examples are named as existing on a common horizon. It joins them across their apparition or emergence as nominal entities. Such a dimension, a horizon beyond the American scene of denial and proscription or any global-level operation of the same, in the context of our reflection on the discourse of "The Conservation of Races," names the entitlement for an African American historical subject on the global level or in the context of modern historicity as a whole.

At the epistemic level, the presentation of this relation, here outlined in formal terms but also indexing the thematic aspects remarked above of the figure of Japan and the figure of the African American, announces the titular claim that guides Du Bois's discourse in this eleventh paragraph and in this address as a whole: the proclamation of an African American historical entity at the end of the nineteenth century. And, it announces all the epistemic implications that would follow therefrom: the authority to claim a name, of self-identification; the right to narrate a form of becoming under the heading of this nominalization; a remark, in a practical theoretical political sense of the power to participate in the marking or re-marking of distinction in the order of the symbolic, principally of the relation to an other (even of self as other), or along the stress lines of both difference (say, in America) and commonality (with, say, Japan).

Yet the formulation of this relation also proposes a scene of entitlement for the imagination of a Japanese historical entity that would remain yet to come at the end of the nineteenth century. For, having suggested that Du Bois operates this reference to Japan to assist in the elucidation of the dimension in which an African American historicity can be recognized, it is necessary to reemphasize the whole rhythm of this procedure. It is first the case, shall we say, that he operates a double sense or vision—and we are at the textual and chronological point in Du Bois's itinerary wherein it is *first* being adduced as a theoretical enunciation or statement and will explicitly follow in a matter of paragraphs—that he will call Negro or African American in order to look beyond the American scene to another horizon, in which and according to which, he can recognize another historical profile he will call Japan. Du Bois thus claims to recognize and affirm Japan in terms of the matter of the historiographical as in the midst of the struggle or striving to propose a future that would be otherwise than either the past or the present-as-past. In this latter instance, he would not only name Japan's affirmation of a futural rendering of itself as the terms of locution by which he is affirming his own openness to such; it is also the case that what he is affirming in Japan and which he claims to recognize therein is a differential mode of becoming that he is also recognizing as specifically his "own" or as the mode of historical becoming of the African American. That is to say, on the basis of his own sense of the historial problematic that has been given to the Negro race (in his sense) in America, Du Bois proposes to recognize the character of the principal problematic that has taken shape in modern history for the Japanese.

In the rhetorical style of Du Bois's presentation of these two examples in the paragraph as a whole, now understood as the mode of joining its formal and thematic aspects, the differences affirm each other: they announce a horizon of the common by way of this articulation of difference.

However, two critical marks must remain here.

One might be a riposte to the most declared terms of Du Bois's formulation: a persisting premise or promise of the "one," the "full," the "true." We must acknowledge a conundrum here: how can one deny these values of orientation? One cannot do so simply, as in the form of an absolute and final declaration. For even to disavow them, one must operate with them. Thus, we read Du Bois's *practice* in his discourse both with and beyond the limits of his own, perhaps necessary, *declarations*. His text resolutely attends to the structure of a temporal passage that constitutes the making of historicity. This sustains a fundamental caution in the domain of the African American situation—then and now. It is also thus the scene of the generosity of his discourse in the text at hand.

Another concerns the example of Japan. Through the metaleptic operation we have followed in the eleventh paragraph of "The Conservation of Races," by way of the example of Japan, Du Bois proposes an affirmation of the possibility of difference as the basis for the recognition of the common or the same. Du Bois formulates the entitlement of Japan's historial status as rooted in a dimension of differential becoming that would distantiate any postulation of a pure genesis or the premise of a telos as a pure finality. This form of recognition of a given historicity would stand already as a riposte to any idea of absolutely replete historial being as sense of self or subject.

IV. CODA

All of this has been on the track of formulating an epistemic entitlement by which to recognize a historiographical figure under the heading of the Negro—and of course, specifically the Negro American in the United States. By way of a certain practice of reading, what I have adduced so far in this passage through the text of Du Bois, specifically a sheaf comprising four paragraphs from the address "The Conservation of Races," is an order of discourse that can be gathered up as a general theoretical proposition. At this level of his practice, as thought, a specific conceptualization of the historicity that inscribes African Americans can be rendered. This is a distinct conception that understands the general structures of historicity that produces the African American as a historial figure as having the always previous infrastructural organization of a certain intermingling and intermixture as its root or ground. (And of course, in this domain every concept metaphor and every term inscribed by discourse is a heavily marked citation. As such it can never be ultimate according to the decision that would inscribe it in theoretical discourse. Hence no quotation marks in the previous sentence.) According to the alogical logic we have begun to adduce here, the entity, the singular, or the instance, are nameable or recognizable only in its articulation as such a heterogeneous form. According to such a thought, form takes shape in the asymmetrical reciprocity of a secondary rhythm, an organization of the second-time, in which "the root of rhythm is its central unit of change" (notably as we have the thought from Cecil Taylor, as annotated from the outset of part II). We have, thus far, been able to propose in our own register of theoretical intervention that such a thought guides Du Bois when he affirms the historial figure of the Negro in general, and the Negro American in the United States in particular, circa 1900, as yet to deliver its "full" message to the world.

A NOTE ON IMPLICATION

We have also been able to recognize two implications beyond that direct titular problematic. On the one hand, I have suggested that this whole gesture of thought directs Du Bois's critical challenge to all those who might begin in the domain of matters African American with the premise that there is always already an analytically replete America to which any practice therein called Negro, or its ensemblic synonyms, should be understood as an appendage or derivation. Instead, by way of his thought of the historial institution of the Negro as American, Du Bois is able to operate the concept metaphor of a certain "warp and woof" as definitively marking the character of the historicity in general that makes it so that such a figure—America, even the very idea of such, as material idea—could be announced at all (Du Bois 1903b, 262–63, chap. 14, para. 25). On the other hand, I have proposed that by way of a certain theoretical gesture, a metaleptic operation, Du Bois was able to adduce a dimension of historicity whose organization relativized both the American scene and the global scenography of his historical present. According to this dimension of historicity, the structure of that which is at stake in the present and yet to come, Du Bois could propose a profound common by which to relate the two historial figures of the Negro American and the Japanese. He was able to name a sense of horizon in which the differential becoming of the future in both figures, the Negro and the Japanese, and in general, could be affirmed as the basis for a future beyond the limits of either the past or the present in any sense.

It was on the basis of this general thought of the status of the differential form of the duration that is the future—or even the future of the future—that Du Bois could insist upon the necessity of announcing an African American historial figure in the America of the present at the end of the nineteenth century and in the future in general.

A NOTE ON IDEALIZATION

It is such an orientation that guides him in the remainder of the essay in his formulations on the future of race differences in his sense. And the specific course that he will propose that the Negro take in the future is given when he writes, in the twelfth paragraph, of the need of the African American to "unswervingly follow Negro ideals." This follows just beyond where we have broken off our tracking of Du Bois's text.

Still, how should we understand this orientation to "Negro ideals," according to the path of elaboration we have been following here? If we take the phrase "Negro ideals" as the name for a problem of existence, then it directs us to a theoretical formulation of the question of *problem*. In this sense, thinking with Du Bois's text of the 1890s, the Negro American, whatever that might be, would pursue a certain "conservation" only as there is such a problem—that of the affirmation of originary possibility—in that historical form. It would be given or not in the historical devolution of freedom. One could then propose a horizon in which the *problem of the Negro* has no such form, that is, has no form. The crucial measure here is that the "*duty*" of "*conservation*" is not categorical or oppositional. The duty in question is the conservation of a difference in both registers of the Negro and the American. One maintains the difference of self that is the path of the announcement of the Negro, as American, as *also* the imperative to hold forth an originary movement of idealization under the heading of the Negro. It is this commitment that sets afoot the terms of the dilemma of subjectivation—the imperative of the maintenance of a heading called Negro outlines a sense of double commitment or double identification, forms of the general figure of intermingling and intermixture that we have adduced in Du Bois's discourse—which he will describe as the very sense as experience of the African American as a subject of historicity. Yet such maintenance of limit is otherwise than any sense of an absolute or a pure finality. *It is a constituted name of the passage beyond or to the thought of an outside.* This is the precise epistemic bearing for contemporary discourse in my own time that I have come to recognize in Du Bois's conceptual and theoretical labor of the end of the nineteenth century and the turn to the twentieth century, for example from 1894 to 1904, the time of the essays of "The Conservation of Races," "Strivings of the Negro People," *The Souls of Black Folk: Essays and Sketches* and the immediate textual aftermath of that accomplishment (see also Chandler 2014, 15–19).

This thought would disrupt at its root any premise or presumption of purity that a putative America might proclaim for itself. This would especially be so if such an implicit heading of purity were as "white" in the specific context of the historicity of the figure of America. Beyond such, though, it would name a thought of both sides of the limit, of the immanent movement of the illimitable as the concatenation of an always previous difference. Understood as the heading of a problem, such a formulation remains radical in our time.[20]

In order to further annotate this thought, I now propose a transposition in which we may bring the question that we have tracked on the level of historicity in general in an early text of Du Bois into dialogue with a contemporary formulation of the problem of practice, of practice understood as art, specifically the practice of the making of music, a form of poïesis in a sense we can recognize from the itinerary of Cecil Taylor. Such practice is at best an outcropping that arises within the topography of an ongoing critical inhabitation of sense (or, we may be permitted to the problematization as a *tropo*graphy). In a certain recognition of Taylor's practice, specifically then, we can propose the general thought that the constituted takes shape only in the address of a problem. It is perhaps in this sense that "form is possibility." At best, then, the formulation of a solution to a problem takes place, if at all, only as another form of problem. We can propose it as the appearance of the singular by way of the blind of repetition. In this sense that which appears only announces the impossible possibility of that which is yet to come. In an essential sense there is no origin, as simple. There is only the appearance of genesis: a structure of originary displacement in which historical form acquires its organization only in the ineluctable differentiation that the arrival of a form induces in the structure that would announce its origination. It is the alogical logic of the appearance of the second time. Such is a principal concept metaphor for the temporal or genetic structure according to which historicity acquires its organization. Certainly this proposes that historicity is always organized through the "warp and woof" of an irreducible and ceaseless passage of the same and the different. It also proposes that there can be a first time only through its configuration in the announcement of the second time. But it proposes that the rhythm of this relation is not according to the irreducible kernel of the same as an idea of form; rather, "the root of rhythm is its central unit of change," an asymmetrical "irregular rhythm," and it does not, as such, state its theme, that is, declare its form as a final idea. Such a statement would always be after the fact, in its wake, in the form of an announcement of the second time. Its form, if at all, would be as problem. This, then, would characterize the historicity, the making of "ideals," that is the emergence of an "African American" historial profile. As Taylor writes astride the movements of the 1960s, it is "subculture becoming major breath" and, yet, "a naked fire gesture" (Taylor 1966).

Approached according to these formulations, Du Bois's thought of the making of Negro ideals is such that its appearance can only take place in the form of the temporal figure of the double or of a doubling—the structured repetition that alone would make possible the constitution of an origin, a so-called origin. For this reason, this thought should be understood less under the heading of the ideal as an idea, or an ideal as pure form, and more by way of a transposition that recognizes the announcement of a possible ideal as the immanent movement of problematization of existence as a way. If we simply retain the name of ideals now as one mark among others, but following here also the discursive context of our discussion of Du Bois—then it is at best only a name for something that is at stake as a difficulty within a *historical* present—as such it is an immanence that marks the possibility of a passage beyond an existing limit, as the yet impossible.

Such would be the path or track by which all those who come late to the threshold of historicity would announce themselves—always otherwise and this just might include every *one*. Always already displaced from origin, such would be the status for any inhabitation of an originary displacement. If it will have been, ever, any inhabitation, it would yet be announced, if at all, as another origin, or better, a re-incipit, a reinauguration, of world, the beyond, which takes the form of another world in this world here and now.

So, what, then, is the implication for contemporary theoretical practice in the general field of studies concerned with the heading "African American" of this passage through the early thought of Du Bois? There are two—one concerning Du Bois's discourse, the other concerning our own. With regard to Du Bois, this passage suggests that his thought must be engaged *first affirmatively* if there is to be an engagement as such. In this way the limits of his discourse might be able to provoke our own epistemological production. That is, there must be a certain fidelity of the letter, first, if we are not to say just whatsoever we wish from our place of an already decided preference in relation to his texts. In this manner, the inhabited limits of his discourse can provoke our own practice as a transgression of those limits. I prefer to call this a form of hyperbolic repetition. For us the question is, how should we approach the problem of the relation of intellectual generations? The approach I have proposed here, which is certainly not the only one in the general sense, maintains that a *paleonymic problematic* (by which I mean the question: how does a supposed new thought engage its inheritance of old words, ideas, concepts, or theoretical premise, which it receives as perhaps already apparently worn out or outworn) is inscribed in every dimension of such a relation. Therefore, at the present, in our own time—which should perhaps be understood as a certain turning point in theoretical production in the field of African American matters as well as in the field of matters entailing the African Diaspora (whatever is such) more generally (not to gainsay the study of all that is at stake under the heading Japan)—what is a fortiori demanded is a profound resting or abiding with the difficulties posed for any practice of thought in any such domain. For the difficulties attendant to the domains just remarked in general could be metaphorized as fault lines running through the epistemic bedrock of our time. Yet, paradoxically in the dimension of existence that is announced in the form of the historial, such lines of concatenation may yet be understood to mark the passage of transposable force. They may yet be understood to mark both sides of a limit. In this sense they could yet become ore-lines for the future practices of thought.

Is there not a heading for this possibility, a critical and desedimentative inhabitation of the historically given, already announced within the practices that have taken shape on the stitched seam of a historicity we can properly call African American? Accepting the inscriptions of both W. E. B. Du Bois and Cecil Taylor here, we can propose that the problem of existence in this domain has never been simply a matter of the persistence of the ideal—whether as philosophy or religion—or the problem of its maintenance. It has also always been a matter of an affirmation of possibility in the break, or irruption, of historical devolution. And, among contemporary thinkers, the work of both Hortense Spillers and Fred Moten comes forth here (Spillers 2003a; Moten 2003). It is in this sense that one can recognize that a theoretical negotiation of this problematic must proceed not only by way of a strict calculation—which it must do—but also by way of the work of the infinitesimal forms of mundane inhabitation. Such heterogeneous practice might be best understood as the practice of an art. In this specific sense, the forms of historicity by which the problem at hand has been engaged yield "form [as] possibility": techniques of suspension of both "double-consciousness" or the sense of "invisibility," on the one hand, or "the bridge" or "the leap," on the other; a fundamental acknowledgment of a practical privilege for the "architectural" figure of the cantilever in form or gesture in general, the practice of the "cut" as a motive of repetition in any order of the social, including the so-called aesthetic, or, the "extravagance of laughter," for example. Such forms, as possibility alone, can name the dimension of existence that can sustain the practice of the metaleptic mode and the organization of force that is hyperbolic repetition. Such for Du Bois. Such for Taylor. What remains at stake, then, for a critical or desedimentative form of practice is not the question of the right or true theory: it is now the question of a carrying forth of the *task* of theoretical labor (Spillers 2003b).

And, then. Might not a certain Europe of the future, our future, for example, and now not only a certain America, recognize its inheritance from the historial profile of a *Negro or African* America? And if so, perhaps in the first rank would be the thought of one W. E. B. Du Bois? Might not another Japan, for example, of the future, reimagine the sense of its own historiality along a track that would profoundly dissemble the yet still powerful pertinence of Du Bois's inimitable concept metaphor, "the *problem* of the color line" (my emphasis), and instead affirm the terms of that still hyperbolic figure of the double: not only the Japanese American at 1897 but also the African American Japanese or Japanese African American at 2007)?"[21] Such a thought as possibility at each of the last two turns of the centuries has now become actual and general—astride the onset of the third decade of this so-called twenty-first century—more than a century and a quarter after Du Bois's first solicitation and yet also remains, still, at stake and beyond even such a sense of then and now.

These are examples. Apparently staid. Perhaps. For it is the case that for those who would presume that one can adjudicate such nominalization from the outside ("no, no, not me, not *my* name" or "no, no it is not so *simple*"), there is no neutral outside of *this* game and its essential possibility. The concatenation does not simply start with these terms. It is, necessarily, their very possibility: and, such it is, in every stage of the reflex in which one would inhabit its passage. In the movement of reciprocal articulation, a dynamic of always parenthetical referentiality is set afoot, the logic of which ultimately destabilizes the premise of the ostensible repleteness of the terms it operates. At the root, we shall we say.

Such is the unstable line that remains most intractable in contemporary thought in this global dimension: to recognize that one's most fundamental and specific historial formation might well be grounded in a constitutive passage through the other, even and perhaps especially, if that other is understood as the radical other—let us say, here, the enemy.[22] Such is the relation of that apparently anachronistic problematic of the African American to the most contemporary forms of thought in our time. Such concatenation is the form, if there is such at all, of both limit and passage. Such is the movement of the whole process as it is always at stake in the distended form of a here and a now. This is the epistemic scene of the future for theoretical labor in our own time in the context of the world of the first generation of the third millennium of this epoch of the modern (Adelson 2017). Perhaps we are not wont to have proposed here that we may think our problematic anew by way of the practical theoretical example of Cecil Taylor, reinscribing herein a tensile thread of the legacies given in the thought of our time, yet also writing once again—always a second time—with the persisting example of the thought opened in the early discourses of one W. E. B. Du Bois.

AFTERTHOUGHT

It might be said that still, in our own time—even as we are abreast of the massive resurgence and affirmative transformation at once of our understanding of all things of Africa, both of its continental provenances and of its Diaspora, most certainly including matters African American, that has been afoot during the past half-century and more—it remains that a fundamental de-sedimentation of the most deeply embedded premises of contemporary thought with regard to differences among supposed groups of humans, gathered as they have been under the heading of the concept of race, are radically at stake for us, our time, our future, our worlds. If so, the annotations of the early work of W. E. B. Du Bois in the present study may be given an additional remark, at once general and theoretical, with some regard to discourses that may be understood as of philosophical provenance.

From the last quarter of the eighteenth century within certain discourses of Europe and the Americas and the Caribbean the idea of the transcendental (a thought that would pertain to all times and all places and for all, without reduction to any particular, as empirical, example) has been proposed and elaborated to sustain in thought the premise of the supposed universal or, ultimately, of the supposed absolute. Yet, a practice otherwise than a pathway determined by such premise may be possible. For, if there is at stake for thought that which we may call the transcendental, it is never simply given, there, available as a presumption, rather it must be constituted. This is to say, if there is such as the transcendental, it has historicity or, better, is *of* historicity. This is also to say, thus, there is also a transcendental historicity. Finally, by way of or as this historicity the supposed transcendental must be understood as always, a mark, an inscription, a position—on the bias, as it were—radically otherwise than the neutral, the ultimate simple, or the supposed absolute and simple general.

It is this thought, with all of its difficulty, tremulous for thought in our time, by way of matters that I inscribe here as African American, in the general sense, another path and passageway to another sense of the general, perhaps, that I have sought to sustain in the annotations of this study.

NOTES

PART I: ON PARAGRAPH FOUR OF "THE CONSERVATION OF RACES"

Dedication: Robert Bernasconi—along with his contribution to contemporary philosophical thought, a certain rethinking of the problematic that has in the past been named under the heading of ethics—has for two whole generations now sought in a manner that is fundamentally scholastic as well as theoretical to bring into relief the constitutive status of the history of the concept of race, including with regard to both Africa and the African Diaspora, in the promulgation of modern philosophy that has proceeded by way of its European elaboration. I dedicate the present discourse in respect, especially to his initiative of the two decades adjacent to the turn to the twenty-first century.

A portion of part I of this study was published in CR: *The New Centennial Review* 14.3.

1 As I remark elsewhere, with regard to my usage of the term *historial*, the theoretical concern is to propose the interest of a step toward something just beyond a simple or naive historicism in the strict sense, when one seeks to address a thought of possibility, to propose the thought of some order beyond the given, the very possibility of an entity that may be understood as given in its existence by emergence, becoming, maintenance, duration, denouement, in the idioms at once of a singularity and a perduration or possible idealization (Chandler 2021a).

2 Alfred A. Moss Jr., in *The American Negro Academy: Voice of the Talented Tenth* (Moss 1981), gives us a detailed account of the preparations and event of this first meeting of the Academy and its context and immediate aftermath. In preparation for the founding session, several addresses on the purpose and goals of the new organization were solicited. W. E. B. Du Bois was asked to speak on the topic of "The Duty of Cherishing and Fostering the Intellect of the Race." Three others were invited to speak: B. T. Banner on "The Special Qualities that Our Race Can Give to the Civilization of the Country," but illness kept him away; J. W. E. Bowen on "The Unique Opportunity for the Growth and Development of the Negro Intellect" and W. H. Crogman on "The Special Work of the Educated Professors Aside from the Beaten Path of Their Vocations," but neither could attend due to prior commitments. A. P. Miller replaced Bowen. Kelly Miller spoke instead of Crogman. And Alexander Crummell gave the opening address. According to Moss, eighteen founding members were present on the occasion at A. P. Miller's Lincoln Memorial Congregational Church, including eight of the nine Washington-based members—John W. Cromwell, Alexander Crummell, Francis J. Grimké, Walter B. Hayson,

John A. Johnson, John L. Love, Albert P. Miller, Kelly Miller—and ten members from other locales—Matthew Anderson, Charles C. Cook, Levi J. Coppin, W. E. B. Du Bois, William H. Ferris, George N. Grisham, W. T. S. Jackson, Lewis B. Moore, William S. Scarborough, and Richard Robert Wright. However, the academy specifically did not include women, even as the matter was directly posed at its opening meeting (Moss 1981, 31, 35–57, esp. 38, 40–41). The documents collected by Moss in the preparation of his study are now deposited in the archives of the Virginia Theological Seminary. See also the account by David Levering Lewis (Lewis 1993).

3 The idea of nature here entails that (at a determinate instance of its lineal possibility) whatever is named under the heading of nature is a closed realm of necessity. In my understanding of his account of the project of a science of the human, Michel Foucault describes such an idea as of a precritical moment persisting into the second-half of the eighteenth century in an ongoing epistemological projection within Europe, a projection that nonetheless was already in epistemic decline under the force of the critical projection of Immanuel Kant (Foucault 1973, 1966). But, in truth, it may have found renewed maintenance within Kant's critical discourse, at stake within and, in turn, placed at stake, his thought on teleology, despite the legible internal contradictions that rendered it incoherent (Kant 2001c, 2007b). R. A. Judy, in his early 1990s reading of a precritical statement about "the Negro" by Kant, had already suggested the contradictory implication of such a maintenance for thought in terms of the architectonic of the critical project (Judy 1993, 108–46; 1991). However, to my understanding Judy does not remark the 1788 essay on teleology. I consider that 1788 essay to encode a pivotal theoretical formulation, the most fulsome summary articulation, of the problematization by Kant with regard to his conceptualization of human difference and its ostensible implication for critical thought, prior to his complicated late efforts to reengage the teleological problematic in his Third Critique (Kant 2000).

4 The *scholastic* lead here was taken by Robert Bernasconi, who beginning in the late 1990s undertook to excavate Kant's writings on the concept of race and bring them to the English-speaking discussion. Here, one should notice his own interpretation of this discursive formation, especially on the place of Kant therein (Bernasconi 2001). That scholastic work included first of all his organization of the first complete translation and publication of several key essays on this concept by Kant from the 1770s and 1780s, above all the 1788 essay now translated under the title "On the Use of Teleological Principles in Philosophy" (Kant 2001c, 2001b, 2007b). It also includes, secondarily, Bernasconi's bibliographic excavation and initiative to reprint many eighteenth-century texts on the idea and problematic of so-called race in general in a fashion that for the first time made them relatively available to a general scholarship in our contemporary moment, presented as an entire anthology comprising eight lengthy volumes (Bernasconi 2001). We should annotate here, however, along with the immediately previous note, that the first systematic attention to Kant's thought of "the Negro" in the contemporary English-speaking context in a theoretical manner that is quite pertinent to the itinerary of engagement with the discourse of Du Bois was in the work of R. A. Judy dating from the early 1990s (Judy 1991; 1993, 108–46).

5 Among others, one can cite the survey from more than two generations ago by the late paleontologist Stephen J. Gould (Gould 1996) and the signal anthology that was prepared a generation past by Evelynn Maxine Hammonds and Rebecca M. Herzig (Hammonds and Herzig 2008). On the relation of the American discourse of the mid-nineteenth century to the question of an anthropology, along with William R. Stanton's work of more than three generations ago, the comparatively more recent work of Scott Michaelsen should be noted (Stanton 1960; Michaelsen 1999).

6 It may be noted here that when republished in April 1903 as the ninth chapter of *The Souls of Black Folk: Essays and Sketches,* the book version of the text of the 1901 essay is without its epistemologically frame-setting first locution. Perhaps Du Bois understood the frame as already provided by the 1903 book as a whole, notably its forethought (Du Bois 1903e, 164–65).

7 The literature that could be cited here is substantial and growing. I reference just a handful of texts that indicate the character of the most specific horizon of discussion and intervention that I wish to remark, a certain "phenomenological" tradition: on Kant (Judy 1993, 108–46; Bernasconi 2001, 2002); on Hegel (Saussy 1993; Bernasconi 1998; Pope 2006); on Husserl (Derrida 2003, 1978c, 1992,); on Heidegger (Derrida 1989; Lacoue-Labarthe 1989; Fynsk 1993, 230–49). And, then, arising at is does from a different and somewhat earlier discursive field of intertextual reference, the signal work, respectively, of Cornel West (West 1987, 1988) and David Theo Goldberg (Goldberg 1993), each marking distinct horizons of political perspective, the former by way of a thought of hegemony developed proximate to the discourse of Antonio Gramsci and the latter by way of a tight critique of the fundamental limits of a liberal horizon of political and moral thought across the modern era.

8 Perhaps the late 1960s essay "Nietzsche, Genealogy, History" is another turning place in Foucault's itinerary where such a questioning of the staidly transcendental figure of Europe (and, at times, "the West") in this theoretical discourse could have been located or appended—even if initially only as a substantial afterthought that could later have acquired its own epistemological and rhetorical standing—but for all appearances it did not occur (Foucault 1998).

9 And, an explanation of the bearing of this difficulty could no doubt be extended in a number of directions and on a number of planes. I cite here three exemplary interrelated, if differing, examples across the post-1960s period, from this same horizon of discourse, adjacent if you will, on the bias: the joint writings of Gilles Deleuze and Felix Guattari over the decade and a half following 1968, the writing of Giorgio Agamben notably of the last decade of the twentieth century, and the joint work of Michael Hardt and Antonio Negri announced at the opening of the first decade of the twenty-first century (Deleuze and Guattari 1987; Agamben 1998; Hardt and Negri 2000).

10 The statement of a quite supple historicism in the work of George Stocking (Stocking 1982), operating primarily with regard to an internal disciplinary problematic, that of anthropology in the United States, in which Du Bois as a figure of thought scarcely appears, would be one kind of example. The project of a history of ideas that presumes the unity of the historicity I have just placed in question, such as that of Quentin

Skinner (Skinner 2002, esp. 57–90), would be another; and herein, the reinscription of the premises of Skinner's approach in the work of David Scott (Scott 1999) in a formulation of horizon that the latter would present as "after coloniality" should be noted. The scholastically persistent and passionately engaged work on the figure of Du Bois by Adolph Reed (Reed 1997) and Ross Posnock (Posnock 1998), respectively, can each stand as an example—differing in their commitments—that exhibits both approaches and pertains to our specific line of discussion. We might say that the issue here can be put into a conditional: if contextualization, then it is always both too much and never enough. There is no such thing as contextualization proper. There are only contextualizations—always in the plural. If so, then a performative inhabitation of the texture of discourse—which is as unavoidable as it is irreducible—is the only form of passage to a claim of context that can be simultaneously responsible to the partiality of the partial and a possible thought of the limits of the limit. It will always have been an immanent inhabitation of the text. Assumed as a project, such practice would be another path to a somewhat different thought of historicity—in particular that which is in question here—now.

11 Thus, it can be said that the ongoing excavation and making available of texts and the revising of the most elemental outline of the history of the discourses of race in European discourses generally—especially philosophical and scientific—since the eighteenth century is of the utmost scholastic importance in our contemporary scene. In this regard, ongoing efforts to bring forward these texts in reprint and translation is a fundamental contribution to the effort of critical thought in this domain. One can note for, example, two projects coming to full postulation astride this century (Bernasconi 2001; Hammonds and Herzig 2008). Thus, our ability to reconstruct the immanent production of the ensemblic conceptualization of the object of thought called race—as seme, idea, and concept, or mark in general—throughout its necessarily confounded and truncated epistemologization remains still sharply limited in the contemporary situation. A certain ongoing historicization of Europe across the modern period remains apposite (Heng 2018).

12 In "The Study of the Negro Problems," prepared and presented as a lecture to the American Academy of Political and Social Science in the Autumn of 1897, Du Bois says, "Finally, if we would rally to this common ground of scientific inquiry all partisans and advocates, we must explicitly admit what all implicitly postulate—that the Negro is a member of the human race, and as one who, in the light of history and experience, is capable to a degree of improvement and culture, is entitled to have his interests considered according to his numbers in all conclusions as to the commonweal" (Du Bois 1898, 17, para. 36; see also 2015i, 90 para. 36).

13 Robert Bernasconi has made the compelling proposition that Blumenbach may have been guided in his theorization of race by his epistemological inhabitation of Kant's formulation, perhaps revising and extending his earliest formulations as he more clearly engaged the implication of Kant's propositions on the use of teleological principle during the latter two decades of the eighteenth century (cf. Bernasconi 2001). This argument is in contradistinction to the hitherto dominant understanding

of this relation. The full consideration of this intervention for how we understand Kant's status in the historicity of the concept of race remains to be elaborated.

14. I thank Robert Bernasconi for a question that he posed to me almost two-and-a-half decades past, on the occasion of a discussion of an initial version of my engagement with this fourth paragraph, that called this dimension of Du Bois's argument into a certain relief.

15. Du Bois uses national groups, or semi-national regional groups, of various kinds as the referent terms here, in this essay. Groups called by such names as "Scandinavian," "Zulu," "Slav," "Chinese," "Sicilian," "Egyptian," "Bushman," "Tartar," "European," "Hottentot," "Roman," and, of course, "Negro." Du Bois's use implies his inscription in the idea that there is such a thing as national character. However, what seems much more crucial here is Du Bois's thought that there is no coherent physical mark, or concatenation of such, on which one could ground a recognition or identification of such a group. His listing of attributes as connected with such groups notwithstanding because the attributes remain confused. It is the referent, national groups or some such group, that is presupposed as already distinguished by Du Bois. He will, of course, attempt to show that such distinction is grounded in history rather than nature.

16. To the extent that he follows Moses on the point, Robert Gooding-Williams risks the same obscurity (Gooding-Williams 1996, 54 n. 5).

17. Consider in this context Georges Canguilhem on the question of ideology and truth in the history of science; each are always inextricably simultaneously at stake in any science (Canguilhem 1988a, 1–23; 1988b, 33–45).

18. This theoretical formulation is both repeated and expanded just three years later in 1900 in a signal essay examining the potential uses of census data in the study of the Negro, wherein programmatically situates two different levels of generality of study, macroscopic and microscopic (Du Bois 1982, 70). And then, seven years later, this thought is echoed in his most important summary account of the work of the Atlanta Conferences in the study of the Negro (Du Bois 1904). It should also be noted that in the essay of 1900, while interpretation is explicitly formulated as a necessary dimension of the microscopic level generally, he does not thematize a separate category for such study altogether. However, according to a theoretical protocol that would render such thematization of interest, it can be proposed on the basis of Du Bois's thought therein, for he clearly marks the limit of even the typical microlevel "social study" in this domain: "they can after all measure only the more powerful economic and social forces and must largely omit the deeper spiritual and moral impulses" (Du Bois 1982, 70). *The Philadelphia Negro: A Social Study* of 1899 is the exemplary example of such a microlevel study (Du Bois and Eaton 1899). *The Souls of Black Folk: Essays and Sketches* of 1903 is an example, perhaps, of another order of study, a practice of interpretation, one that we are perhaps within rights to describe as at the cutting edge of such practices latter recognized as comprising a whole approach in the human sciences (Du Bois 1903c; cf. Chandler 2014, 38–39).

19. A systematic account of the metaphorics of "blood" in Du Bois's discourse, in particular of the turn of the twentieth century, might yet be undertaken. Yet it should

proceed as an open—rather than pre-judged—approach to the theoretical registers in which they are produced therein. It ought remain open to the most fundamental paradoxes posed therein for critical thought.

20 In the little known, relatively brief, but nonetheless astute essay from 1900 noted above on the use of census data to study the problem of the Negro, as annotated above, Du Bois speaks of "impulses" as a reflexive practice. There he remarks "the deeper spiritual and moral impulses" as excessive to the typical descriptive form of "social study" (Du Bois 1982, 70). It can be shown that this essay is in all truth indicative of an essential theoretical disposition for Du Bois that has bearing on our contemporary understanding of both the history of modern social thought (all ethnological disciplines) at the turn to the twentieth century and any fulsome understanding of the history of African American studies. I hope to elaborate this understanding elsewhere, in a separate study of Du Bois's broad projection of an African American studies.

21 Proximate to the turn to the twentieth century, Du Bois quotes this phrase often. It is from the penultimate line from the closing stanza of the closing untitled section, commonly known as the "Epilogue" in the long poem, *In Memoriam A. H. H.*, by Alfred, Lord Tennyson (1809–1892), a requiem for his friend Arthur Henry Hallam, composed over seventeen years and first published anonymously in 1849 (Tennyson 1982).

22 And then, a bit later, in critically discussing Heidegger's proposition from the same moment, the 1930s, of the animal as being "poor in world," hence not "of spirit" (which is in fact a thought that is very close to some aspects of nineteenth-century discourses of Europe and America about a putative "Negro"), Derrida remarks "a certain anthropocentric even humanist teleology" that operates in a complicated fashion in this dimension of Heidegger's thought. He then cautions: "I do not mean to criticize this humanist teleology. It is no doubt more urgent to recall that, in spite of all the denegations or all the avoidances one could wish, it has remained *up till now* (in Heidegger's time and situation, but this has not radically changed) the price to be paid in the ethico-political denunciation of biologism, racism, naturalism, etc. If I analyze this 'logic,' and the aporias or limits, the presuppositions or the axiomatic decisions, above all the inversions and contaminations, in which we see it becoming entangled, this is in order to exhibit them and formalize the terrifying mechanisms of this program, all the double constraints that structure it. Is this unavoidable? Can one escape this program? No sign would suggest it, at least neither in 'Heideggerian' discourses nor in 'anti-Heideggerian' discourses. Can one transform this program? I do not know. In any case, it will not be avoided all at once and without reconnoitering it right down to its most tortuous ruses and most subtle resources" (Derrida 1989, 55–56, emphasis in the original French text; 1990b, 69–70).

23 The itinerary of engagement with the thought of Du Bois in the work of the philosopher K. Anthony Appiah can be taken as an apposite and signal example. In the first stage of this engagement, marked textually at the mid-1980s, Appiah stringently criticized Du Bois for failing to carry to completion, as he phrased it, an argument against the idea of race. Here, see Kwame Anthony Appiah, "The Uncompleted Argument: Du Bois and the Illusion of Race" (Appiah 1985), which was slightly revised and reprinted as

"Illusions of Race" in *In My Father's House: Africa and the Philosophy of Culture* (Appiah 1992a). However, in the second stage of this engagement, marked at the inception of the 1990s, in the closing chapter of *In My Father's House*, he was led to affirm the possibility of a "non-racialist pan-Africanism" (Appiah 1992b, 173–80). This thought, as formulated by Appiah, seems to bear no theoretical advance beyond the protocols that were adduced in Du Bois's discourse of the 1890s—especially the texts of the middle months of 1897 when "The Conservation of Races" and "Strivings of the Negro People" were produced—the time when Du Bois arrived at his first independent formulation of the so-called Negro problem. The question might be put as to whether it should have led to Appiah's hesitation at the time of that reissued formulation, that is in the first instance of his engagement with Du Bois, if not even to a theoretical revision, of his headline denigration of the position of Du Bois that had been presented in the earlier presentation of the essay, which had been essentially reprinted at the opening of the book. It is thus only a surprise of circumstance to the present practitioner that in its eventuality Appiah was led, a generation or so later, at the beginning what might be termed a third stage of his engagement with Du Bois, to praise the nineteenth-century thinker as perhaps an exemplary "rooted cosmopolitan" (Appiah 2005). (I thank the musician and thinker Tobias Nette, of Berlin, for bringing this last reference and citation to my attention sometime in 2008, by epistolary notation.)

24 The passage quoted in extenso above appears in revision as follows: "So dawned the time of Sturm und Drang: storm and stress to-day rocks our little boat on the mad waters of the world-sea; there is within and without the sound of conflict, the burning of body and rending of soul; inspiration strives with doubt, and faith with vain questionings. The bright ideals of the past,—physical freedom, political power, the training of brains and the training of hands,—all these in turn have waxed and waned, until even the last grows dim and overcast. Are they all wrong,—all false? No, not that, but each alone was over-simple and incomplete,—the dreams of a credulous race-childhood, or the fond imaginings of the other world which does not know and does not want to know our power. To be really true, all these ideals must be melted and welded into one. The training of the schools we need to-day more than ever,—the training of deft hands, quick eyes and ears, and above all the broader, deeper, higher culture of gifted minds and pure hearts. The power of the ballot we need in sheer self-defence,—else what shall save us from a second slavery? Freedom, too, the long-sought, we still seek,—the freedom of life and limb, the freedom to work and think, the freedom to love and aspire. Work, culture, liberty,—all these we need, not singly but together, not successively but together, each growing and aiding each, and all striving toward that vaster ideal that swims before the Negro people, the ideal of human brotherhood, gained through the unifying ideal of Race; the ideal of fostering and developing the traits and talents of the Negro, not in opposition to or contempt for other races, but rather in large conformity to the greater ideals of the American Republic, in order that some day on American soil two world-races may give each to each those characteristics both so sadly lack" (Du Bois 1903a, 10–11, para. 12).

25 The pioneering work of Manning Marable, first gathered in summary more than three generations ago (for his own engagement was lifelong, its intellectual formation rooted in the watershed era of the 1960s), remains the best study and guide in opening any engagement with this fundamental dimension of Du Bois's work (Marable 1986).

26 I acknowledge here an original interlocution, by telephone, with R. A. Judy whose remark of this 1956 letter led to my studied attention of it—perhaps two-and-a-half decades ago. Yet I also acknowledge here that Herbert Aptheker, in an interview of almost two hours, patiently answered my questions, pertaining in part to this text, in early February 1998 at his home in San Jose, California. A tape recording of this conversation is in my possession. During that conversation he described his own sense of Du Bois's concern with the order of question posed in the 1956 letter. Aptheker's recollections were always marked for me by a concern on his part with a fundamental dimension of practical questions that operated within the mutual terms of their relation.

PART II: ON THE QUESTION OF THE ILLIMITABLE IN THE THOUGHT OF W. E. B. DU BOIS

Dedication: Through the course of friendship sustained across more than a whole generation of time, and more, the example of the practice of Cecil Taylor, at the time of this writing (astride the opening decade of this century), more than any other, made possible the elaboration that is offered in these annotations. His way in the making of music was an example in every sense of the possibility that I understand Du Bois to have proposed. Part II is dedicated thus to his memory, with respect to his way in making life.

1 The specific line of reference is to Kant's attempted exposition of a principle of teleology as rendering available a ground within pure practical reason for a philosophical concept of race during the years of his promulgation of the critical project (Kant 2007b, 2001c). The two principal scholars in the English-speaking context who from the 1990s each in different ways strongly directed our attention to Kant's texts on the general problematic of the Negro, or the concept of race, are Ronald A. T. Judy (1991) and Robert Bernasconi (2001, 2002, 2006). My own approach is somewhat different, proceeding as it does by way of the thought of Du Bois on the modern epoch as a whole. It brought me to a central concern with Kant's account of teleology in relation to his entire architectonic. It is my hope to offer elsewhere a further consideration of Kant's problematization on its own terms, notably including the Third Critique (Kant 1998, 2000).

2 This phrase, "secondary rhythm," appears in Du Bois's essay, unpublished during his lifetime, "Sociology Hesitant," dating most likely from the late winter or early spring of 1905. The typescript of the essay can be found in the W. E. B. Du Bois Papers, now in the main available on microfilm (Du Bois 1905[?]). In October of 2003 I was privileged to hear a rich exploration by Alexander Weheliye of the motif of the "secondary rhythm" in Du Bois's essay at a conference celebrating the centenary of *The Souls of*

Black Folk held at Northwestern University and organized by Dwight McBride and Robert Gooding-Williams. Although I had noted the motif of the "double," as well as its correlate "secondary," in Du Bois's earliest writings, it was my subsequent work to annotate Du Bois's essay for a contemporary republication that led me to elaborate the interwoven thought of the "second time" and that of a "secondary rhythm," as offered herein (Du Bois 2015g).

3 Likewise, elsewhere, I have offered an annotation of Du Bois's itinerary of thought with reference to such general problematization, of both theoretical and intellectual practice and historical eventuality or historicity (Chandler 2014, 46–56).

4 This is so, even as the first position named here had, *in Europe* and concerning *négritude*, an exemplar in Jean-Paul Sartre. See the relevant citations in "*L'expérience vécue du Noir*," chapter 5 of Frantz Fanon's *Peau noire, masques blancs,* originally developed on its own in 1952 in Lyons, France, under the heading that might be best put in English as "the lived sense of the 'black'" with quotation marks (Fanon 1952, 88–114, or 2001).

5 Another engagement in this discussion proposed that we might reposition the terms by which the issue could be approached, namely, that Du Bois's thought in the 1897 essay indicated a fundamental conundrum, one that might remain so for thought in our own time. However, that position went forward without commentary in the scholarship. On the occasion of a presentation of such a discussion at the conference "The Academy and Race: Toward a Philosophy of Political Action," organized by Kevin Thomas Miles and sponsored jointly by the departments of philosophy and Africana studies at Villanova University, March 8–10, 1996, the notations and engagement from Lucius T. Outlaw were apposite (Chandler 1996). That disposition is the general and guiding approach elaborated throughout this study.

6 The formulation "futural form" is affirmatively expropriated from Judith Butler's incisive mediation on the politics of the performative in our time (1997, 147). Among other things, she addresses the way in which thought always and necessarily maintains within its elaboration an openness to its futural form as a mark of its performative incipit. In developing his thought from a reading of Du Bois's previously unpublished essay "Sociology Hesitant," specifically of what he remarks as Du Bois's interventionary citation of Immanuel Kant's idea of the "asymptote of the hyperbola," Judy (2000) called for a certain hyperbolic "thinking with" Du Bois in a superbly audacious manner. In a short meditation on the inaugural figure, not just the "word" "between" as it occurs at the outset of the first chapter of *The Souls of Black Folk*, in seeking to remark that which must have preceded such enunciation, Du Bois's practice was noted as "producing a hyperbolic force," a locutive gesture, an inventive intervention, that adduces by rhetorical simulation the character of an experience of a scene of dissimulation (Chandler 1993).

7 The reference here is to the appendix to the transcendental dialectic in the *Critique of Pure Reason* (Kant 1998).

8 A reading of the conceptual and rhetorical movements of this paragraph is offered in part I of the present study. Yet the entire paragraph should be recalled to mind here: "Although the wonderful developments of human history teach that the grosser physical differences of color, hair and bone go but a short way toward explaining the different

roles which groups of men have played in Human Progress, yet there are differences—subtle, delicate and elusive, though they may be which have silently but definitely separated men into groups. While these subtle forces have generally followed the natural cleavage of common blood, descent and physical peculiarities, they have at other times swept across and ignored these. At all times, however, they have divided human beings into races, which, while they perhaps transcend scientific definition, nevertheless, are clearly defined to the eye of the Historian and Sociologist" (Du Bois 1897a, 2015b).

9   Derrida proceeds to this thought by way of his annotation of the pathway of Edmund Husserl (c. 1935). The phrase is from the earliest major published work by Derrida, originally issued in 1962, *Edmund Husserl's Origin of Geometry: An Introduction* (Derrida 1978c, 131; 1974, 141). At the juncture in his text from whence I quote, he is declaring an immanent sense of telos that he has adduced in an elaboration of Husserl's discussion of the "origin of geometry." Likewise, this whole reference to Derrida's own pathway must be also indexed, in its eventuality, to Friedrich Nietzsche's second essay in his *On the Genealogy of Morality* (1884) (Nietzsche 1998). It is a thought in which this immanent opening is the essence of historicity. This problematic is the very path by which Derrida developed his thought of the "trace" or "supplement." It was the problematic of an inaugural form of historicity for African Americans, especially as formulated by Du Bois in "The Conservation of Races" and "Strivings of the Negro People," both dating from 1897, that guided me from the inception of my own engagement with the texts of Derrida (Chandler 2014, 62–67). It is in this sense that I emphasize the question of historically given "problem" and propose a thought of problematization as the scene of fundamental theoretical labor.

10 Here I recall Edward Said's rich meditation on this performative problematic. In his angle of attention, Said emphasizes that in order for a coherent historiographical *narration* to become possible, some titular authority must be accepted as its referent. For him, the decisive ground of this acceptance is always material, having to do with the organization of resource, production, and labor. Without such an assumed reference, the events or experiences, especially the uniqueness of such, for a given historical subject remain just beyond narration, just beyond coherent or ensemble symbolization. A refusal to acknowledge such reference operates as if it would effect an epistemological evacuation. Although it is not simply coextensive with it, this epistemological violence is always part of a more general violence, of which material and physical destruction is usually an immediate and ongoing actuality. For Said, in the example with which he was concerned in his essay, the status of Palestinians at the end of the twentieth century, the material ground of reference noted above always entails the question of state power. See his decisive essay "Permission to Narrate" (Said 1984).

11 The seventeenth paragraph reads in full: "If we carefully consider what race prejudice really is, we find it, historically, to be nothing but the friction between different groups of people; it is the difference in aim, in feeling, in ideals of two different races; if, now, this difference exists touching territory, laws, language, or even religion, it is manifest that these people cannot live in the same territory without fatal collision; but if, on the other hand, there is substantial agreement in laws, language and religion; if there

is a satisfactory adjustment of economic life, then there is no reason why, in the same country and on the same street, two or three great national ideals might not thrive and develop, that men of different races might not strive together for their race ideals as well, perhaps even better, than in isolation. Here, it seems to me, is the reading of the riddle that puzzles so many of us. We are Americans, not only by birth and by citizenship, but by our political ideals, our language, our religion. Farther than that, our Americanism does not go. At that point, we are Negroes, members of a vast historic race that from the very dawn of creation has slept, but half awakening in the dark forests of its African fatherland. We are the first fruits of this new nation, the harbinger of that black to-morrow which is yet destined to soften the whiteness of the Teutonic to-day. We are that people whose subtle sense of song has given America its only American music, its only American fairy tales, its only touch of pathos and humor amid its mad money-getting plutocracy. As such, it is our duty to conserve our physical powers, our intellectual endowments, our spiritual ideals; as a race we must strive by race organization, by race solidarity, by race unity to the realization of that broader humanity which freely recognizes differences in men, but sternly deprecates inequality in their opportunities of development" (CR 11–12, para. 17).

12 Yet to come were Du Bois's projections of an "encyclopedia africana," circa 1910, and the "Star of Ethiopia" pageant, circa 1912 (cf. Du Bois 1915; 1983 [1915]). Each projection exfoliates the basic thetic disposition already articulated by him in the text under discussion here, "The Conservation of Races" (Du Bois 1915; 1983 [1915]).

13 Du Bois was in dialogue with Franz Boas at this precise juncture in time, as the latter had just visited Atlanta University and participated in the Atlanta conference for the study of the Negro for that year (Du Bois 1906, 19, and see 19–21). What should be clear from the essay at hand is that the principles of Du Bois's formulations in 1906 were already operating in 1897. This is the question of an entire other annotation.

14 Jeremy Pope proposed the irreducibility of the force of an "Egyptian" historial figure in the constitution of Hegel's philosophical idea of "Greece" *and* simultaneously, still more fundamentally, the necessity and means, perhaps in part by way of the thought of Du Bois, of developing a whole other sense of historicity in order to recognize an Egypt that is seen in a manner that would be more open to its historial becoming (Pope 2006).

15 In exemplary work, Scott Trafton has illuminated the ambiguity on a general cultural plane that nonetheless attends any position in such a debate, especially the malleability and volatility of the figure of Egypt in nineteenth-century discourses in the United States (Trafton 2004). Too, however, in line with my annotations in part I on the limits in twentieth-century European discourses that indexed the problem of the example attendant to the question of the human, I note here that a question of a certain eighteenth-century European discourse on ancient Egypt is one of two principal examples of ideogrammatic writing to which Jacques Derrida takes reference in his study *Of Grammatology* (the other example is ancient and contemporary China) in questioning a modern western European conception of writing as such is encoded in the thought of Jean Jacques Rousseau's essay on the origin of languages (Derrida

1976b, 78–81; Rousseau 2009). This problematic is at once exemplary, irruptive, and futural in contemporary philosophy and thought on a global scale of reference astride the third decade of the twenty-first century.

16   Although it can only be noted here, it is of considerable scholastic and epistemological import that the first major academic archaeological excavations of the civilization of ancient Kush was afoot at almost the exact time of Du Bois's initial efforts toward a reformulation and projection anew of the problem of the status of ancient civilizations of northeast Africa, notably of the Nile river basin. Yet, that scholarship dismissed out of hand that the domains in question had a genesis among peoples of the continent who would be understood as African or Negro. Yet, too, as noted above, over the past half century, especially since the opening decade of this century, the problem of understanding this domain has initiated transformations in the study of ancient history that could well prove revolutionary in a general sense, that is globally, for our understanding (cf. Emberling and Williams 2020).

17   This formulation of problem is not to gainsay the supple and sustained articulation of historial sense of an African provenance in North "America" that has articulated since the sixteenth century in the historicity of all that has come to be known as Canada.

18   I thank Masako Nakamura for calling my attention to the pattern of Du Bois's autobiographical references to Japan, in particular the Meiji era, during our conversations at the 2006 annual meeting of the Japan Association for American Studies held at Nanzan University in Nagoya, Japan.

19   I index here a dimension yet to be cultivated, an entire domain, of interlocution of matters African American and of Japan, even as there is an entire archive, several in fact, that has yet to be properly cultivated (Chandler 2012a). Too, I wish to link this thought to a certain "dimension" of historicity remarked by Nicole Waligora-Davis as pertaining to what I am led to remark as an abiding sense of hope, even in the face of the given as a form of persisting limit (Waligora-Davis 2006).

20   The whole theme of *duty*—which is above all about the demands given by history to those who might undertake to intervene in its devolution—is of such general bearing in Du Bois's thought that it would stand elaboration on its own terms. For example, it runs throughout *The Souls of Black Folk: Essays and Sketches* (Du Bois 1903c). It is also the premise of the text that could be considered the theoretical coda of that book, the essay on the "talented tenth" (Du Bois 2015j). Here allow me to note this theme, the first positioned in relation to religion, the latter in terms of the status woman, in the work of two scholars on the nineteenth and early twentieth centuries, respectively, on the South Asian subcontinent (Guha 1997; Spivak 1988a).

21   With this latter date, I retain here an index of the moment of the writing of this discourse, 2004 to 2007, inscriptions which I shared in both fact and thought with Cecil Taylor. Perhaps it is apposite thus to recall the performances of Taylor in Japan, in 2007, in Miyagi prefecture but, notably, his collaboration with Yosuke Yamashita at Suntory Hall in Tokyo (Taylor and Yamashita 2007). Likewise in 2013, on the occasion of Taylor's receipt of the Kyoto Prize in Arts and Philosophy, for which he invited the dancer Min Tanaka to perform with him for the prize ceremony and workshop in

Kyoto (Chandler 2018). Taylor's historic first visit to Japan in 1973, with Jimmy Lyons and Andrew Cyrille, is documented on two recordings (Taylor 1973a, 1973b).

22 And, here, I recall the dialogue from my experience with five scholars: first, in gesture, in this instance, Gil Anidjar, then also Kendall Thomas and Etienne Balibar, and, finally, on another register, Fred Moten and the late Jacques Derrida, at the conference "tRaces: Deconstruction and Race" held at the University of California at Irvine in April 2003. The conference was organized by David Theo Goldberg and Dragan Kujundzic, who, beyond all differences, made the conversation of that time possible.

REFERENCES

Adelson, Leslie A. 2017. *Cosmic Miniatures and the Future Sense: Alexander Kluge's 21st-Century Literary Experiments in German Culture and Narrative Form*. Berlin: De Gruyter.
Agamben, Giorgio. 1998. *Homo Sacer: Sovereign Power and Bare Life*. Translated by Daniel Heller-Roazen. Stanford, CA: Stanford University Press.
Ajayi, J. F. Ade, ed. 1989. *General History of Africa VI: Africa in the Nineteenth Century until the 1880s*. Berkeley: University of California Press.
Althusser, Louis. 1970. *For Marx*. Translated by Ben Brewster. New York: Vintage.
Appiah, Kwame Anthony. 1985. "The Uncompleted Argument: Du Bois and the Illusion of Race." *Critical Inquiry* 12 (1): 21–37.
Appiah, Kwame Anthony. 1986. "The Uncompleted Argument: Du Bois and the Illusion of Race." In *"Race," Writing, and Difference*, edited by Henry Louis Gates Jr., 21–37. Chicago: University of Chicago Press.
Appiah, Kwame Anthony. 1989. "The Conservation of 'Race.'" *Black American Literature Forum* 23 (1): 37–60.
Appiah, Kwame Anthony. 1992a. "Illusions of Race." In *In My Father's House*, 28–46.
Appiah, Kwame Anthony. 1992b. *In My father's House: Africa in the Philosophy of Culture*. New York: Oxford University Press.
Appiah, Kwame Anthony. 2005. "Ethics in a World of Strangers: W. E. B. Du Bois and the Spirit of Cosmopolitanism." *Berlin Journal: A Magazine for the American Academy in Berlin* 11 (Fall): 23–26.
Aptheker, Herbert. 1955. *History and Reality*. New York: Cameron Associates.
Aptheker, Herbert. 1989. *The Literary Legacy of W. E. B. Du Bois*. White Plains, NY: Kraus International.
Aristotle. 1966. *Metaphysics*. Edited and translated by Hippocrates G. Apostle. Grinnell, IA: Peripatetic Press.
Aristotle. 1975. *The Nicomachean Ethics*. Translated by Hippocrates G. Apostle. Dordrecht: D. Reidel.
Austin, J. L. 1975. *How to Do Things with Words*. 2nd ed. Edited by James O. Urmson and Marina Sbisà. Cambridge, MA: Harvard University Press.
Bernasconi, Robert. 1998. "Hegel at the Court of the Ashanti." In *Hegel after Derrida*, edited by Stuart Barnett, 41–63. London: Routledge
Bernasconi, Robert. 2001. "Who Invented the Concept of Race? Kant's Role in the Enlightenment Construction of Race." In *Race*, edited by Robert Bernasconi, 11–36. Malden, MA: Blackwell.

Bernasconi, Robert. 2002. "Kant as an Unfamiliar Source of Racism." In *Philosophers on Race: Critical Essays*, edited by Julie K. Ward and Tommy L. Lott, 145–66. Oxford: Blackwell.

Bernasconi, Robert. 2006. "Kant and Blumenbach's Polyps: A Neglected Chapter in the History of the Concept of Race." In *The German Invention of Race*, edited by Sara Eigen and Mark J. Larrimore, 73–90. Albany: State University of New York Press.

Bernasconi, Robert, ed. 2001. *Concepts of Race in the Eighteenth Century*. 8 vols. Bristol, UK: Thoemmes.

Blumenbach, Johann Friedrich. 1791. *Über den Bildungstrieb*. Göttingen: Johann Christian Dieterich.

Blumenbach, Johann Friedrich. 2001a. *Concepts of Race in the Eighteenth Century*. Vol. 4, *De generis humani varietate nativa/Johann Blumenbach*. Edited by Robert Bernasconi. Bristol, UK: Thoemmes.

Blumenbach, Johann Friedrich. 2001b. *Concepts of Race in the Eighteenth Century*. Vol. 5, *Über die natürlichen Verschiedenheiten im Menschengeschlechte/Johann Blumenbach*. Edited by Robert Bernasconi. Bristol, UK: Thoemmes.

Blumenbach, Johann Friedrich, Thomas Bendyshe, Karl Friedrich Heinrich Marx, Pierre Flourens, Rudolf Wagner, and John Hunter. 1865. *The Anthropological Treatises of Johann Friedrich Blumenbach*. Edited by Thomas Bendyshe. London: Published for the Anthropological Society by Longman, Green, Longman, Roberts, and Green.

Boas, Franz. 1911. *The Mind of Primitive Man: A Course of Lectures Delivered before the Lowell Institute, Boston, Mass., and the National University of Mexico, 1910–1911*. New York: Macmillan.

Boas, Franz. 1989. *The Shaping of American Anthropology, 1883–1911*. Edited by George W. Stocking. Chicago: University of Chicago Press.

Bonnet, Charles. 2019. *The Black Kingdom of the Nile*. Cambridge, MA: Harvard University Press.

Butler, Judith. 1997. *Excitable Speech: A Politics of the Performative*. New York: Routledge.

Canguilhem, Georges. 1988a. *Ideology and Rationality in the History of the Life Sciences*. Translated by Arthur Goldhammer. Cambridge, MA: MIT Press.

Canguilhem, Georges. 1988b. *Idéologie et rationalité dans l'histoire des sciences de la vie: Nouvelles études d'histoire et de philosophie des sciences*. 2nd ed., revised and corrected. Paris: J. Vrin.

Chandler, Nahum Dimitri. 1993. "Between." *Assemblage: A Critical Journal of Architecture and Design Culture*, no. 20 (April): 26–27.

Chandler, Nahum Dimitri. 1996. "The Economy of Desedimentation: W. E. B. Du Bois and the Discourses of the Negro." *Callaloo* 19 (1): 78–93.

Chandler, Nahum Dimitri. 2012a. "Introduction: On the Virtues of Seeing—At Least, but Never Only—Double." Special Issue. Toward a new parallax: Or, Japan—in another traversal of the Trans-Pacific. *CR: The New Centennial Review* 12 (1) (Spring): 1–39.

Chandler, Nahum Dimitri. 2012b. "A Persistent Parallax: On the Writings of W. E. Burghardt Du Bois on Japan and China, 1936–1937." Special Issue. Toward a new parallax: Or, Japan—in another traversal of the Trans-Pacific. CR: *The New Centennial Review* 12 (1)(Spring): 291–316.

Chandler, Nahum Dimitri. 2014. "Of Exorbitance: The Problem of the Negro as a Problem for Thought." In *X: The Problem of the Negro as a Problem for Thought*, 11–67. New York: Fordham University Press.

Chandler, Nahum Dimitri. 2018. "The Coming of the Second-Time." *A-Line: A Journal of Progressive Thought* 1 (3–4), August 30. https://alinejournal.com/category/vol-1-no-3-4/page/2.

Chandler, Nahum Dimitri. 2021. *Toward an African Future—Of the Limit of World*. Albany: State University of New York Press.

Chandler, Nahum Dimitri. 2022. *"Beyond This Narrow Now" Or, Delimitations, of W. E. B. Du Bois*. Durham, NC: Duke University Press.

Crummell, Alexander. 1992. *Destiny and Race: Selected Writings, 1840–1898*. Edited by W. J. Moses. Amherst: University of Massachusetts Press.

Darwin, Charles. 1896. *The Descent of Man and Selection in Relation to Sex*. New edition, revised and augmented. New York: D. Appleton and Co.

Darwin, Charles. 1897 [1859]. *The Origin of Species by Means of Natural Selection; or, The Preservation of Favored Races in the Struggle for Life*. New York: D. Appleton and Co.

Deleuze, Gilles, and Félix Guattari. 1987. *A Thousand Plateaus: Capitalism and Schizophrenia*. Translated by Brian Massumi. Minneapolis: University of Minnesota Press.

Derrida, Jacques. 1974. Introduction. In Husserl, Edmund, *L'origine de la géométrie: Traduction et Introduction*. Translated by Jacques Derrida. 2nd ed., 3–171. Paris: Presses Universitaires de France.

Derrida, Jacques. 1976a. "Linguistics and Grammatology." In *Of Grammatology*, 27–63. Baltimore, MD: Johns Hopkins University Press.

Derrida, Jacques. 1976b. *Of Grammatology*. Translated by Gayatri Chavravorty Spivak. Baltimore, MD: Johns Hopkins University Press.

Derrida, Jacques. 1978a. *Edmund Husserl's "The Origin of Geometry": An Introduction*. Edited by David B. Allison. Translated by John P. Leavey. Stony Brook, NY: Nicholas Hays.

Derrida, Jacques. 1978b. "From Restricted to General Economy: A Hegelianism without Reserve." In *Writing and Difference*, translated by Alan Bass, 251–77. Chicago: University of Chicago Press.

Derrida, Jacques. 1978c. Introduction to "The Origin of Geometry." In *Edmund Husserl's "The Origin of Geometry": An Introduction*, edited by David B. Allison, translated by John P. Leavey, 25–153. Stony Brook, NY: Nicholas Hays.

Derrida, Jacques. 1978d. "Violence and Metaphysics: An Essay on the Thought of Emmanuel Levinas." In *Writing and Difference*, translated by Alan Bass, 79–153. Chicago: University of Chicago Press.

Derrida, Jacques. 1982a. "Différance." In *Margins of Philosophy*, translated by Alan Bass, 1–27. Chicago: University of Chicago Press.

Derrida, Jacques. 1982b. "The Ends of Man." In *Margins of Philosophy*, translated by Alan Bass, 109–36. Chicago: University of Chicago Press.

Derrida, Jacques. 1982c. "Signature, Event, Context." In *Margins of Philosophy*, translated by Alan Bass, 307–30. Chicago: University of Chicago Press.

Derrida, Jacques. 1983. "Geschlecht: Sexual Difference, Ontological Difference." *Research in Phenomenology* 13 (1): 65–83.

Derrida, Jacques. 1986. *Glas*. Translated by John P. Leavey Jr. and Richard Rand. Lincoln: University of Nebraska Press.

Derrida, Jacques. 1987. "The Laws of Reflection: Nelson Mandela, in Admiration." Translated by Mary Ann Caws and Isabelle Lorenz. In *For Nelson Mandela*, edited by Jacques Derrida and Mustapha Tlili, 11–42. New York: Seaver.

Derrida, Jacques. 1989. *Of Spirit: Heidegger and the Question*. Translated by Geoffrey Bennington and Rachel Bowlby. Chicago: University of Chicago Press.

Derrida, Jacques. 1990a. "Force of Law: The 'Mystical Foundation of Authority.'" *Cardozo Law Review* 11 (5–6): 919–1045.

Derrida, Jacques. 1990b. *Heidegger et la question: De l'esprit, Différence sexuelle, différence ontologique (Geshlect I), La main de Heidegger (Geshlect II)*. Paris: Flammarion.

Derrida, Jacques. 1992. *The Other Heading: Reflections on Today's Europe*. Translated by Pascale-Anne Brault and Michael B. Naas. Bloomington: Indiana University Press.

Derrida, Jacques. 2002a. "Declarations of Independence." Translated by Tom Keenan and Tom Pepper. In *Negotiations: Interventions and Interviews, 1971–2001*, edited and translated by Elizabeth Rottenberg, 46–54. Stanford, CA: Stanford University Press.

Derrida, Jacques. 2002b. "Force of Law: The 'Mystical Foundation of Authority.'" In *Acts of Religion*, edited by Gil Anidjar, 230–98. New York: Routledge.

Derrida, Jacques. 2003. *The Problem of Genesis in Husserl's Philosophy*. Translated by Marian Hobson. Chicago: University of Chicago Press.

Derrida, Jacques. 2005. *Rogues: Two Essays on Reason*. Translated by Pascale-Anne Brault and Michael B. Naas. Stanford, CA: Stanford University Press.

Derrida, Jacques. 2007. "The Laws of Reflection: Nelson Mandela, in Admiration." Translated by Mary Ann Caws and Isabelle Lorenz. In *Psyche: Inventions of the Other*, vol. 2, edited by Peggy Kamuf and Elizabeth Rottenberg, 63–86. Stanford, CA: Stanford University Press.

Du Bois, W. E. B. 1894[?]. "The Afro-American." W. E. B. Du Bois Papers, MS 312 (Series 3, subseries C), Special Collections and University Archives, University of Massachusetts-Amherst Libraries.

Du Bois, W. E. B. 1897a. "The Conservation of Races." American Negro Academy Occasional Papers 2. Washington, DC: American Negro Academy.

Du Bois, W. E. B. 1897b. "Strivings of the Negro People." *Atlantic Monthly* 80 (August), 194–98.

Du Bois, W. E. B. 1898. "The Study of the Negro Problems." *Annals of the American Academy of Political and Social Science* 11 (1): 1–23.

Du Bois, W. E. B. 1900. "The Present Outlook for the Dark Races of Mankind." *A.M.E. Church Review* 17 (2): 95–110.

Du Bois, W. E. B. 1901. "The Relation of the Negroes to the Whites in the South." *Annals of the American Academy of Political and Social Science* 18 (1): 121–40.

Du Bois, W. E. B. 1903a. "Of Our Spiritual Strivings." In *The Souls of Black Folk: Essays and Sketches*, 1–12. Chicago: McClurg.

Du Bois, W. E. B. 1903b. "The Sorrow Songs." In *The Souls of Black Folk: Essays and Sketches*, 250–64. Chicago: McClurg.

Du Bois, W. E. B. 1903c. *The Souls of Black Folk: Essays and Sketches*. 1st ed. Chicago: McClurg.

Du Bois, W. E. B. 1903d. *The Souls of Black Folk: Essays and Sketches*. 2nd ed. Chicago: McClurg. Electronic edition available at Documenting the American South, University of North Carolina Library, http://docsouth.unc.edu/church/duboissouls/dubois.html.

Du Bois, W. E. B. 1904. "The Atlanta Conferences." *Voice of the Negro* 1 (March):85–90.

Du Bois, W. E. B. 1905[?]. "Sociology Hesitant." W. E. B. Du Bois Papers, MS 312 (Series 3, subseries C), Special Collections and University Archives, University of Massachusetts–Amherst Libraries.

Du Bois, W. E. B. 1915. *The Negro*. Home University Library of Modern Knowledge. New York: Holt.

Du Bois, W. E. B. 1920. *Darkwater: Voices from Within the Veil*. New York: Harcourt, Brace and Howe.

Du Bois, W. E. B. 1935. *Black Reconstruction: An Essay toward a History of the Part Which Black Folk Played in the Attempt to Reconstruct Democracy in America, 1860–1880*. New York: Harcourt, Brace and Co.

Du Bois, W. E. B. 1947. *The World and Africa: An Inquiry into the Part Which Africa Has Played in World History*. New York: Viking.

Du Bois, W. E. B. 1968. *The Autobiography of W. E. B. Du Bois: A Soliloquy on Viewing My Life from the Last Decade of Its First Century*. Edited by Herbert Aptheker. New York: International.

Du Bois, W. E. B. 1973. *The Correspondence of W. E. B. Du Bois*. Vol. 3, *Selections, 1944–1963*. Compiled and edited by Herbert Aptheker. Amherst: University of Massachusetts Press.

Du Bois, W. E. B. 1975a. *Darkwater: Voices from Within the Veil*. Complete Published Works of W. E. B. Du Bois. Edited by Herbert Aptheker. Millwood, NY: Kraus-Thomson Organization.

Du Bois, W. E. B. 1975b. *Dusk of Dawn: An Essay toward an Autobiography of a Race Concept*. Complete Published Works of W. E. B. Du Bois. Edited by Herbert Aptheker. Millwood, NY: Kraus-Thomson Organization.

Du Bois, W. E. B. 1975c. *The Negro*. Complete Published Works of W. E. B. Du Bois. Edited by Herbert Aptheker. Millwood, NY: Kraus-Thomson Organization.

Du Bois, W. E. B. 1976a. *Black Reconstruction: An Essay toward a History of the Part Which Black Folk Played in the Attempt to Reconstruct Democracy in America, 1860–1880*. Complete Published Works of W. E. B. Du Bois. Edited by Herbert Aptheker. Millwood, NY: Kraus-Thomson Organization.

Du Bois, W. E. B. 1976b. *The World and Africa: An Inquiry into the Part Which Africa Has Played in World History*. Complete Published Works of W. E. B. Du Bois. Edited by Herbert Aptheker. Millwood, NY: Kraus-Thomson Organization.

Du Bois, W. E. B. 1980a. *The Papers of W. E. B. Du Bois, 1803 (1877–1963) 1979*. Microfilm. Compiled and edited by Herbert Aptheker and Robert C. McDonnell. Sanford, NC: Microfilming Corp. of America.

Du Bois, W. E. B. 1980b. "Sociology Hesitant." In *The Papers of W. E. B. Du Bois, 1803 (1877–1963) 1965*. Microfilm. Compiled and edited by Herbert Aptheker and Robert C. McDonnell, reel 82, frames 1307–12. Sanford, NC: Microfilming Corp. of America.

Du Bois, W. E. B. 1982. "The Twelfth Census and the Negro Problems." In *Writings by W. E. B. Du Bois in Periodicals Edited by Others*. Vol. 1, 1891–1909. Complete Published Works of W. E. B. Du Bois. Compiled and edited by Herbert Aptheker, 69–72. Millwood, NY: Kraus-Thomson Organization.

Du Bois, W. E. B. 1983 [1915]. "'The Star of Ethiopia." In *Writings in Periodicals Edited by W. E. B. Du Bois. Selections from The Crisis*. Vol. 1, 1911–1925. Complete Published Works of W. E. B. Du Bois. Compiled and edited by Herbert Aptheker, 114–15. Millwood, NY: Kraus-Thomson Organization.

Du Bois, W. E. B. 2010. "The Afro-American." *Journal of Transnational American Studies* 2 (1). https://escholarship.org/uc/item/2pm9g4q2.

Du Bois, W. E. B. 2012. "The Meaning of Japan (1937)." Special Issue. Toward A New Parallax: Or, Japan—In Another Traversal of the Trans-Pacific. CR: *The New Centennial Review* 12 (1): 233–55.

Du Bois, W. E. B. 2015a. "The Afro-American." In *The Problem of the Color Line at the Turn of the Twentieth Century: The Essential Early Essays*, compiled and edited by N. D. Chandler, 33–50. New York: Fordham University Press.

Du Bois, W. E. B. 2015b. "The Conservation of Races." In *The Problem of the Color Line at the Turn of the Twentieth Century: The Essential Early Essays*, compiled and edited by N. D. Chandler, 51–66. New York: Fordham University Press.

Du Bois, W. E. B. 2015c. "The Development of a People." In *The Problem of the Color Line at the Turn of the Twentieth Century: The Essential Early Essays*, compiled and edited by N. D. Chandler, 243–70. New York: Fordham University Press.

Du Bois, W. E. B. 2015d. "The Present Outlook for the Dark Races of Mankind." In *The Problem of the Color Line at the Turn of the Twentieth Century: The Essential Early Essays*, compiled and edited by N. D. Chandler, 111–38. New York: Fordham University Press.

Du Bois, W. E. B. 2015e. *The Problem of the Color Line at the Turn of the Twentieth Century: The Essential Early Essays*. Compiled and edited by N. D. Chandler. New York: Fordham University Press.

Du Bois, W. E. B. 2015f. "The Relation of the Negroes to the Whites in the South." In *The Problem of the Color Line at the Turn of the Twentieth Century: The Essential Early Essays*, compiled and edited by N. D. Chandler, 189–208. New York: Fordham University Press

Du Bois, W. E. B. 2015g. "Sociology Hesitant." In *The Problem of the Color Line at the Turn of the Twentieth Century: The Essential Early Essays*, compiled and edited by N. D. Chandler, 271–84. New York: Fordham University Press.

Du Bois, W. E. B. 2015h. "Strivings of the Negro People." In *The Problem of the Color Line at the Turn of the Twentieth Century: The Essential Early Essays*, compiled and edited by N. D. Chandler, 67–76. New York: Fordham University Press.

Du Bois, W. E. B. 2015i. "The Study of the Negro Problems." In *The Problem of the Color Line at the Turn of the Twentieth Century: The Essential Early Essays*, compiled and edited by N. D. Chandler, 77–98. New York: Fordham University Press.

Du Bois, W. E. B. 2015j. "The Talented Tenth." In *The Problem of the Color Line at the Turn of the Twentieth Century: The Essential Early Essays*, compiled and edited by N. D. Chandler, 209–42. New York: Fordham University Press.

Du Bois, W. E. B., ed. 1906. *The Health and Physique of the Negro American: Report of a Social Study Made under the Direction of Atlanta University; Together with the Proceedings of the Eleventh Conference for the Study of the Negro Problems Held at Atlanta University, on May the 29th, 1906*. Atlanta, GA: Atlanta University.

Du Bois, W. E. B., and Isabel Eaton. 1899. *The Philadelphia Negro: A Social Study, by W. E. B. Du Bois; Together with a Special Report on Domestic Service by Isabel Eaton*. Publications of the University of Pennsylvania. Series in Political Economy and Public Law, no. 14. Philadelphia: University of Pennsylvania.

Ehret, Christopher. 2016. *The Civilizations of Africa: A History to 1800*. Charlottesville: University Press of Virginia.

Emberling, Geoff, and Bruce B. Williams, eds. 2020. *The Oxford Handbook of Ancient Nubia*. New York: Oxford University Press.

Fanon, Frantz. 1952. *Peau noire, masques blancs*. Paris: Éditions du Seuil.

Fanon, Frantz. 2001. "The Lived Experience of the Black." In *Race*, edited by Robert Bernasconi, 184–202. Malden, MA: Blackwell.

El Fasi, Mohamed, ed. 1988. *General History of Africa III: Africa from the Seventh to the Eleventh Century*. Berkeley: University of California Press.

Fisher, Marjorie M., Peter Lacovara, Salima Ikram, and Sue D'Auria, eds. 2012. *Ancient Nubia: African Kingdoms on the Nile*. Foreword by Zahi Hawass. Photographs by Chester Higgins Jr. Cairo: American University in Cairo Press.

Fortune, T. Thomas. 2008. "The Afro-American (1890)." In *T. Thomas Fortune, the Afro-American Agitator: A Collection of His Writings, 1880–1928*, edited by Shawn Leigh Alexander, 215–20. Gainesville: University Press of Florida.

Foucault, Michel. 1966. *Les mots et les choses: Une archéologie des sciences humaines*. Paris: Gallimard.

Foucault, Michel. 1972. *The Archaeology of Knowledge and the Discourse on Language*. Translated by A. M. Sheridan Smith. New York: Harper and Row.

Foucault, Michel. 1973. *The Order of Things: An Archaeology of the Human Sciences*. Translated by Alan Sheridan. New York: Vintage.

Foucault, Michel. 1978. "M. Foucault to zen: Zendera taizai-ki." Dialogue with Sogen Omori. Transcribed, compiled, and edited by Christian Polac. Translated by Kiyoyasu Sato. *Shunjū* 197 (August-September): 1–6.

Foucault, Michel. 1980a. *The History of Sexuality*. Vol. 1, *An Introduction*. Translated by Robert Hurley. New York: Vintage.

Foucault, Michel. 1980b. "Right of Death and Power over Life." In *The History of Sexuality*, vol. 1, *An Introduction*, translated by Robert Hurley, 135–59. New York: Vintage.

Foucault, Michel. 1997a. "Polemics, Politics, and Problematizations: An Interview with Michel Foucault." By Paul Rabinow. Translated by Lydia Davis. In *Essential Works of Foucault, 1954–1984*, vol. 1, *Ethics: Subjectivity and Truth*, edited by Paul Rabinow, 111–19. New York: New Press.

Foucault, Michel. 1997b. "Preface to *The History of Sexuality*." Vol. 2. Translated by William Smock. In *Essential Works of Foucault, 1954–1984*, vol. 1, *Ethics: Subjectivity and Truth*, edited by Paul Rabinow, 199–205. New York: New Press.

Foucault, Michel. 1997c. "What Is Enlightenment?" Translated by Catherine Porter. In *The Politics of Truth*, edited by Sylvère Lotringer. 101–34. New York: Semiotext(e).

Foucault, Michel. 1998. "Nietzsche, Genealogy, History." Translated by Sherry Simon and Donald F. Bouchard. In *Essential Works of Foucault, 1954–1984*, vol. 2, *Aesthetics, Method, and Epistemology*, edited by James D. Faubion, 369–92. New York: New Press.

Foucault, Michel. 1999. "Michel Foucault and Zen: A Stay in a Zen Temple (1978)." Conversation with Sogen Omori. Transcribed, edited, and compiled by Christian Polac. Translated by Richard Townsend. In *Religion and Culture*, edited by Jeremy R. Carrette, 110–14. New York: Routledge.

Foucault, Michel. 2003. *"Society Must Be Defended": Lectures at the Collège de France, 1975–76*. Edited by Mauro Bertani. Translated by David Macey. New York: Picador.

Fynsk, Christopher. 1993. *Heidegger: Thought and Historicity*. 2nd ed. Ithaca, NY: Cornell University Press.

Goldberg, David T. 1993. *Racist Culture: Philosophy and the Politics of Meaning*. Cambridge, MA: Blackwell.

Gooding-Williams, Robert. 1996. "Outlaw, Appiah, and Du Bois's 'The Conservation of Races.'" In *W. E. B. Du Bois on Race and Culture: Philosophy, Politics, and Poetics*, edited by Bernard W. Bell, Emily Grosholz, and James B. Stewart, 39–56. New York: Routledge.

Gould, Stephen Jay. 1996. *The Mismeasure of Man*. Rev. ed. New York: Norton.

Gould, Stephen Jay. 2002. *The Structure of Evolutionary Theory*. Cambridge, MA: Harvard University Press.

Guha, Ranajit. 1997. "Colonialism in South Asia: A Dominance without Hegemony and Its Historiography." In *Dominance without Hegemony: History and Power in Colonial India*, 1–99. Cambridge, MA: Harvard University Press.

Hammonds, Evelynn M., and Rebecca M. Herzig, eds. 2008. *The Nature of Difference: Sciences of Race in the United States from Jefferson to Genomics*. Cambridge, MA: MIT Press.

Hardt, Michael, and Antonio Negri. 2000. *Empire*. Cambridge, MA: Harvard University Press.

Heidegger, Martin. 1962. *Being and Time*. Translated by John Macquarrie and Edward Robinson. New York: Harper and Row.

Heidegger, Martin. 2000. *Introduction to Metaphysics*. Translated by Gregory Fried and Richard Polt. New Haven, CT: Yale University Press.

Heng, Geraldine. 2018. *The Invention of Race in the European Middle Ages*. Cambridge: Cambridge University Press.

Holt, Thomas C. 1998. "W. E. B. Du Bois's Archaeology of Race: Re-reading 'The Conservation of Races.'" In *W.E.B. DuBois, Race, and the City: "The Philadelphia Negro" and Its Legacy*, edited by Michael B. Katz and Thomas J. Sugrue, 61–76. Philadelphia: University of Pennsylvania Press.

Husserl, Edmund. 1969. *Formal and Transcendental Logic*. Translated by Dorion Cairns. The Hague: Martinus Nijhoff.

Husserl, Edmund. 1999. *The Idea of Phenomenology: A Translation of Die Idee der Phänomenologie: Husserliana II*. Translated by Lee Hardy. Dordrecht: Kluwer Academic.

Huxley, Thomas Henry. 1896a. *Collected Essays*. 9 vols. New York: D. Appleton and Co.

Huxley, Thomas Henry. 1896b. *Evolution and Ethics and Other Essays*. New York: D. Appleton and Co.

Huxley, Thomas Henry. 1896c. *Man's Place in Nature and Other Anthropological Essays*. New York: D. Appleton and Co.

Jefferson, Thomas. 1999 [1776]. "The Declaration of Independence [as amended and adopted in Congress], July 4, 1776." In *Thomas Jefferson, Political Writings*, edited by Joyce O. Appleby and Terence Ball, 102–5. New York: Cambridge University Press.

Judy, Ronald A. 1991. "Kant and the Negro." *Surfaces* 1. https://id.erudit.org/iderudit/1065256ar.

Judy, Ronald A. 1993. *(Dis)forming the American Canon: African-Arabic Slave Narratives and the Vernacular*. Minneapolis: University of Minnesota Press.

Judy, Ronald A. 2000. "Introduction: On W. E. B. Du Bois and Hyperbolic Thinking." *Boundary 2: An International Journal of Literature and Culture* 27 (3): 1–35.

Kant, Immanuel. 1997 [1788]. *Critique of Practical Reason*. Edited and translated by Mary J. Gregor. New York: Cambridge University Press.

Kant, Immanuel. 1998 [1781]. *Critique of Pure Reason*. Edited and translated by Paul Guyer and Allen W. Wood. New York: Cambridge University Press.

Kant, Immanuel. 2000 [1790]. *Critique of the Power of Judgment*. Edited by Paul Guyer. Translated by Paul Guyer and Eric Matthews. New York: Cambridge University Press.

Kant, Immanuel. 2001a. "Idee zu einer allgemeinen Geschichte in weltbürgerlicher Absicht." In *Schriften zur Ästhetik und Naturphilosophie: Texte und Kommentar*, vol. 1, edited by Manfred Frank and Veronique Zanetti, 321–38. Frankfurt am Main: Suhrkamp.

Kant, Immanuel. 2001b. "On the Use of Teleological Principles in Philosophy (1788)." Translated by J. M. Mikkelsen. In *Race*, edited by Robert Bernasconi, 37–56. Malden, MA: Blackwell.

Kant, Immanuel. 2001c. "Über den gebrauch teleologischer prinzipien in der Philosophie." In *Schriften zur Ästhetik und Naturphilosophie: Texte und Kommentar*, vol. 1, edited by Manfred Frank and Veronique Zanetti, 381–414. Frankfurt am Main: Suhrkamp.

Kant, Immanuel. 2007a. "Idea for a Universal History with a Cosmopolitan Aim (1784)." Translated by Allen W. Wood. In *Anthropology, History, and Education*, edited and translated by Robert B. Louden and Günter Zöller, 108–20. New York: Cambridge University Press.

Kant, Immanuel. 2007b. "On the Use of Teleological Principles in Philosophy (1788)." Translated by Günter Zöller. In *Anthropology, History, and Education*, edited and translated by Robert B. Louden and Günter Zöller, 195–218. New York: Cambridge University Press.

King, Martin Luther, Jr. 1970. "Honoring Dr. Du Bois." In W. E. B. Du Bois, *Dusk of Dawn: An Essay toward an Autobiography of a Race Concept*, vii–xvii. New York: Schocken.

Kirkland, Frank M. 1992–1993. "Modernity and Intellectual Life in Black." *Philosophical Forum* 24 (1–3): 136–65.

Ki-Zerbo, Joseph, ed. 1981. *General History of Africa I: Methodology and African Prehistory*. Berkeley: University of California Press.

Lacoue-Labarthe, Philippe. 1989. "Transcendence Ends in Politics." In *Typography: Mimesis, Philosophy, Politics*, edited by Christopher Fynsk, 267–300. Cambridge, MA: Harvard University Press.

Lewis, David Levering. 1993. *W. E. B. Du Bois: Biography of a Race, 1868–1919*. New York: Henry Holt.

Lott, Tommy L. 1992–1993. "Du Bois on the Invention of Race." *Philosophical Forum* 24 (1–3): 166–87.

Lott, Tommy L. 2001. "Du Bois's Anthropological Notion of Race." In *Race*, edited by Robert Bernasconi, 59–83. Malden, MA: Blackwell.

Marable, Manning. 1986. *W. E. B. Du Bois: Black Radical Democrat*. Boston: Twayne.

Matsumura, Wendy. 2015. *The Limits of Okinawa: Japanese Capitalism, Living Labor, and Theorizations of Community*. Durham, NC: Duke University Press.

McGann, Karen, et. al., dir. 2019. *Africa's Great Civilizations*. PBS mini-series. Narrated by Henry Louis Gates Jr. San Francisco: PBS.

Michaelsen, Scott. 1999. *The Limits of Multiculturalism: Interrogating the Origins of American Anthropology*. Minneapolis: University of Minnesota Press.

Mokhtar, Gamel el Din, ed. 1981. *General History of Africa II: Ancient Civilizations of Africa*. Berkeley: University of California Press.

Moses, Wilson Jeremiah. 1989. *Alexander Crummell: A Study of Civilization and Discontent*. New York: Oxford University Press.

Moses, Wilson Jeremiah. 1993. "W. E. B. Du Bois's 'The Conservation of Races' and Its Context: Idealism, Conservatism and Hero Worship." *Massachusetts Review* 34 (2): 275–94.

Moss, Alfred A., Jr. 1981. *The American Negro Academy: Voice of the Talented Tenth*. Baton Rouge: Louisiana State University Press.

Moten, Fred. 2003. *In the Break: The Aesthetics of the Black Radical Tradition*. Minneapolis: University of Minnesota Press.

Niane, Djibril Tamsir, ed. 1984. *General History of Africa IV: Africa from the Twelfth to the Sixteenth Century*. Berkeley: University of California Press.

Nietzsche, Friedrich. W. 1991. *Zur Genealogie der Moral: Eine Streitschrift*. Frankfurt am Main: Insel.

Nietzsche, Friedrich. W. 1998. *On the Genealogy of Morality: A Polemic*. Translation and notes by Maudemarie Clark and Alan J. Swensen, with an introduction by Maudemarie Clark. Indianapolis, IN: Hackett.

Ogot, Bethwell A., ed. 1992. *General History of Africa V: Africa from the Sixteenth to the Eighteenth Century*. Berkeley: University of California Press.

Outlaw, Lucius T., Jr. 1996a. "Against the Grain of Modernity: The Politics of Difference and the Conservation of 'Race.'" In *On Race and Philosophy*, 135–57. New York: Routledge.

Outlaw, Lucius T., Jr. 1996b. "'Conserve Races?': In Defense of W. E. B. Du Bois." In *W.E.B. Du Bois on Race and Culture: Philosophy, Politics, and Poetics*, edited by Bernard W. Bell, Emily Grosholz, and James B. Stewart, 15–37. New York: Routledge.

Pope, Jeremy W. 2006. "Ägypten und Aufhebung: G. W. F. Hegel, W. E. B. Du Bois, and the African Orient." *CR: The New Centennial Review* 6 (3): 149–92.

Pope, Jeremy W. 2014. *The Double Kingdom under Taharqo: Studies in the History of Kush and Egypt, c. 690–864 BC*. Leiden: Brill Academic.

Posnock, Ross. 1998. *Color and Culture: Black Writers and the Making of the Modern Intellectual*. Cambridge, MA: Harvard University Press.

Ratzel, Friedrich. 1896–1898. *The History of Mankind*. 3 vols. Translated by A. J. Butler. Introduction by E. B. Tylor. New York: Macmillan.

Reed, Adolph L. 1997. *W. E. B. Du Bois and American Political Thought: Fabianism and the Color Line*. New York: Oxford University Press.

Rousseau, Jean-Jacques. 2009. "Essay on the Origin of Languages: In Which Melody and Musical Imitation Are Treated." Translated by John T. Scott. In *Essay on the Origin of Languages and Writings Related to Music*, edited by John T. Scott, 289–332. Hanover, NH: University Press of New England.

Said, Edward. 1984. "Permission to Narrate: Edward Said Writes about the Story of the Palestinians." *London Review of Books*, 16–29 February, 13–17.

Sartre, Jean-Paul. 1956. *Being and Nothingness: An Essay on Phenomenological Ontology*. Translated with an introduction by Hazel E. Barnes. New York: Philosophical Library.

Saussy, Haun. 1993. "Hegel's Chinese Imagination." In *The Problem of a Chinese Aesthetic*, 151–88. Stanford, CA: Stanford University Press.

Scott, David. 1999. *Refashioning Futures: Criticism after Postcoloniality*. Princeton, NJ: Princeton University Press.

Shimabuku, Annmaria. 2018. *Alegal: Biopolitics and the Unintelligibility of Okinawan Life*. New York: Fordham University Press.

Skinner, Quentin. 2002. *Visions of Politics*. Vol. 1, *Regarding Method*. Cambridge: Cambridge University Press.

Spillers, Hortense J. 2003a. *Black, White, and in Color: Essays on American Literature and Culture*. Chicago: University of Chicago Press.

Spillers, Hortense J. 2003b. "The Crisis of the Negro Intellectual: A Post-date." In *Black, White, and in Color: Essays on American literature and Culture*, 428–70. Chicago: University of Chicago Press.

Spillers, Hortense J. 2006. "The Idea of Black Culture." *CR: The New Centennial Review* 6 (3): 7–28.

Spivak, Gayatri Chakravorty. 1988a. "Can the Subaltern Speak?" In *Marxism and the Interpretation of Culture*, edited and with an introduction by Cary Nelson and Lawrence Grossberg, 271–316. Urbana: University of Illinois Press.

Spivak, Gayatri Chakravorty. 1988b. "Subaltern Studies: Deconstructing Historiography." In *Selected Subaltern Studies*, edited by Ranajit Guha and Gayatri Chakravorty Spivak, 3–32. New York: Oxford University Press.

Stanton, William R. 1960. *The Leopard's Spots: Scientific Attitudes toward Race in America, 1815–59*. Chicago: University of Chicago Press.

Stocking, George W. 1982. *Race, Culture, and Evolution: Essays in the History of Anthropology*. Chicago: University of Chicago Press.

Taylor, Cecil. 1966. "Sound Structure of Subculture Becoming Major Breath/Naked Fire Gesture." Liner notes in *Unit Structures*. LP BST 84237. Los Angeles: Blue Note Records.

Taylor, Cecil. 1973a. *Akisakila*. PA-7067. With Jimmy Lyons and Andrew Cyrille. Tokyo: Trio Records.

Taylor, Cecil. 1973b. *Solo*. PA-7067. Tokyo: Trio Records.

Taylor, Cecil, and Yosuke Yamashita. 2007. *4 Hands: Cecil Taylor and Yosuke Yamashita in Concert*. Directed by Shirai, Yasuhiko, and Katsuya Shirai. Tokyo: 4 Hands Films.

Tennyson, Alfred, Lord. 1982. *In Memoriam*, edited by Susan Shatto and Marion Shaw. Oxford: Oxford University Press.

Trafton, Scott. 2004. *Egyptland: Race and Nineteenth-century American Egyptomania*. Durham, NC: Duke University Press.

Waligora-Davis, Nicole. 2006. "W. E. B. Du Bois and the Fourth Dimension." *CR: The New Centennial Review* 6 (3): 57–90.

West, Cornel. 1987. "Race and Social Theory: Towards a Genealogical Materialist Analysis." In *The Year Left: An American Socialist Yearbook*, vol. 2, edited by Mike Davis, 74–90. London: Verso.

West, Cornel. 1988. "Marxism and the Specificity of Afro-American Oppression." In *Marxism and the Interpretation of Culture*, edited and with an introduction by Cary Nelson and Lawrence Grossberg, 17–33. Urbana: University of Illinois Press.

INDEX

Absolute Truth, at Harvard turned away from search for, 73
"Academy and Race," a conference, Villanova University, March 8–10, 1996. *See also* Miles, Kevin Thomas, 155
Adolph Reed, 150
affirmative engagement, 141
Africa, 1, 2, 4, 25, 71; ancient Kush, 156
African American: African American Japanese, or Japanese African American, 143; dilemma, "Can I be both?," 121; discourse, and contemporary thought, 97; example of, 95; historical example of, 129; historicity, 88; intelligentsia, 7, 13, 17, 113
Agamben, Giorgio, 149
Ajayi, J. F. Ade, 124
Alfred, Lord Tennyson, 64; *In Memoriam A. H. H.*, 116, 152; "make one music as before, but vaster," 65; "one far off Divine event," 64, 112
alogical logic, 106, 108, 137; or the movement of a secondary rhythm, 84; of the second time, 106
Althusser, Louis, 95
ambiguity of physical character, mixture, crossing, exceptions, and qualification, 102
America, 65
American Academy of Political and Social Science, 55, 150; *Annals* of, 13 American Indians, 98
American Negro Academy (ANA), 3, 6, 7, 43, 68, 72, 76, 113, 121, 134, 147. *See also* "The Conservation of Races"
American Reconstruction, 131; and Meiji Restoration, 130
Americas, the, 1, 25, 145
anacrusis, 85
anaphora, 134
Anderson, Matthew, 148

Anidjar, Gil, 159
Appiah, K. Anthony, 77, 86, 152–53
Aptheker, Herbert, 131, 154; January 10, 1956, letter from W. E. B. Du Bois, 73 Aristotelian categories, 104
Aristotle: metaphysics, 104; *Nicomachean Ethics*, 104
association (external), theoretical concept of, 135. *See also* dissociation (internal); illimitable
asymmetrical reciprocity of sameness and difference, theoretical concept of, 48. *See also* intermingling
"Asymptotes of the Hyperbola," 73
Atlanta Conference for the Study of the Negro Problems, 151, 157; Eleventh conference, 12
Atlanta University, 74
Austin, J. L., 59, 93
autobiographical: and historiographical, 82

Balibar, Etienne, 159
Baltic states: and essentially all of the "eastern" countries of "Europe," 135
Banner, B. T., 147
Bantu: ancient culture of, 122; the Bantus as kind of people, 98 Berlin conference, 1
Bernasconi, Robert, 30, 148, 149, 150, 154
bias: a thought on the bias, 72
biologism, 66, 152
Black Reconstruction: An Essay Toward a History of the Part Which Black Folk Played in the Attempt to Reconstruct Democracy in America, 1860–1880: the 1935 historical study by W. E. B. Du Bois, 57
blood, 63, 101; the metaphorics of "blood" in Du Bois's discourse, 151
Blumenbach, Johann Friedrich, 22, 36, 150

Boas, Franz, 35, 56; Atlanta conference for the study of the Negro: 1906, 157; "Human Faculty as Determined by Race," 35; *The Mind of Primitive Man*, 35
Bonnet, Charles, 124
Bowen, J. W. E, 147
Browne, Francis Fisher, 19, 70
Bushmen: of Africa, 98; the Bushman, 22, 151
Butler, Judith, 93; "futural form," 155

Canada, 158
Canguilhem, Georges, 151
Caribbean, 145
Carnegie Hall, 26
chance, 51, 61; and law: in human conduct, 74; and Law, 73
Chinese, 22, 32, 151
civil war, 118
civilization, 117
cohesiveness and continuity: of race groups in the sense of history, 102
color, 101
common history: traditions, impulses, formulation in paragraph five, 100
conservation, 75, 139
"The Conservation of Races," 3, 4, 6, 7, 8, 10, 12, 16, 19, 20, 23, 24, 36, 38, 52, 54, 60, 61, 64, 65, 68, 72, 75, 82, 93, 94, 97, 107, 113, 120, 125, 126, 134, 135, 139, 153, 156, 157; no pure term, in the account of present races, in paragraph nine of 1897 essay, 98–100; paragraph two, 16; paragraph three, 17, 18, 72, 126; paragraph four, 18, 22, 34, 44, 78, 155; paragraph five, 18, 45, 49, 50, 58, 105, 107, 120; paragraph six, 49, 50, 57, 58, 63; paragraph seven, 68; paragraph eight, 97–100; paragraphs eight and nine, 95; paragraph nine, 61, 66, 100–111; paragraphs nine and ten, 61; paragraph ten, 64, 111–116; paragraphs ten and eleven, 95; paragraph eleven, 71, 117–37, 129; paragraph twelve, 71; paragraph seventeen, 125, 156–157; paragraphs seventeen and eighteen, 72; phrase "eye of the Historian and Sociologist" in, 45, 54, 107; "race in the sense in which History tells us," 102; racial difference in human history, 99; roles which men have played in Human Progress, 120; theoretical production in, 67; theoretical production in, as nascent theory of general possibility of intermingling, 76, 77; "What is the real distinction between," 100; "What is the real meaning of Race?," 21; "whole process" as the movement of, 144; as formulated in paragraph nine, 109; "whole process" as history of race differences theorized in paragraph nine, 101. *See also* Du Bois, W. E. B.
constitution of the world, 38, 53
contextualization, 87, 150
Cook, Charles C., 148
Coppin, Levi J., 148
cranial measurements, 101
criteria, 31, 45, 49, 64; of race: four such criteria: color: hair, cranial measurements and language, 31
criterion, 31
critique of essentialism: of the 1980s and 1990s, 75
Crogman, W. H., 147
Cromwell, John W., 6, 147 crossing, 109
Crummell, Alexander, 6, 7, 75, 147
culture: concept of, 95
Cyrille, Andrew. *See* Taylor, Cecil, 59
Czech, 98

Darwin, Charles, 22, 36, 43
Declaration of Independence: of the United States of America, 93 declaration(s): theoretical: in relation to practice(s), 135
Deleuze, Gilles, 149
Derrida, Jacques, 12, 26, 37, 59, 66, 93, 95, 104, 114, 149, 159; "*Destruktion*" and Heidegger, 66; Edmund Husserl's *Origin of Geometry: An Introduction*, 156; "The Ends of Man," 26; *Of Grammatology*, 157; *Heidegger et la question: De l'esprit* (*Of Spirit: Heidegger and the Question*), 66, 68; and humanist teleology and Heidegger, 152; not unilaterality of subjectivity and idea of spirit, 66; opposition to fascism, 66; opposition to "nazism," 66; spirit, 66; "ultra-transcendental," 59; unprecedented responsibilities of thought and action in opposition to fascism, 67
desedimentation, as theoretical practice, 103, 145; of the concept of race: in our time, 94; general labor of: as theoretical labor in critical thought, 81; and Jacques Derrida, 66; of thought, 92

determinate indetermination" as theoretical concept, 48. *See also* "intermingling"
diaspora: African, 145
difference, 49; among humans, 43; an order of organization of, 45; general order of, 52
differences, 52; with an s, 50
differences and subtle forces, 53, 58
differences in men: recognizes, to recognize such, 72
differentiation, as theoretical concept of: of spiritual and mental differences, 72. *See also* intermingling
discourses of the spirit: in European thought from Kant to Heidegger, 83
dissociation (internal), as theoretical concept of, 128, 135. *See also* association (external); illimitable
double: the motif of: in Du Bois's earliest writings, 155
"double-consciousness," 142. *See also The Souls of Black Folk: Essays and Sketches*
Dragan Kujundzic, 159
Du Bois, W. E. B.: "The Afro-American": circa 1894, 3; *Darkwater: Voices from Within the Veil*, 56; a fragment of his fundamental discourse, 75; his practice: in relation to his declarations, 135; idea of family in, 62; intermingling, 77–78; January 1956 letter, 74; *The Negro*, 98; *The Philadelphia Negro: A Social Study*, 9, 15, 151; philosophical (and scientific and secular), as Du Bois's practice, his commitment, 43; "The Present Outlook for the Dark Races of Mankind," 14; "the problem of the twentieth century is the problem of the color line," 118; project of African American studies, 152; *also* "The Study of the Negro Problems"; "The Relation of the Negroes to the Whites in the South," 13; "The Twelfth Census and the Negro Problems": signal 1900 essay, 151, 152; *The World and Africa: An Inquiry into the Part Which Africa Has Played in World History*, 57. *See also* "The Conservation of Races"; "The Present Outlook for the Dark Races of Mankind"; *The Souls of Black Folk: Essays and Sketches*; "Strivings of the Negro People"
Durkheim, Émile, 35, 56
Dutch, 98
duty, 121, 139, 158

"Duty of Cherishing and Fostering the Intellect of the Race": Du Bois's topic for first American Negro Academy (ANA) meeting, 147. *See also* American Negro Academy (ANA); "The Conservation of Races"
duty to conserve, 72. *See also* "The Conservation of Races"
dynamic infrastructure, 50. *See also* intermingling

Egypt, 124; ancient, 122, 123, 124
Egyptian, 22, 32, 151; ancient civilization of Egypt, 122; Egyptian civilization, 117; Egyptians, 98; historical figure of: and Greece, 157
El Fasi, Mohamed, 124
Emberling, Geoff, 124; and Bruce Williams, 158
"encyclopedia Africana": W. E. B. Du Bois's project of, 157
English: English and Teuton: represent the white variety of mankind, 101; English nation: stood for constitutional liberty, 112; includes the Scotch: the Irish: and the conglomerate American, 98; people: the English of Great Britain, 98
Enlightenment, 11
enunciation, 123
Esquimaux, 98
essence, 29
essentialism, 91
Ethiopia, 124; ancient Negro civilization of, 122
Europe, 1, 3, 4, 25, 65, 71, 123, 145, 148, 155; discourses of: since the seventeenth century, 105; European, 9, 22, 23, 24, 27, 151; European eidos, 25; European philosophy, 20 evolutionary theory. *See* Gould, Stephen Jay
example, 82; the two examples of Japan and matters Negro American, 136

family, 62
Fanon, Frantz, 155; *L'expérience vécue du Noir*: chapter 5 of Fanon's *Peau noire: masques blancs*, 155
Ferris, William H., 75, 148
fifteenth century: 1441, 1 figure of an "X," 110
First World War, 57 Fisher, Marjorie M., 124
forces, 49, 52
formulation of a problem: W. E. B. Du Bois's discourse as thus relevant to our time, 119

INDEX · 175

Fortune, T. Thomas, 3, 76, 131
Foucault, Michel, 26, 37, 95, 148, 149; *The Order of Things*, 26
freedom, 41, 61
French horizon of discourse: situation, *problématique*, bio-power, *différance*, 95 Freud, Sigmund, 35, 56, 83
Fynsk, Chrisopher, 149

German, 22, 33, 98; Germany, 3, 26; as nation: for science and philosophy, 112
gift: "gift of story and song": as one of three gifts of the Negro to America, 125; "gift of sweat and brawn": as one of three gifts of the Negro to America, 125; "gift of the Spirit": as one of three gifts of the Negro to America, 125; the three gifts: gifts of the Negro to America, 125
globalized war across boundaries: proclaimed as both categorical and hierarchical, 118
Goldberg, David Theo, 149, 159
Gooding-Williams, Robert, 77, 86, 151, 175
Gould, Stephen Jay, 149; conception of historicity: evolutionary theory, 106
Gramsci, Antonio, 149
Greece: ancient: supposed as replete, 123; Greek: ancient thought of, 29; legacies of ancient Greek, 79
Grimké, Archibald, 6
Grimké, Francis J., 6, 147
Grisham, George N., 148
ground, 61, 67, 111
Guattari, Felix, 149
Guha, Ranajit, 158. *See also* South Asian subcontinent

Hammonds, Evelynn Maxine, 149, 150
Hardt, Michael. *See* Negri, Antonio, 149
Hayson, Walter B., 147
Hegel, G. W. F., 25, 26, 83, 89, 139
Heidegger, Martin, 26, 59, 66, 83, 149; the animal as "poor in world," 152. *See also* Derrida, Jacques (*Heidegger et la question*)
Heng, Geraldine, 150
Herzig, Rebecca M., 149, 150
Hindoos: of Central Asia, 98; includes traces of widely differing nations, 98
historia: concept of, 95; historial, 1, 5, 23, 29, 32, 123, 147; idea of, and entitlement of Japan's historial status, 136; historial character: in relation to physical characteristics, 96; historicism, 27, 149; historicity, 14, 88, 105; historiographical: and autobiographical, 82; historiography: as the narrative of this itinerary of intermingling and intermixture, 111; history of ideas, 27; as the itinerary of intermingling and intermixture, 111; a term susceptible to multiple desedimentations, 95
History: at Harvard, W. E. B. Du Bois turned to the study of, 73
Holocaust, 25, 118
Holt, Thomas, 86
horizon, 61, 66
Hottentot, 22, 151
human: the idea of, 25, 28; specific level of difference among: 52; specific organization of the same, 52. *See also* intermingling
Husserl, Edmund, 26, 35, 37, 56, 83, 149; and Jacques Derrida, 156; transcendental *epoché*, per Derrida's formulation, 59
Huxley, Thomas Henry, 22, 36

idea, 60; or *eidos*, 59; in Immanuael Kant's sense of idea, 37
idea of race, 8, 21, 23, 30. *See also* human
idea of the human, 27. *See also* human
ideal, 97; concept, 113; idealization, 37; ideals, 69, 113, 115, 143; ideals of life, 61, 101, 112, 114; ideals of the American Republic: end of chapter one of *The Souls of Black Folk Essays and Sketches*, 143
illimitable: (external) association: (internal) dissociation, 135; movement of "intermingling": intermixture, and crossing: as race in history, 111; passage beyond, or to, the thought of an outside, 139
illusions of reason: transcendental illusions, 59. *See also* idea; Kant, Immanuel
indeterminate determination, 48, *also* intermingling individualism, 58
inequality: as something one deprecates, 72
infinitely, 105
integration of physical difference, 109. *See also* intermingling intellectual clearinghouse, 6, 7
intentionality, 61
interlocution, 102

"intermingling," 35, 38, 41, 42, 44, 75, 83, 96, 111, 113, 127; difference as the heterogeneous structure of sameness and difference, 110; and intermixture, 50; movement of: bespeaks an irreducible opening within the order of necessity, 111; as a radical: order of the movement of difference, 110; a theory of the general possibility of "intermingling" among humankind, 77
intermixture, 111; and "intermingling," 50

Jackson, W. T. S., 148
James, William, 73; Jamesian Pragmatism, 72–73
Japan, 128, 132, 133, 134, 135, 136, 158; Emperor of Japan, 129; the example of Japan, 237; Meiji era, 128; Meiji Restoration, 130, 132
Japan Association for American Studies, 158
Japanese, 117, 122, 134, 138
Japanese African American: or African American Japanese, 143
Japanese and African American as historical examples, 128
Japanese example, 122; Japanese historical example, 128
Jefferson, Thomas, 83, 89; Declaration of Independence, 93
Jews, 25
Johnson, John A., 148
Judy, R. A., 87, 148, 149, 154; first systematic attention to Kant's thought of "the Negro," 148

Kant, Immanuel, 11, 25, 26, 36, 59, 89, 104, 148, 154; appendix to the transcendental dialectic, 11, 59; critical sense, 37; *Critique of Pure Reason*, 11; essay of 1788 translated as "On the Use of Teleological Principles in Philosophy," 11, 148; "The Determination of the Concept of Race," 11; ideas of reason: constitutive and regulative use of, 59
Ki-Zerbo, Joseph, 124
King, Rev. Martin Luther, Jr., 26
kinship, 38
Kirkland, Frank M., 86
krités: as activity of *krínein*: to separate, 30; as determination of *kritérion*, 30; to judge, 30
Kush: an ancient civilization of Nubia, 123, 124; an ancient civilization of the southern Nile: of autochthonous development, 124; ancient: which the Greeks knew as Nubia: Kerma to Meroë, 124
Kyoto, 159

Lacoue-Labarthe, Phillippe, 149
law, 51; law and chance: in human conduct, 74; "Law and Chance," 73
Lewis, David Levering, 148
Lincoln Memorial Church: in Washington, D.C.: *also* Miller, Arthur P., 3
literature and art: in relation to ideals: *also* ideals, 114, 115
Lott, Tommy, 86
Love, John L., 75, 148
Lyons, Jimmy, 159. *See also* Taylor, Cecil

Magyar, 98
Man: concept of: and its epistemological derivative the human, 95; the idea of, 25
Marable, Manning, 154
Mason, Otis T., 35
mathesis, 105
Matsumura, Wendy: 133. *See* Okinawa
McBride, Dwight, 175
McGann, Karen, 124
Meiji era, 158; Meiji Restoration: and the American Reconstruction after the American Civil War, 130
metalepsis: metaleptic operation, 137
Michaelsen, Scott, 149
Miles, Kevin Thomas, 155
Miller, Albert P., 75, 147, 148
Miller, Kelly, 75, 76, 147, 148
Mokhtar, Gamal el Din, 124
Mongolian, 101; includes Chinese, Tartar, Corean, and Japanese, 98; Mongolians: of Eastern Asia, 98; represent the yellow variety of mankind, 101
Moore, Lewis B., 148
Moses, Wilson Jeremiah, 7, 43, 86
Moss, Alfred A., Jr, 7, 43, 75, 147, 148
Moten, Fred, 142, 159
movement of "transcending" differentiation, 113. *See also* intermingling

Nakamura, Masako, 158
narrative: capsule narrative, 100; narrative of race in history: as process of intermingling, of intermixture, and crossing, 111

National Association for the Advancement of Colored People (NAACP), 6
natural laws, 19. *See also* "The Conservation of Races," paragraph three; law
naturalism, 66, 152
nature: idea of, 148; as not essentially closed structure: as described in "The Conservation of Races" paragraphs four, nine, and ten, 102
necessity, 41
Negri, Antoni, and Michael Hardt, 149
négritude: in Europe, 155
Negro, 151; as a group: as a "race," 93; ideals, 71, 140; Negroes of Africa and America, 98; Negroes represent the black variety of mankind, 101; Negroid Mediterranean culture, 122; as perhaps: the most indefinite of all, 98; race, 117
Negro American: in America, 2; contribution, 119; intelligentsia, 1, 3, 9; leadership, 10, 19; Negro ideals: in the making of America, 124
Negro problem: as half-named, 14; as plural: as in problem(s), 4; in the United States, 3
Niagara Movement, 6
Niane, Djibril Tamsir, 124
Nietzsche, Friedrich, 35, 83; *On the Genealogy of Morality*, 35, 156; section of enumerated as 13, 59
Nile River, 124
Nishida, Kitaro, 131
non-simple: as theme in the essay "The Conservation of Races," 99. *See also* "The Conservation of Races"
Nubia: especially the ancient civilization of Kush, 123, 124. *See also* Africa; Egypt; Kush

Ogai, Mori, 131
Ogot, Bethwell A., 124
Okinawa, 133; Japan, 132. *See* Japan
ontology, 89; ontological, 48, 88, 112; W. E. B. Du Bois's affirmation wrongly supposed as, 121. *See also* paraontology
order of the same: the general order of, 52. *See also* "intermingling"; necessity
origin: origin of the origin: *also* historia: *also* alogical logic, 114; originary complication: *also* historia: *also* alogical logic, 91; originary difference: *also* historia, 91

Outlaw, Lucius T., 77, 86, 155

paleonymy: paleonymic practice, 44, 81; paleonymic problematic, 141
paraontology: paraontological: Du Bois's affirmation better understood as: *also* paleonymy, 88, 121, 122; practice of, 89, 90, 106. *See also* ontology; paleonymy
"perhaps," 38
phaenomenon, 20, 23, 33
philosophy: as in "human philosophy" or philosophical understanding of the human, 93; philosophical discourse, 21; "whole question of race in human philosophy," 126
physical: in paragraph nine of "The Conservation of Races" described as "race identity and common blood," 103; physical characteristics: in relation to historial character, 96; physical differences of humans: and race differences, 102; physical race lines, 105
physics, 51
Poland, 135; Pole, as in the Polish, 98
Pope, Jeremy, 124, 149; historical figure of Egypt for G. W. F. Hegel, 157
possibility, 68
Powell, John Wesley, 35
"The Present Outlook for the Dark Races of Mankind," 14; "the problem of the twentieth century is the problem of the color line," 118
problematization, 47; "problem of the color line," 14, 25, 92, 143, *also* W. E. B. Du Bois, problem of the Negro as a general problem for fundamental thought, 104

race: concept of, 2, 4, 8, 10, 23, 24, 28, 34, 45, 94, 96, 116, 120, 151; as not ontological, 64; critical logical work on the concept of: in paragraphs four through six of 1897 essay, 111; deeper differences are spiritual, psychical, difference: paragraph nine, 101; differentiation of spiritual and mental differences: paragraph nine, 101; function of: up to the present time, 117; integration of physical differences: given in paragraph nine, 101; movement of development as not onto-logical, 104; origins and destinies of races, 100; the past of, 97; physical distinctions not explain deeper differences, 101;

race difference: not ontological: too easily called such, 102; race differences, 6, 101; race identity and common blood, 105; race in human philosophy, 18; races: the future of, 97; races are historical entities, 99; racial groups, 9. *See also* paraontology

racism, 152

Ratzel, Friedrich, 22, 36

repetition, 114

Roma, 25

Roman, 22, 151

Romance nations, 98, 101; includes Frenchman, Italian, Sicilian: and Spaniard, 98; stood for literature and art, 112

Ross Posnock, 150

Royce, Josiah, 73

Russia, 135; Russian, 98

Said, Edward: "Permission to Narrate," 156

Santayana, George, 73

Sartre, Jean-Paul, 95, 155

Saussy, Haun, 149

Scandinavian, 32, 98, 151

Scarborough, William S., 43, 75, 148

science and philosophy: in relation to ideals: *also* ideals, 114, 115

Scott, David, 150

Second World War: aftermath of, 91

secondary: the motif of, in Du Bois's earliest writings, 155; "second time," *also* alogical logic, 144; "secondary rhythm" in Sociology Hesitant," 154

sedimentation, 103

self-organization, 72

self-reflexivity, 61, 63

Semites, 101; Semitic people: of Western Asia and Northern Africa, 98

Shimabuku, Annmaria, 133. *See also* Okinawa

Sicilian, 22, 32, 151

Skinner, Quentin, 149–150

Slav, 22, 32, 101, 151; Slavs of eastern Europe, 98

slavery, 25

Slovenia, 135

sociological and historical races of men, 112. *See also* "The Conservation of Races"; "intermingling"

sociology, 51; as the "measurement of the element of Chance in Human Action," 73; at Harvard W. E. B. Du Bois turned to study of, 73; in January 1956 Du Bois letter: as "measurement of Chance in Human Action," 73; as Science of "limits of Chance in human conduct": in "Sociology Hesitant": 1904, 74; "Sociology Hesitant," 51, 155; "Sociology Hesitant," an unpublished fragment of theoretical criticism by Du Bois, 75; the posthumously published essay "Sociology Hesitant," 52, 54; sociology as science of "limits of Chance in human conduct," 74

Soseki, Natsume, 131

The Souls of Black Folk: Essays and Sketches, 13, 14, 15, 37, 56, 66, 71, 125, 135, 139, 151, 154–155; Æschylus mentioned in, 71; "double-consciousness," 142; chapter one first as 1897 essay, 14, 65, 69, 70, 131, 139, 153; "meaning of 'swift' and 'slow' in human doing," 126; ninth chapter of, and the 1901 essay version of that chapter, 149; "Of the Sorrow Songs," chapter fourteen of, 15, 16, 19, 70–71, 127; "Of Our Spiritual Strivings," chapter one of, 125, 128, 153; one sentence from the closing chapter the book, 126; Shakespeare mentioned in, 71; "sphinxes on the shores of science," 71; "swift and slow in human doing," 71; "warp and woof," 138, 140. *See also* Du Bois, W. E. B.; "Strivings of the Negro People"

South Asian subcontinent: two scholars on nineteenth and early twentieth centuries of, 158

South Sea Islanders, 98

sovereignty, 26

Spillers, Hortense, 24, 142; "The Idea of Black Culture," 57

spirit: spiritual: and physical difference: as common history, common laws and religion, 103; a conscious striving together for certain ideals of life, 103, differences, 96, 105; as infinitely transcending the physical, 103; *also* "intermingling," 112; psychical, 106; as race differences, 102; and social difference, 112; spiritual and mental differences, 110

Spivak, Gayatri Chakravorty, 158

Stanton, William R., 149

Star of Ethiopia, the pageant: W. E. B. Du Bois's projection of, 57. *See also* Kush

status: and the concept of race, 8

Stocking, George, 149
strife, 100
striving, 18, 61, 62, 115
"Strivings of the Negro People," 1897 essay: as chapter one of *The Souls of Black Folk*, 14, 65, 69, 70, 131, 139, 153; reference to "Sturm und Drang" in, 69; "sits in its accustomed seat" (as quotation from Shakespeare) in, 70. See also Du Bois, W. E. B.; *The Souls of Black Folk: Essays and Sketches*. See also "The Study of the Negro Problems," 1897 essay: "the fourth division" as described in, 55, 150; written in late summer or autumn, 1897, 107; written in the same year as "The Conservation of Races," 107; written in late summer or autumn, 1897, 107. See also Du Bois, W. E. B.
synonymia, 134
synonyms, 138

talented tenth, 158
Tanaka, Min: performance with Cecil Taylor: at Kyoto Prize award ceremony events, Kyoto, Japan, 158
Tartar: as a people, 22, 33, 151
Taylor, Cecil, 37, 81, 85, 140, 142, 143, 144; "form is possibility," 81, 142; historic first visit to Japan in 1973: with Jimmy Lyons and Andrew Cyrille, 159; Kyoto Prize in Arts and Philosophy, 158; "naked fire gesture," 140; performance with Yosuke Yamashita: at Suntory Hall in Tokyo, Japan, 158; performances in Japan, Miyagi prefecture, Tokyo: and at Kyoto Prize ceremony, 158; "the root of rhythm is its central unit of change," 137; "subculture becoming major breath," 140
telos, 114; telic, 60
Teuton, 98, 101; Teutons, 98
theological (and religious and sacred): as Alexander Crummell's practice, 43; as not W. E. B. Du Bois's practice, 43

theoretical: theoretical decision, 94; theoretical discourse, 94; theoretical labor, 95; titular question, 102
Thomas, Kendall, 159
totalitarianism, 66
Toussaint L'Ouverture, 71
traditional logic: logic of noncontradiction, 60
Trafton, Scott: historical figure of Egypt for nineteenth-century America, 157
transcendental, 27, 145; in paragraph nine, 101; transcend, 103; transcendental historicity: transcending, 104, 106, 111; Trotter, William Monroe, 6; *also* ultra-transcendental, 145
truth: concept of, 5

ultra-transcendental, 59. See also Derrida, Jacques: *Of Grammatology*
University of Pennsylvania, 74

variety of mankind: between these are many crosses and mixtures: *also* race: *also* intermingling, 101
Virginia Theological Seminary, 148

Waligora-Davis, Nicole, 158
wars of colonization, 118 Washington, Booker T., 6, 131 "we the people," 93
Weber, Max, 35, 56, 83
Weheliye, Alexander, 154
West, Cornel, 149
Wilberforce University, 3
Williams, Bruce. 124, 159. See also Emberling, Geoff
Wright, Richard Robert, 75, 148

Yamashita, Yosuke: performance with Cecil Taylor: at Suntory Hall in Tokyo, Japan, 158. See also Taylor, Cecil

Zamboes: of America, 98
Zulu, 22, 32, 151

www.ingramcontent.com/pod-product-compliance
Lightning Source LLC
Chambersburg PA
CBHW051126160426
43195CB00014B/2356